MODERN HUMA

TEXTS

(formerly D

VOLUME 61

Editor
DAVID D. GEORGE
(Hispanic)

CONFIGURING COMMUNITY: THEORIES, NARRATIVES, AND PRACTICES OF COMMUNITY IDENTITIES IN CONTEMPORARY SPAIN

D1614396

CONFIGURING COMMUNITY: THEORIES, NARRATIVES, AND PRACTICES OF COMMUNITY IDENTITIES IN CONTEMPORARY SPAIN

by

PARVATI NAIR

MANEY PUBLISHING
for the
MODERN HUMANITIES RESEARCH ASSOCIATION
2004

Maney Publishing
for the
Modern Humanities Research Association

ISBN 1 904350 14 3

© The Modern Humanities Research Association 2004

Copies may be ordered from Publications Sales, Maney Publishing, Hudson Road, Leeds LS9 7DL, UK; e-mail mhra@maney.co.uk. Further information about the activities of the MHRA and individual membership can be obtained from the Honorary Secretary, Dr David Gillespie, Department of European Studies and Modern Languages, University of Bath, Bath BA2 7AY, UK, or from the website at www.mhra.org.uk.

Produced in England by
MANEY PUBLISHING
HUDSON ROAD   LEEDS LS9 7DL   UK

For Mark

CONTENTS

ACKNOWLEDGEMENTS

This book is a reworking of my doctoral dissertation, which I completed in 2001. My sincere thanks go to Jo Labanyi for the rigour, thought, and encouragement that she offered as supervisor of my thesis. It was an immense privilege to have entered the research process under her guidance. The department of Language Studies, London Guildhall University assisted me with financial aid for travel to Spain between 1996 and 2000 and with a semester's sabbatical which enabled me to write up. I also acknowledge the assistance of the Central Research Fund, University of London for a travel grant that financed fieldwork for my final chapter. The Spanish Research Seminar group at Birkbeck College gave me much worthwhile feedback on my work, for which I am grateful. Warm thanks to Isabel Santaolalla for generous help at times when I have needed it. My thanks also go to colleagues at the School of Modern Languages at Queen Mary, University of London, in particular to Omar García for help at crucial moments. Needless to say, I am very grateful to the many people whom I interviewed in the course of this research project, most especially Núria Andreu, Bernardo Atxaga, and Julio Llamazares, and to those numerous members of NGOs and other groups and organizations in Spain who offered me their time and assistance.

I thank the external examiners of my thesis, Mark Allinson and Paul Julian Smith, for invaluable suggestions and new insights which I have tried to incorporate here. Similarly, I thank Chris Perriam for much useful advice. My thanks also go to Catherine Davies for her suggestion that I submit this dissertation to the MHRA for their consideration. Most especially, I am grateful to David George of the MHRA for his patience, support, and meticulous assistance in re-shaping this dissertation.

Close friends and family have played a very important role in the course of my writing the thesis and subsequently turning it into a book. In particular, I thank Kanishka Chowdhury, Berta Gaya, and Antonio Sánchez, friends who warmly endured, at one stage or another, the vagaries of this project. I am extremely grateful to my parents for the moral and practical support that they have given me throughout. At every stage, their interest and their encouragement have been invaluable. My thanks also go to my son, Jamie, for so much fun along the way and for ensuring, as only a child can, that the anxieties of writing were kept in check by the joy of seeing him grow alongside and so much beyond the thesis. This book is for Mark McGlynn, whose theoretical insights, patience, and unstinting support both helped me to imagine this project and sustain its momentum.

INTRODUCTION

In sharp reversal of the monolithic imagination of national identity projected for so long by the culturally levelling discourses of Francoism, Spanishness, for the past two decades, has been actively constructed in terms of multiplicity and synchronicity. Any location of identity thus rests on the historically contingent axes of temporal and spatial parts. In this scattered and fragmented cultural landscape, the modern imagination of nation necessarily cedes to a more ambivalent vision of collective identity, one that allows for a more adept navigation through the disjuncture of postmodernity. Ironically, therefore, this has meant the return to the concept of community. While the nation continues to be an important point of reference for collective identity, it is no longer by any means the sole available imagination of the latter that circulates in popular discourse. The emphases on local, regional, and transnational affiliations means that collective identities co-exist within overlapping parameters and no single definition can override any other. My principle hypothesis in this book is that contemporary, postmodernist Spain has experienced a resurgence of community, which both cuts across and is prioritized over nation; equally, the term is ambivalent, transferable across contexts and, as such, presents a reworking of its stable connotations in premodern or traditional usage.

This research project began as an attempt to analyse narrative and identity in contemporary Spain. My aim had been to examine the role of a range of narratives in the construction of cultural identity at communal level since the transition to democracy, bearing in mind the diverse socio-cultural and economic changes, which have taken place in Spain over the past one hundred years. In particular, I was concerned with the effects on narratives of identity of the steep, though uneven, acceleration of modernity in the second half of the twentieth century, with the attendant increase in migration from rural to urban areas, resulting in the weakening of rural life and localized communities. My original focus took as its historical basis the gradual erosion of primary orality[1] over the nineteenth and twentieth centuries and aimed to examine contemporary narratives in diverse media from this perspective. I quickly realized, however, that an analysis of narrative and identity focusing on the contemporary period at communal, as opposed to individual, levels was inextricably tied to the question of what exactly constitutes a 'community' in present-day Spain. Given the proliferation of multi-layered discourses of identity that prevail in Spanish and most other cultural contexts today, the notion of 'community' defies any single definition. Yet, in Spain, as much as or more than in most other countries, the word 'community' abounds and is seen to function in diverse and even contradictory senses. Since the transition to democracy (1975–82), Spain has been a nation of seventeen different autonomous 'communities' or regions, it gained membership of the European Community and has become an active participant in continental and global socioeconomic links leading to still more vague and de-localized constructions of 'community'. Concurrently, organic definitions or understandings of community as 'home' continue to fuel the cultural imaginary, thereby charging the notion with an emotive force that is widely present in political rhetoric. Divergences thus emerge between the contingent practices of community and its many imagined, and often essentialized,[2] contours.

My aim, therefore, is to problematise the concepts, narratives, and practices of community identity in the context of contemporary Spanish culture. I shall do so by analysing texts dating from 1985 onwards in a range of cultural media. By focusing upon the concept of community in examples of literature, film, and music, I hope to draw out the complexities and ambivalences present in discourses and narratives of community identities across diverse media. In order to achieve this, I shall map a range of cultural texts and media onto overlapping theoretical frameworks drawn from several disciplines. The question of community identity will therefore be examined from varied theoretical and interdisciplinary perspectives, examples of which are issues of loss, memory, history, narration, and displacement in ethnography, sociology, cultural studies, and philosophy. The spatial and temporal contextualization of the formulation of community identity is central to each analysis, so that community as a concept may be understood to be contingent upon the impermanent, axial intersections of space and time, rather than as rooted or stable. Equally important for each of the chapters is an understanding of the larger cultural backdrop to the texts in question, provided by Spain's uneven involvement in the processes of modernity, an engagement that has experienced sharp acceleration over the past twenty years as Spain has aligned itself with the rest of Western Europe. To date, no research project has taken up the question of community identities in Spain from an interdisciplinary theoretical framework. While this issue has clearly been the focus of studies on Spanish nationalism and contemporary politics (see, for example, Alonso Zaldívar and Castells [1992]) and plurality in terms of contemporary communal or social identities has also been explored in the context of postmodernity in Spain (see the last section of Graham and Labanyi [1995]), no in-depth analysis is as yet available of the cultural significance of the resurgence of community as such in contemporary Spain. The use of theory here and the choice of texts across cultural paradigms is a deliberate effort to understand community in diverse perspectives and contexts.

To varying degrees, the research methodology used for writing each chapter has consisted of textual analyses constructed within interdisciplinary theoretical frameworks, combined, where relevant, with fieldwork, mainly in the form of interviews with key informants who were either central to the construction of the 'text' in question or who could provide useful background information. While some of these interviews were taped, with varying degrees of success (Llamazares, Córdoba prison), others (Atxaga, Gutiérrez, Andreu) were not and I always took notes either during the interview or shortly thereafter. The decision to tape or not depended largely on what suited interviewees or appeared appropriate, possible, or unobtrusive under the circumstances. The logic behind this research approach lies in a deliberate attempt to locate this analysis in the disciplinary border zones of cultural studies and contemporary ethnography. In the late twentieth century — and early twenty-first — increasing postmodernist intertwining of text and lived practice has led, in my opinion, to blurred distinctions between these two disciplines, so that community, no longer the theoretical preoccupation or product solely of anthropology, is at once tangible and abstract, imagined and lived, often in contradictory and competing ways. Equally, cultural studies can itself be viewed as having emerged not so long ago from the poststructuralist and postcolonial encounters of ethnography and textual studies. Therefore, my aim is also to locate this disciplinary overlap in a larger context of the humanities through the above-mentioned reliance upon interdisciplinary theory, so that shared theoretical concerns may be viewed from different disciplinary perspectives, presenting diverse discourses of knowledge as interconnected.

Each of the following chapters is an attempt to configure community in the context of contemporary Spanish culture. The 'texts' that have been chosen range in medium, but all raise issues concerned with identity at the level of community, as opposed to just that of the individual. Various discursive strands are explored in the course of the five chapters, so as to facilitate a multi-stranded approach to the analyses of community. In so doing, key aspects of identity at communal level are brought to the fore: cultural memory and amnesia, location and landscape, identity as plural, even contradictory, narratives or 'voices', essential as opposed to floating identity, liminality and contingency, ethnicity, the question of borders and transgression, displacement and cultural politics. Furthermore, an interdisciplinary theoretical framework has been brought to bear upon the texts in question, with, in general, two theorists working alongside one another in each case. However, given the numerous, undeniable anthropological explorations and uses of the term 'community', various contemporary ethnographic approaches to community identity, based upon ethnography's own contemporary re-assessments of its disciplinary project, will be explored. These, nevertheless, will be associated with theorists from other disciplines, so as to provoke a dialogic relation between diverse disciplines and media through analysis. It is hoped that this — perhaps unconventional — approach will serve to turn the theory, not only into a framework for the text, but also to turn the text into a space where theory can bounce off theory. Moreover, culture viewed through 'double-frames' becomes in-between and inconclusive. Community, in this light, is liminal, in constant emergence.

Not surprisingly, this study will aim to be open-ended: if cultural analysis is to be effective, then it must track culture's own reinventiveness.

1. Here I am borrowing Walter Ong's term, bearing in mind the distinctions he makes between primary orality as localized forms of narrative transmission and secondary orality, which is reliant upon technology for its transmission, as delocalized and a byproduct of modernity's emphasis upon technology.
2. My use of the term 'essentialism' or 'essentialized' denotes an ahistorical and closed stance that occludes dialogue or negotiation.

CHAPTER 1

COMMUNITY THEORIZED

No doubt it would be worthwhile to attempt a base definition of 'community' as currently in use, so as to establish a clear starting point for this research project. However, it is important to bear in mind that the term 'community' has long defied explicit definition in modern usage and a clear starting point thereby becomes problematic in itself. For this very reason, and because the commonly-shared premodern connotations of the term endow it with a solid sense of location whereby it has often provided a firm field of research in the social sciences, it has long been the focus of attention of numerous researchers in anthropology, sociology, and philosophy. Widely used, frequently invoked and almost always elusive, 'community' has received numerous, often contradictory, definitions over the past decades.

Perhaps, as a starting point for this project, it would be useful to turn to Nigel Rapport and Joanna Overing's section on community in their book *Social and Cultural Anthropology: The Key Concepts* (2000: 60–65), where they begin by referring to Robert Redfield's work, *The Little Community, and Peasant Society and Culture* (1960):

Among the more renowned attempts [to define community] remains that of Robert Redfield (1960:4), who identified four key qualities in community: a smallness of scale; a homogeneity of activities and states of mind of members; a self-sufficiency across a broad range of needs and through time; and a consciousness of distinctiveness. (2000: 60)

The title and date of Redfield's work almost immediately locate his definition as relevant to localized, perhaps rural, communities, linking it more to premodern connotations of the term and structuralist understandings of culture than to any present-day connotations. Clearly, Redfield views community as dependant upon stability of space and linearity of time, bounded by a common belief among members in what makes them different or separate. As I hope the following sections will show, each of the qualities that Redfield highlights in 'community' has been rendered problematic by shifts in contemporary culture, forcing attention onto the underlying processes of modernity which have so irrevocably shaken the certainties of space and time.

1. MODERNITY/POSTMODERNITY

This exploration of community identity rests on the notion that postmodernity should be viewed not as a break with modernity or as a historical sequel to it, but rather as an accelerated complication of the latter's motley encounters with tradition, in other words, as the cultural climate of late capitalism. Furthermore, and very importantly in the Spanish context, the uneven spread of modernity leads to the coexistence of modernity and postmodernity in the same time-frames, giving rise to hybridity and plurality resulting from encounters with alterity. Equally, the impetus for such ambivalence can be found in modernity's focus on social progress, a key feature of which is the inevitability of displacement. Viewed in temporal and spatial terms, the experience of modernity as travel brings with it fragmentation, a process that is more readily associated with postmodernity. Quoting Marx's statement that being modern means living in a world where 'all that is solid melts into air' (1982: 15), Marshall Berman, in his seminal work on modernity of that title, describes modernity in the following way:

The maelstrom of modern life has been fed from many sources: great discoveries in the physical sciences, changing our images of the universe and our place in it; the industrialization of production, which transforms scientific knowledge into technology, creates new human environments and destroys old ones, speeds up the whole tempo of life, generates new forms of corporate power and class struggle; immense demographic upheavals, severing millions of people from their natural habitats, hurtling them half-way across the world into new lives. . . (1982: 16)

The unmistakeable emphasis here is on modernity as change or transformation, modernity as movement and upheaval. Also worth noting is Berman's statement that modernity speeds up the 'tempo of life', bringing destruction in its wake at the same time as it forges new ground. For Berman, therefore, modernity is experienced as contradiction, a paradoxical coexistence of disintegration and renewal, rootless uncertainties and the driving need to make oneself at home:

The process of modernization, even as it exploits and torments us, brings our energies and imaginations to life, drives us to grasp and confront the world that modernization makes, and to strive to make it our own. I believe that we and those who come after us will go on fighting to make ourselves at home in this world, even as the homes we have made, the modern street, the modern spirit, go on melting into air. (1982: 348)

Berman's exploration of modernism and modernization as the twin processes of modernity highlights the activation brought on by the latter to the imagination. In particular, he states that the modernist engages in the imagination of the past as a way of refiguring the present, constructing newness from ghosts. Yet, modernity's project of social progress entails a discursive disavowal of the past, one that refuses to acknowledge the many reworkings of memories and past traces that fuel the very processes of modernity:

If modernism ever managed to throw off its scraps and tatters and the uneasy joints that bind it to the past, it would lose all its weightand depth, and the maelstrom of modern life would carry it helplessly away. It is only by keeping alive the bonds that tie it to the modernities the past — bonds at once intimate and antagonistic — that it can help the moderns of the present and the future to be free. (1982: 346)

The complex and contradictory process of modernity as at once a distancing from the past and an effort of approximation to the past is brought to light when Berman's above statement is juxtaposed with Leo Strauss's claim that:

Modernity started from the dissatisfaction with the gulf between the is and the ought, the actual and the ideal (1975: 91)[1]

Central to modernity, then, is the ambiguity which is derived from the juxtaposition or coexistence of a repudiation of the present as the result of history and the nostalgia for the same. Implicit here is the restlessness that is central to modern identities, a mobility that speaks both of searching for lost pasts and for new, better ways of being. A chief characteristic of modernity, then, is mobility accompanied by the contingency that leads to ambivalences.

The notion of contingency is not conventionally associated with modernity. Indeed, the generally accepted view is that modernity replaced ecclesiastical authority with scientific certainties. The normalizing discourses of modernity which seek to separate and categorize cultural and other spheres, such as science, art, morality, law, etc. can, however, also be viewed as expressions of the fragmentation inherent to modernity.[2] At the same time, they can be read as attempts to construct stability and order in unstable and mobile contexts. Modernity's totalizing drive and the metanarratives that it puts forth, as analysed by Foucault and Lyotard, must then be considered in the light of modernity experienced increasingly as both promise and crisis. The postulation of unities, therefore, results more from abstract or imagined systems of meaning for the moderns rather than from lived experience, which confronts the struggle for knowledge with its limits. Indeed, the contingency of modern life arises from the fragmentation of temporal and spatial frameworks and hence from the splitting of unities. Furthermore, such fragmentation increases the divide between imagined unities and dispersed realities, challenging the bases upon which discourses of knowledge are constructed.

As Gerard Delanty argues, strong resonances of postmodernity can therefore be found in modernity. By viewing postmodernity as a continuation of the modern project, Delanty stresses that postmodernity is not a break with modernity, but rather 'a deepening of the reflexive and sceptical moment of the modern itself' (2000: 5). Delanty also argues that modern discourses of self and power establish limits and possibilities for the self, constructing identity through doctrines of self-determination which nevertheless are affirmed by reference to the Other:

The modern quest for identity and community can be seen as the medium by which self and other are actualized. The self receives its affirmation of identity only by reference to an unknowable other, be it God, exotic or primitive peoples, nature, a myth or primordial origins, adversaries of war, the mad, the poor, criminals. For modernity, this was a project of mastery, for self-determination was also a project of determination of the Other. (2000: 3)

He goes on to state that postmodernity should be viewed, not in terms of a rupture with modernity, but in terms of a shift in the prioritization of Self over Other, whereby the foregrounding of the latter leads to increased historical preoccupations, reflexivity and the preoccupation with the past that is less readily associated with modernity:

If the Holocaust marked the culmination of the modern quest for mastery and the determination of the Other by the self, postmodernity as a post-colonial and post-Holocaust discourse forces us to see the self through the eyes of the Other. In this reversal in the priority of Self and Other, subjectivity is reconstituted around a new responsibility for history and nature. (2000: 3)

These shifts in the constitution of subjectivity can be translated at communal level in terms of a shift of emphasis from society to community. Thus, modernity's insistence upon nationhood and society, as opposed to the imagined premodern groupings of community in the 'organic' sense,[3] alters with the reflexivity brought on by awareness of contingency. Indeed, postmodernity can perhaps be considered as a stage of evolved reflexivity resulting from the awareness of the impossibility of modernity's attempts to establish wholeness or unity. The ensuing focus on the particular, the urge to rescue the fragments of identity before they are dispersed, turns the postmodern stress onto community as a new form of citizenship which allows for the contingent and the fragmented. Despite the scatterings of postmodernity, the imagination of community then overtakes modernity's focus on the national or the social; unlike the modern nation, however, postmodern communities must be imagined as incomplete, open-ended, and contested. Furthermore, these communities can be imagined in multiple ways and along diverse planes. Elaborated out of plural and differential identities, postmodern communities offer positions in increasingly mediated local and global spaces.

Over twenty years ago, Raymond Williams wrote in his *Keywords* that since the nineteenth century, a polarity has been established between community and society. While community was viewed as immediate and constructed out of direct relationships, society emerged from structured or organized relations. This binary can no longer be so clearly applied to the two notions, nor can they be so easily separated. Membership of society can no longer be said to eclipse community; indeed, any society could be said to consist of overlapping and shifting communities. In the last decade alone, the accessibility and connectivity afforded by the world wide web, the sharp acceleration of globalization and increased transnational flows of capital and human resources foreground community as a key feature of a fast-expanding supra-societal and global imaginary: to quote John Tomlinson, 'To discuss globalization, then, is inevitably to engage with the discourse of modernity' (1999: 32). Community refigured through multi-dimensional configurations emerges as a central aspect of this globalized late modernity.

GLOBALIZATION

The concept of community as explored in this book, therefore, relies to a large extent on an understanding of globalization as a key feature of accelerated modernity/postmodernity. Jan Aart Scholte states that there is widespread confusion regarding the exact meaning of the word 'globalization' and argues that there are five broad definitions of this term that should provide a basis for understanding. Firstly, globalization can be perceived as cross-border relations between countries, leading to situations of exchange and interdependence. Secondly, the term also refers to the removal of:

government-imposed restrictions on movements between countries in order to create an 'open', 'borderless' world economy [. . .] Evidence for such 'globalization' in recent decades can be found in the widespread reduction or even abolition of regulatory trade barriers, foreign-exchange restrictions, capital controls and (for certain citizens) visas. (2000: 16)

This point is of obvious relevance when considering Spain's membership of the European Union, whereby Europeanization takes on the shape of localized (i.e. Europe-wide) 'globalization' in an effort to construct and fortify a continental identity. Thirdly, Scholte states that globalization has been equated with universalization, whereby cultures synthesize to produce a hybrid but universal cultural experience. Clearly, this view is problematic simply because it oversimplifies the contingencies of local contexts by regarding globalization as a homogenizing process. In fourth place, he argues that globalization can be understood as Americanization or Westernization, whereby the structures of modernity are spread across the globe, destroying local cultures and, with this, the ability of non-Western cultures to exist independently: 'globalization in this sense is sometimes described as an imperialism of McDonald's, Hollywood and CNN' (2000: 16).[4] Equally, this view too is problematic since it has been argued that globalization decentres the West through its emphasis on connectivity (Tomlinson 1999: 92)[5]. In fifth place, Scholte states that globalization can be equated with deterritorialization or, to use his term, 'supraterritoriality' (2000: 16). In this sense, globalization alters conventional links between communities and geographical zones, no longer mapping community or society in terms of space. This shift away from spatial contours challenges and overcomes the traditional roles of borders, frontiers, and other forms of enclosing identity within given terrains or fields.

It is also clear that globalization is closely linked with growing consumerism and reliance upon technology. As such, it is both the result of the acceleration of late modernity and a key contributor to this acceleration. In this context, globalization is often linked to increased fragmentation at sub-national and transnational levels, causing ethnic groups and other particularisms to champion their causes in increasingly multicultural societies across the globe. Thus, while viewed as homogenizing in terms of patterns of commodities and consumption, globalization equally causes particularisms, often constructed in essentialized terms, to rise to the fore. The relevance of globalization to a contemporary analysis of community identities (the plural here being particularly apt in the given context) lies in this phenomenon. Collective affiliations become central consequences of globalization, turning community into a social imperative, but fundamentally altering its conventional patterns. Furthermore, these new emerging communities pose challenges to national sovereignty, depriving the latter of any absolute totalizing powers. Not until the spread of globalization in the latter half of the twentieth century did community pose a threat to nation. Up to this point in time, collective or communal identities were generally accepted as subservient to national affiliation, turning the latter into what Rupert Emerson called 'the terminal community' (1960: 95). The subsequent acceleration of modernity, however, together with the increasing accessibility of technologies of transnational communication, has dislodged community from the confines of national territory, forcing nations to confront their inability to function as ultimate communities through acknowledgement and acceptance of nonterritorial transworld communities.

Clearly, globalization shifts the problems to be considered in community analysis, problematizing links between communal affiliations and space, forcing issues of locality and culture to be reexamined. The absolute salience of locality diminishes with globalization, but nevertheless, the latter does not translate into any definitive rupture with space as the trope of identity. In this sense, while globalization vastly extends possibilities for communities, it does not necessarily imply a severance with spatial dimensions. Rather, globalization problematizes the spatial, causing it to be the focus of reflexivity, altering the essentialism conventionally assigned to land, place or landscape. In a chapter titled 'Spacializing Feminism: Geographic Perspectives', Linda McDowell makes the following statement:

In these postmodern, post-positivist, self-reflexive times, when ideas about positionality, location, borders and margins are the hot words on the lips of every social and feminist theorist. . .it may seem curious to be writing about the need to spatialize feminism or feminist theory. (1996: 28)

This attempt to construct the spatial through theorizing perhaps illustrates a growing preoccupation with detachment from locality. Equally, the process of globalization entails changes to the local brought on by links with afar, thus altering land or landscape as a stable, unchanging and defining feature of communal identity. Anthony Giddens states that:

Globalization concerns the intersection of presence and absence, the interlacing of social events and social relations 'at distance' with local contextualities. We should grasp the global spread modernity in terms of an ongoing relation between distanciation and the chronic mutability of local circumstances and local engage-ments. (1991: 21–22)

By establishing definitions of globalization that focus on the abstract through terms such as 'absence/presence', etc., Giddens highlights the time–space problematic of this phenomenon. For Giddens, modernity is inherently a process whereby spatial dimensions are increasingly disembedded from place, conceived instead in symbolic terms and abstract, imagined relations. Stating that 'the widespread use of mechanical timing devices facilitated, but also presumed, deeply structured changes in the tissue of everyday life' (1991: 71), Giddens points to modernity's major disruption of pre-modern chronotopes with the subsequent construction of an imagined global temporality that coincides with varying degrees of independence from spatial moorings.

The complex connectivity that accompanies globalized modernity, neverthe-less, does not detract from the urge to 'make oneself at home in the modern world', as Berman notes. Giddens argues that modernity should equally be viewed in this light, exploring the drive to 're-embed', or to construct roots — be it through discourse or practice — against the onslaught of mobility, as a condition of modernity. Thus for the moderns, mobility, on the one hand, is accompanied by the need to construct 'essentials' as a way of countering the fragmentation brought on by travel and abstract connections. The attempts at 're-embedding', then, can be read in the light of modernity's increasing experience of deterritorialization, a process whereby place–culture relationships are shifted through globalization.

DETERRITORIALIZATION

In his chapter on deterritorialization, Tomlinson (1999) borrows Néstor García Canclini's definition of this term as 'the loss of the "natural" relationship of culture to geographical and social territories' (1999: 107). In addition, we should note Giddens's development of the modern relationship with place as 'phantas-magoric' or abstract, imagined, reconstructed, and free from reliance upon face-to-face interaction between people within the confinement of given settings. As Gisela Brinker-Gabler states, deterritorialization can be understood in its many strands as a complex process whereby boundaries of all sorts, those of land

serving here as metaphors, are shifting, porous, and mediated, rendering identity
ambivalent and poised for change, though desiring or invoking stability:

Negotiating rupture, marginalization and differing communities destabilizes subject
positions and creates various new shifting sites: the exile and the immigrant, the
resistant re/unified subject who transcends the new unity by creating an alternative
community and the ambivalent re/unified subject who constantly crosses borders,
traversing boundaries. (1997: 288)[6]

The ambivalence experienced through globalized cultural conditions manifests
itself in diverse ways, an example being the influence of increasingly abstract or
distanciated forces or entities on local places, such as the arrival of chain stores
selling the same stock, decided upon in far away locations, to diverse
neighbourhoods or the links made possible to remote parts of the world by
connection to the internet. Established contrasts between proximity and distance
thereby alter, destabilizing the binaries that have offered structure to knowledge
and identity and placing ambivalence onto the latter. Indeed, it is possible to
argue that globalization affects these former categories not just through its
mobilization en masse of people and capital, but also because of the alterations
it brings to locales. With culture lived as movement, stable, 'essentialized' places
are turned into wayside stops, routes of passage, points on a larger itinerary of
impermanence. Furthermore, the extensive grip of capitalism across the globe,
the imprint of transnational corporations on particular spaces threatens to turn
these into non-distinct points which all appear much the same as one another.
The loss of particularity thus is unsurprisingly a major area of debate for
theorists of globalization. However, as Tomlinson points out, such globalized
modernity layers itself over and around the daily interactions of locals with one
another and with place: 'real places and non-places intertwine and tangle
together in modern societies' (1999: 111). New technologies, for example, such
as the mobile phone or cable television, allow local communities greater intra-
connectivities as well as opening them up to contact and influences from
elsewhere. Equally, established cultural practices may continue in the midst of
these changes. The ensuing plurality allows populations of local spaces the
ability to imagine and construct through a variety of practices participation in
local and trans-locale affiliations. Furthermore, it should be borne in mind that
the extent to which this is possible or practised will inevitably vary both
according to contextual contingencies and the shared histories, cultural memories, and communal practices of various points on the globe, not to mention their
varying positions in the global economic hegemonies. Deterritorialization, thus,
implies a complex form of interaction between different levels or paces of
modernity, unevenly spread across the globe and experienced to differing degrees
in different places. The unevenness of this process, its local variations and
constructions point to the relevance of theories of hybridity to an understanding
of globalization. The disengagement from land as the defining trope of

communal identity translates, therefore, not merely to movement away from 'origins' or landscape but also to the attempts to construct or imagine 'origins', i.e. essentialisms, mapped onto multiple, many-dimensional 'scapes' through incomplete, hybrid mediations.

Hybridity

Temporal intersections and connections, together with spatial dislocations and cross-locations, which challenge conventional discourses of modernity as the end-point of a continuous and linear social development are present in the earlier mentioned work of Néstor García Canclini, whose work on hybridity is central to an understanding of uneven experiences globalization. By theorizing the concept of hybridity, Canclini illustrates the coexistence in Latin America of traditions from the past and an unevenly spread modernity. By locating Latin America in this hybrid, or in-between space, Canclini precludes any linear vision of cultural processes. Tradition, as cultural memory which persists via practices in the present, interacts in complex ways with the modern, as constructed by nations, to produce a globalized modernity where specific cultures and places are ambiguously located. The traditional, therefore, is resignified in its journeys across contexts, particularly in the light of mass migration to urban centres. In this way, narratives or practices of memory are both kept alive across time and space and updated to new callings. The concept of hybridity, therefore, is central to experiences of deterritorialization, and culture itself becomes border-line. In his descriptions of the border town of Tijuana, Canclini names it both as a place of transit, intersections, and marginality and a modern, cosmopolitan city with a strongly defined identity. The fusion of the local with what lies outside the borders gives rise to cultural identity, so that, as Canclini states,'the hybridizations described [. . .] bring us to the conclusion that today all cultures are border cultures' (1995: 261). Furthermore, he goes on to state that:

There is yet another way in which the obliquity of the symbolic circuits allows us to rethink the links between culture and power. The search for mediations and diagonal ways for managing conflicts gives cultural relations a prominent place in political development. (1995: 261)

The possibilities opened up by hybridity in terms of empowerment must rely, then, on the traditional as cultural memory being resignified through its interaction with modernity across contexts. Indeed, as Pnina Werbner states in her introduction to *Debating Cultural Hybridity* (1997), the concept of hybridity is itself the result of the theoretical shift from modernity to postmodernity, the formulation of which denotes the self-reflexivity and precarious identities of ambivalent late modernity. Canclini avails of this move in theory to state with hindsight that, in fact, 'for being the land of pastiche and bricolage [i.e. Latin America], where many periods and aesthetics are cited, we have had the pride of being postmodern for centuries' (1995: 6). In this sense, hybridity results from the embrace of the traditional together with the modern in all its guises, an embrace which also rise to the postmodern. What is more, these are not seen as opposed positions or as successive stages in culture, but as co-existing and mutually implicated, despite inherent contradictions.

In the conclusion to his chapter on deterritorialization, Tomlinson argues that this latter concept cannot be considered without also calling forth the concept of reterritorialization. He juxtaposes the mobility asigned to modernity with the driving urge to rebuild 'home' elsewhere, to appropriate and to embed. The ambivalence and uncertainties of modernity's migratory experiences render modern subjects vulnerable to temporal and spatial shifts, precarious in their daily survivals. Furthermore, the attempt to reterritorialize must entail degrees of compromises in and adaptations to identity, so that hybridity becomes a feature of complex, contemporary modern existence. In a similar vein, Homi Bhabha too underlines the provisionality of today's living:

[. . .] anxiety is created by enjoining the local and the global; the dilemma of projecting an international space on the trace of a decentred, fragmented subject. Cultural globality is figured in the *in-between* spaces of double frames: its historical originality marked by a cognitive obscurity; its decentred 'subject' signified in the nervous temporality of the trans-national, or the emergent provisionality of the'present'. (1994: 216)

Bearing in mind this notion that modernity and postmodernity are intertwined, double-framed in complex ways through processes of globalization, this statement underlines the ambivalence of identity and some of the tensions as regards space and time that girdle constructions of community in the contemporary age. While the question of belonging becomes ever more poignant with deterritorialization, hybridity, embraced as a strategy of empowerment, offers new avenues for the construction of a communal self. Conventional models provided by the nation-state and citizenship no longer being sufficient to encompass communal identity, cultural belonging becomes conceived along diverse scapes, mapped in the imagination onto abstract affiliations.

DIVERSE ETHNOSCAPES

The destabilization of the self and other unities that has taken place in the course of modernity, and that has accelerated hugely in recent years through globalization, requires the very notion of land or body to be refigured. In this sense, and as stated by Tomlinson above, it is not that space can be dispensed with, but rather that notions of space themselves have to be reinvented. Such re-imagination foregrounds the abstract, turning cultural invention into a key form of updating cultural practice to changing tempos of mobility. Writing on global modernity, Arjun Appadurai states that:

By ethnoscape, I mean the landscape of persons who constitute the shifting world in which we live: tourists, immigrants, refugees, exiles, guest workers and other moving groups and persons constitute the essential feature of the world, and appear to affect the politics of and between nations to a hitherto unprecedented degree. This is not to say that there are not anywhere any relatively stable communities and networks, of kinship, friendship, of work and of leisure, as well as of birth, residence and other filiative forms. But this is to say that the warp of these stabilities is everywhere shot through with the woof of human motion, as more persons and groups deal with the realities of having to move, or the fantasies of wanting to move. (1990: 297)

What becomes clear from the above is that the construction of practiced, experiential spaces is matched by that of invented, discursive spaces. If, as Michel de Certeau has said, 'space is a practiced place' (1986: 117), then boundaries between the practiced and the imagined have blurred, rendering space abstract and overlapping cultural practice with cultural imagination. While mobility and connectivity are conventionally accepted as necessary features of modernity, globalization challenges the notion that movements or links can be unilineal and finite merely through offering web-like extensions of communal affiliations. Furthermore, the uncertainties of identities and positions throw up sites of contestations that turn community into a form of empowerment. The question of power relies inevitably on the construction of discourses and narratives which attempt territorialization as a means to stability.

Given the diverse planes or scapes along which community is now inclined to build itself, it is not surprising to find that the unity until recently assigned to the nation-state is hugely undermined. No longer reliant on the nation as a definer of the limits of identity or as a marker of the boundaries of the playing field, the quest for empowerment embraces hybrid encounters with alterity that exceed the national as routes of travel and engagement with the other. The result is that the concept of citizenship, formerly limited to the nation-state, now exceeds the latter and the imagined belonging that is inherent to it becomes equally applicable to cross- and supra-territorial, discursively invented communities.

COMMUNITY AND CITIZENSHIP

These changes that have come to the fore on a worldwide scale in the late twentieth century require new understandings of the notion of citizenship. From the seventeenth century onwards, the concept of citizenship has been linked inextricably with the emergence of the nation-state in the Western world. As such, it was a European concept that was transported in past centuries to colonized parts of the globe and has undergone changes in the course of modernity's evolutions. The growing transnational mobility of people and capital, the heterogeneity of cultural values and practices, the hybrid products of encounters between formerly unified categories leads to the erosion of the boundaries of the nation-state and to multi-layered allegiances to diverse collective identities. As Stephen Castles and Alistair Davidson state:

Globalization, the increased mobility of people and the burgeoning of new forms of communication make myths of homogeneity unsustainable. Cultural diversity has become a feature of virtually all modern societies. Assimilation is no longer an option because of the rapidity and multidirectionality of mobility and communication [. . .] Answers to the question 'Who is a citizen?' are becoming increasingly difficult. (2000: 127)

The very challenges that the nation-state is facing in contemporary times, most explicitly in democratic societies, forces a refiguring of the concept of citizenship, even as this notion becomes all the more relevant in shifting and fluid environments. In the context of community identities, the present crisis in citizenship poses both ambiguities and possibilities. Nevertheless, as stated earlier, the weakening of the nation's borders does not translate into a complete erosion of the nation as a functioning unit. Importantly, and despite internal and external contradictions, the nation-state continues to function as a community, despite major adaptations to cultural, political, and economic fluxes. In the context of postmodernity, nation-states have increasingly to take into account the diverse processes of community that traverse them, increasing the porosity of borders so that individuals and collectives may reconstitute themselves as new cultural and political actors in Western democratic societies. In the context of Spain, this point is stressed by Jo Labanyi when she states that:

The Spanish nation-state may have been eroded but it is not under threat, precisely because contemporary Spaniards do not have to renounce to their Spanishness to be simultaneously cosmopolitan and (say) Aragonese. What has been done to death — through parodic repetition — is the concept of a unified national identity that politicians and writers — originally liberal, subsequently reactionary — have attempted to impose since the Romantic period. (1995: 405)

These processes of change affecting the notion of postmodern citizenship, which include features of globalization such as deterritorialization, the urge to refigure or invent 'home', the construction of new ethnic, religious, or gender groups, the mobilization of politics and culture, offer new forms of consciousness and identity in the quest for empowerment. Through tactics of full or partial exclusion, they construct political and cultural discourses that may well seem at variance with the interests of a unified nation-state. At the same time, and as explained by the above quote, by allowing their borders varying degrees of porosity, by imagining new forms of citizenship and by adapting to global shifts and contingencies, nations too survive by meeting the challenges of complex, supra-national connections with imagination and flexibility.

As the self-reflexivity of late modernity questions and deconstructs apparent unities, as our sense of place as stable and of time as lasting is turned into imaginary fragments, community transcends nation-state and society, offering solidarity and identity to dispersed collectives in non-hierarchical ways not offered by nations in their roles as imagined communities. Nevertheless, community within a globalized framework must — unlike its pre-modern manifestations — be mobile, nomadic, and often lived 'virtually', given the overall cultural and socio-economic contexts produced by globalization. Equally, discourses of community identity share with those of nation the rhetoric of essentialisms and the fantasy of stability. Like the discourse of nation, community identity is constructed at collective level from a shared imagination of the past and a shared project for the future, presenting the impression of temporal durability and attachment to place. Theories of citizenship or belonging cannot function outside of the concept of community, for the former implies at a most basic level membership of a political community. At the same time, all collective groups or communities are bonded most significantly by the drive for political empowerment, although their politics may not be organized according to national structures. It is primarily in this political sense that a post-national concept of citizenship via community can be developed. Equally, conventional associations of unity, immediacy, and place that are associated with community can undermine globalized post-national citizenship, highlighting its propensity for dispersal.

The structuralist view of identity as difference persists, nevertheless, in postmodernist constructions of community as a key feature of imagining community affiliation. Thus, while practices of community may be open-ended, the impetus of modernist discourse to anchor identity through discourses of differentiation can be discerned through lingering notions of community as entire, integrated, and fenced. Equally pertinent as concepts such as deterritorialization and hybridity to contemporary configurations of community is the myth of community as synonymous with integrity, in both a moral and a physical sense. This myth, constantly challenged by the mobile tactics of survival practised by identity at the level of community, can be traced in its narrative trajectory to religious discourse and almost certainly has its origins there, rather than in any history of premodern times.

COMMUNITY AS MYTH

A tension was noted earlier in this chapter between community and society in the discourses of modernity, whereby the binary opposition between tradition and modernity translates itself into the dualism of community and society. In *Modernity and Postmodernity*, Gerard Delanty describes conventional polarizations of community and society, stating that:

Communities are culturally integrated totalities while society is essentially defined by its parts. Tönnies largely regretted the passing of community — the world of the village and the rural community — and the arrival of society — the world of the city — believing that community could supply the individual with greater moral resources. The idea of community thus suggests a strong sense of place, proximity, totality, while society suggests fragmentation, alienation and distance. (2000: 116)

Not surprisingly, this exoticized, moralistic view of community was also constructed through anthropological discourse, whose modern, colonial perspective on 'primitive' cultures otherized them as holistic, organic totalities. In many ways, this myth of the ideal community speaks of a gathering of individuals, prioritizing the group and establishing defined boundaries through shared values, narratives, and practices. Furthermore, anthropology's colonial position placed community on the margins of modernity, rooting it in place and availing of its essentialisms and cohesion in such a way as to underline modernity's ruptures and fragmentations. The common moral order assigned to the myth of community, its cohesion and the vision of totality that it offers have served, in opposition to society, as an inspiration to modern ideologies and political discourses. To quote Delanty:

Community implies: (1) solidarity, in the sense of a feeling of togetherness, a feeling of collectivity and mutual attachments; (2) trust, as opposed to the secrecy and distance that characterized life in the social; and (3) autonomy, in that community involves the recognition of the value of the person as a social being. (2000: 118)

The imagined polarity between community as solidarity and society as fragmentation or distance begs probing. Bearing in mind the earlier cited work by Berman (as well as Gidden's and Walter Benjamin's theories of the modern city as phantasmagoric), it could be asserted that modernity's idealized memory of community as belonging to a past that is 'beyond' reach expresses the struggle to find temporal anchor in the midst of maelstrom. Clearly, the very demarcations established by modernity's discourses on society also point to the implications of the myth of community as organic entity in the fragmentation of the social fabric. While the development of both concepts of community and society can be located in the historical context of modernity, it is the role of the myth of community in society's own mobilities that provokes curiosity. Modern sociological theory assigned community to the past, yet continued to dwell in the imagination of community in terms of an ideal, unified nation-state and the concept of citizenship. Society, therefore, fell within the confines of a larger community, itself conceived in terms of the nation. In an ironic turn, however, late modernity's dissatisfaction with national confines and the possibilities for identity construction posed by postmodernity once again prioritize community, both because it empowers subjects and offers emotive force through the myth of essentials and because it is a project that foregrounds the particular and the contingent.

THE ORGANIC COMMUNITY

In order to refigure the concept of community identity in the context of postmodernity, it is firstly necessary to clarify the basic tenets of organic or holistic notions of community, so that the myth of community as it persists in the postmodern imaginary may be better understood. Nostalgia for wholeness and the imagination of lost unity is not unusual in Judeo-Christian cultures. The Biblical origins of such imaginings lie clearly in the story of exile from Paradise. Indeed, the myth of community as evoked in many a politician's ideologically-fired rhetoric[7] can be linked to religious evocations of the human condition as exile and, as such, deterritorialization or displacement. Also Biblical in origin is the equation of community with shared morality or integrity, an equation that features largely in perceptions of community as pre-modern or traditional. Furthermore, modernism's construction of community as an 'imagined and holistic past' that preceded it also parallels the nostalgic memory of Paradise pieced together in hindsight after the irreversible experience of rupture. Both visions of totality, whether religious or secular, require community as a concept to be connected to a defined 'place', be it Paradise or the rural village. They also depend on a linear experience of time, whereby the lost wholeness belongs to a past that can only be recalled through memory and regained in its totality at the end of the trajectory to either salvation or utopia. The lived experience of modernity as movement and fragmentation understandably assigned community to the pre-modern past. The spatial and temporal fluxes of postmodernity, however, complicate this view of community, as the past is now juxtaposed and synchronic with the present. Community thereby becomes foregrounded, but clouded in ambiguities.

Theorists of community have attempted to write community into modernity, providing guidelines for its successful construction. Perhaps the best known communitarian is Amitai Etzioni, whose book *The Spirit of Community* (1995) is a vigorous attempt to reinscribe community into social and cultural practice. Etzioni presents community in terms of immediacy or closeness, best expressed through the assumption of social responsibility that exceeds the individual. Etzioni writes of 'virtues' and 'values', his work presenting a clear dichotomy between good and bad. His chapters dedicated to the family and the school as the sites where these virtues and values are best developed highlight the importance of the communalizing process, whereby individuals acquire communitarian values. Furthermore, Etzioni offers a series of practical steps whereby community at various levels — but always envisioned in terms of totality — can form, not least of which being a daily gathering around the dinner table or going for counselling before marrying:

There are, however, ways to encourage young people to enter marriage more responsibly, help sustain and enrich those marriages that are in place, and at the same time reflect the moral voice of the community that marriages are not to be treated as disposable relations. (1995: 78)

The above quote makes it all too clear that, for Etzioni, community is perceived in terms of morality and, as such, his notion fits with the traditional imagination of ideal community. While he repeatedly attempts to take into account irreversible changes from pre-modern times, such as the predominance of urban living, as opposed to rural life, or the triggers of modern capitalist structures, nevertheless, he cannot move beyond a vision of community as morally cohesive totality:

The local community? The national community? . . .communities are best viewed as if they were Chinese nesting boxes, in which less encompassing communities. . .are nestled within more encompassing ones. . .which in turn are situated within still more encompassing ones, the national and cross-national ones [. . . Moreover, there is room for non-geographic communities that criss-cross the others, such as professional or work-based communities.When they are intact, they are all relevant, and all lay moral claims on us by appealing to and reinforcing our values.(1995: 32)

The picture is cosy: community as a nestling box offers emotional security and guaranteed 'belonging'. Furthermore, the moral voice that binds it makes sure that all is 'good' or 'right' and provides clear boundaries and opposition with what is 'bad' or 'wrong'. Despite trying to update community to modernity, Etzioni relies almost entirely on a holistic view of it that echoes the conventional myth of community. There are no obvious provisions here for encounters with alterity, no questioning of the relevance of morality to a steeply inclined, globalized capitalism. Nor is there any obvious understanding of the temporal fragmentation that accompanies postmodernity.

Etzioni's views are interesting, not because of any originality, but because of the fuel they provide to normalizing discourses. Perhaps their most obvious weakness lies in the persistent reliance upon shared morality, a reliance that carries recognizable religious overtones. The question surely arises as to the very feasibility of a common morality within postmodernity. Temporal and spatial fragmentation disperses even the abiding quest or longing for a lost cohesiveness. It also scatters the possibility of a binding morality, foregrounding instead ambivalence and contingency. While the myth of totality may continue to inspire the postmodern imaginary, nevertheless, postmodernist cultural narratives and practices of community must surely come to terms with their incompleteness and malleabilities. Morality, then, cannot be considered a source of cohesion, since postmodernity, by its very definition, confers the plural onto this concept.

The Spanish context is perhaps exemplary of the postmodernist eclipse of society and spotlight on community. It is also exemplary of the impossibility of community as totality or cohesive unit. By dispensing with the notion of moral integrity from community and by incorporating into it instead a flexible concept of citizenship that extends across regional and other circuits, community is turned web-like, a prime vehicle for postmodern cultural politics, denoting cleavage as well as complex interaction. In this sense, an analysis of the contemporary Spanish resurgence of community, viewed through cultural narratives and practices, constructs a place for it not in a local or national imaginary, but in a shifting, unreliable transnational and global reality. Furthermore, the importance of community shifts, thereby, from an imagined longing which, by its very definitions, is unrealizable to diverse, open-ended discourses and practices.

COMMUNITY AS PRAXIS

The two-way relationship between practice and myth can perhaps best be explored in the context of community through an understanding of how this refigured and flexible concept of multi-sited and transnational citizenship functions. Cohen (*The Symbolic Construction of Community,* 1985) insists that while community is imagined, it is nevertheless not imaginary. By viewing community as a symbolic structure, Cohen argues that imagining community translates into an awareness of boundaries, itself necessarily an awareness of contact or overlap between Self and Other. This notion whereby the symbolic only derives significance from relation with and against other symbols has been strongly pursued by French sociologists. In particular, the work of Pierre Bourdieu, more detailed in Chapter 4 of this thesis, stresses the mutual reciprocity of signification through relationships of similarity and difference between individuals and groups that are necessarily sited, i.e., embodied, and temporally defined. Bourdieu's relational theories are best expressed in his development of the concepts of habitus, field, and practice which focus on an ongoing two-way relationship between the objective structures of social fields and the embodied field of the habitus as it engages in everyday practices. By viewing identity as relational, in other words, by considering the Self in the light of its differences from as well as its negotiations and conflicts with the Other, identity is seen to be contextually contingent. Indeed, in his *Practical Reason,* Bourdieu elaborates upon his notion of *distinction,* stating that it 'is nothing other than *difference*, a gap, a distinctive feature, in short, a *relational* property existing only in and through its relation with other properties' (1998: 6). Clearly, Bourdieu is stating here that difference itself is a mask for relation, and vice-versa. This double-layered approach to binaries may serve to illuminate the problems of defining community.

While community identity, viewed as difference, can be thought of in terms of appropriation and embodiment of borders and *space* (or, increasingly in postmodern contexts, *scapes*), it is important to bear in mind that such spatial constructions require mediation, whether these be in terms of capital or empowerment. Equally, the myths of community as essentialized and holistic serve to reinforce what Bourdieu terms the habitus, reifying community whilst, as modes of *distinction,* also serving as a means of mediation with a larger context of spatial and temporal contingencies. It is not surprising, therefore, to find — as the analysis of prison practices of rehabilitation will show — that the myths of community are often divergent from the practices of community. It can be argued that it is through this very divergence of narrative or myth (viewed as the structures that give shape to a collective imaginary) and lived practice — a divergence or difference that can also be viewed as relation — that community identities derive their mobility and their abilities to refigure themselves by cutting across space and time.

COMMUNITY IN SPAIN

The end of the transition to democracy in Spain in 1982, with the establishment of autonomous regional communities whose cultural discourses aim to refigure local identities, was followed not long after by Spain's integration into the European Community. Alignment with Europe had required not only rapid economic acceleration, but had also triggered major cultural shifts. In their article titled 'The Politics of 1992', Sánchez and Graham stress the cultural confusions and upheavals experienced with the speed of change, turning Spain's experiences into a microcosm of global postmodernity. Indeed, they underline what they call 'the confused (and confusing) hybridity' (Graham and Sanchez: 408) that results from the amalgamation of the modern with the postmodern. The uneven modernity in Spain of the early twentieth century quickly being followed by the sense of isolation that accompanied the long years of Francoism exacerbated the inequalities of material and cultural development, so that the initially heady focus on democracy and progress had before long to confront its own instabilities. To quote:

Thus in recent times, accelerating after 1978, Spain has experienced a rapid process of belated modernization [. . .], but, at the same time — precisely because this modernization process has necessarily meant assimilation to a wider European economic and cultural environment — it displays all the social and economic decentring and cultural fragmentation typical of the postmodern era. Indeed, the very speed of change in Spain provides the rest of Europe with a kind of technicolour close-up of a worldwide cultural and economic process. (Graham and Labanyi, 1995: 408)

The hybrid coexistence of multiple timeframes in different parts of the country coincides with the cultural ambiguities resulting from the shift in focus from the national to the regional in internal contexts and, concurrently, from the national to the European at a post-national level. As Graham and Sánchez also point out, however, the Spain of the eighties had not reckoned with the ambivalences and fragilities of the Europe that it had so eagerly joined. Indeed, Spain's giddy entry into postmodernity was followed not long after by major global shifts and realignments. The pace of change across Europe in the last decade or so of the twentieth century brought major changes to worldwide notions of community, borders and territory. 1989 marked the opening of the Iron Curtain and the fall of the Berlin Wall. Only six months later, Eastern European countries had disengaged themselves from Soviet dominance, followed fifteen months later by the historic reunification of Germany. Two years later, the Warsaw Pact dissolved, thirty months after which the Soviet Union became a federation, thus marking an end to the polaric opposition between the superpowers that had framed global perceptions and positions throughout the postwar period. During this whole frenetic period, Western European nations voted in favour of a transnational European Union. The emergence of new regionalisms in Spain, as of new nationalisms in Europe, promoted often very contradictory discourses of community. What becomes clear is that as the long-standing markers of cultural and political identity increasingly revealed their porosity and flexibility in the face of capitalist-oriented economic shifts, so the term community came to be used in diverse contexts, but always as an indicator of stability. In Spain, thus, community became a favoured term as a consequence of an overwhelming disavowal of the Francoist past. Community allowed the recognition of the local, the regional, and the particular in precise contrast to the erasure of these very categories that had been part and parcel of Francoist nation building. Equally, community embraced the nation as a whole, thus perpetuating a sense of national identity, viewed as a 'larger' community. Furthermore, this term also allowed for a sense of continental belonging in terms of Europe, whereby Spain's accelerated economic growth could be viewed as part and parcel of the European project of progress via modernity, in other words, heightened capital flows and technological reliance. Thus, in what might seem to be a contradiction in terms, community, conventionally associated with tradition, came to be a term that was synonymous with Spain's desired progression towards economic, technolo- gical, and cultural emancipation together with its retrieval of hitherto muffled regional identities. Despite these confusions, Spain's successful combination of nation-state and autonomous communities has since often been contrasted with the violent shattering of the former Yugoslavia. In Spain, the writing of new collective identities required not a turn to community as opposed to nation, society, or citizenship, but the ability to somehow rewrite this pre-modern, traditional concept weighted with myth into the fabric of a chequered, hybrid, and restless postmodernity.

Numerous questions come to mind: what are the inter-relationships of nationalisms, communities, and cultural practices? How are communities refigured into and against old metanarratives of identity? How do multicultural subjects transform and rewrite the forms and subjectivities of communities?

How can communities cohere in the face of postmodern incommensurabilities and the irreconcilable differences of culture? Should mobility be written into the refiguring of community, turning it into a 'vehicle' that forges 'cultural routes' instead of a 'home' that establishes a 'cultural field'? How do the myths and imaginations of community diverge, then, from its practices and lived realities? To what extent is the European Community, driven by market-forces, emblematic of capitalism's incursions into and appropriation of the moral integrity attached to traditional communities?

What becomes clear when considering the concept of community in the larger context of contemporary Spanish culture is that it clearly rides the tension between postmodernism and a modern, structuralist imagination of identity as fixed or essential. The invention of tradition through community is nowadays a reflexive act, with culture in its many aspects being used to produce community identities or, at least, the awareness of the loss of rural or past, territorially and morally 'bound' communities, in their many manifestations. Equally, the constantly updated practices of community accompanied by the many rewritings of community in cultural texts speak of the awareness of its incompleteness. While the appeal of community lies largely in the myths it evokes of unity, essentialism, and permanence, nevertheless, the self-awareness that surrounds its constructions results to a great extent from the deliberate search for historical narratives with which to lend temporal weight to postmodernist cultural constructions. As will be seen in this book, various cultural media, such as literature, film, and music, are thereby deployed to reconstruct or invent the past and to provide diverse, and often paradoxical, narrative models of community. In this sense, the construction of community becomes an example of disjunctured and dissonant hybridity, challenging conventional linear notions of history through the coexistence of different time frames. Postmodernist constructions of community, therefore, foreground the synchronicity, as opposed to linearity, of time, by exposing narratives of communal memory as temporal pastiche. Community thus exposes the myths of modernity, with its linear vision of history, through the particularity and contingency of its application.

Despite the flattening out of time, historical memory, which is foundational to any kind of community identity — and, no doubt, whose construction, albeit piecemeal, in a postmodern context is more feasible than achieving any degree of common morality — has been the focus of extensive efforts at recuperation since the transition to democracy. Equally, contemporary cultural products construct community in terms of the tension between essentialism and postmodernism, thereby displaying ambiguities and ambivalences that remain unresolved. Such paradoxes, however, should be viewed in the light of Spain's general ambiguities and the different cultural pulls that are present in terms of globalization, the foregrounding of regional identities and recent Europeanization. In their respective contributions to *Contemporary Spanish Cultural Studies*

(Barry Jordan and Rikki Morgan-Tamosunas 2000), both Hugh O'Donnell and Liz Crolley stress the role of popular culture in the construction of regional community identities. O'Donnell outlines the effect of Catalan soap operas and Crolley examines football as a forum for regional community. The impetus provided by market forces, however, underlies many of these cultural products, inevitably essentializing community as myth. Culture, despite its commodification, thereby becomes a space for imagining communal belongings, but again is frozen and closed. In an introduction to the section on youth and popular cultures in their above mentioned book, Barry Jordan and Rikki Morgan-Tamosunas stress that:

[. . .] whilst in the world of official Spanish politics, notions of community and collective responsibility appear increasingly marginalized given the current neo-liberal economic climate, paradoxically perhaps Spain's *telenovela* continues to provide spaces in which viewers can find a nostalgic outlet for other 'imagined communities'. Here, unlike the world of aggressive individualism and commodity fetishism, values of solidarity respect, tolerance and community appear to survive and prosper. (2000: 264)

The binding morality that those who believe in the integrity of community's temporal and spatial scatterings makes it clear that the myth of essentialized community is unfeasible in practice. Indeed, a closer examination of 'remembered' totalities might reveal the gaps in memory, the cohesive modernist narrative which in hindsight constructs the totality that never really was. In this context, it is worth recalling Arjun Appadurai when he states that 'natives [. . .] people confined to and by the places to which they belong, groups unsullied by contact with a larger world, have probably never existed' (1988: 39).[8] In a similar vein, Delanty argues that modernity is 'itself deeply rooted in the pre-modern world view', but denotes 'the penetration of scepticism into the identity of the self' (2000: 4, 5) that marks the shift to modernity. In terms of community, the heightened reflexivity of postmodernity and contemporary transformations in the social production of space, place, and spatiality in Spain should be taken into consideration in order to discover new possibilities. This means that in today's larger cultural context, community needs to be viewed not in terms of exclusion from the Other via any moral code, but rather, as Delanty aptly points out with reference to postmodern identity and reflexivity, in terms of a prioritization of Other over Self, in other words as engagement and encounter with the Other. Equally, community identities rest not just on shared memories, but also on contested memories and uneven oblivion. What is more, rather than be viewed as 'essence', community needs to be understood in terms of discursive performance or symbolic signification as a channel for encounter with the Other.

In this context, it is worth noting that, while regional communities in Spain may reiterate their identities through the production of culture, equally the latter offer means of connecting with other identities, so that the sense of community at regional level is overlapped by various other possible community identities. Most importantly, the coexistence in Spain of various time frames specifically facilitates the contradictory overlap of essentialized, traditional, and closed communities with new configurations of this term. The postmodern condition, as the hybrid cultural offspring of modernity's uneasy coupling with tradition, is particularly multi-faceted and unpredictable in contemporary Spain, more so than in most other parts of Western Europe: community, as a result, takes on many dissimilar, diverse, and shifting forms.

Indeed, it is precisely because Spain presents so uneven a cultural surface that community has risen to such relevance there. The postmodern coexistence of diverse temporalities often projects culture in confusing and competing ways: television viewers in many of the regional communities, thereby, are offered images which construct and relay apparently contradictory identities, whilst also emphasizing the fluidity of identity. Andalusian television, *Andavisión*, for example, often promotes folkloric and pre-modern identities in terms of culture through programmes which favour purist renderings of flamenco or which focus on local rituals of community, such as the *romerías* at Easter; at the same time, viewers have access to a range of images and discourses which identify them as belonging to communities that are not confined to their sense of place and that often, in fact, exceed it to the extent of cutting across previously closed — and now deliberately porous — national boundaries. What becomes all too apparent are the contradictory and juxtaposed temporal depths experienced in terms of communal belongings, at once shallow and seemingly timeless. Notions of spatial rootings are also profoundly disturbed, linking diverse spatial points through images and technology whilst also affirming the importance of the local. Europeanization thereby adopts the tactics of globalization, both altering local spaces through the medium of technology and disembedding communities from place. New identities are therefore layered onto old ones, despite the essentialisms attached to the latter.

These shifts of time and space in post-Francoist Spain rose in intensity, of course, in the wake of the Francoist modernization of the sixties, which witnessed mounting migration to cities from the countryside. The depletion of the rural areas has without doubt continued to the present-day, leaving even many smaller towns or *pueblos* stripped of a sizeable working population. The demise or abandonment of rural Spain, with all its cultural connotations of stability, rooting, etc. has been explored through numerous cultural texts in recent years. Of relevance here is Icíar Bollaín's film *Flores de otro mundo* (1999), co-scripted with the writer Julio Llamazares.

While this issue of displacement from land or from rural areas will be explored in greater depth in the next chapter, nevertheless, other similar examples abound in contemporary Spain. In only the past decade or so, Toledo, for example, has experienced growing migration to the outward extending suburbs of Madrid, leaving the town itself to numerous passing tourists, some elderly residents, too old to move and often living in old age homes, and to the ghosts of more colourful, medieval times. In this sense, and despite a degree of local life, Toledo has become much of a 'museum town' over the past twenty years, populated through a cultural imaginary that is shared by those who visit the place but then disperse to diverse global points. Deterritorialization, therefore, is central to contemporary Spanish culture, the disembedding of people from place having begun with the displacements brought on by modernity and accelerating sharply over the past few decades.

Though the forced migrancy of modernity transforms the relation of communities to land, nevertheless, many cultural practices and attitudes can be seen to have been transported across contexts. Adaptations to the demands of modern life have not done away, in this sense, with traditional patterns of sociality in Spain. Street life, therefore, assumes an importance that can be measured from both the activities that take place outside and also the amount of time that people spend in common spaces. It is thus not uncommon for older residents of cities, many of whom will have been migrants from rural areas, to bring a chair down from their flats to the pavement in the evening in order to converse with neighbours or passers-by. Such appropriation of public spaces for the sake of gathering with locals can be viewed as the spontaneous and hybrid encounter of tradition with modernity. Similarly, the very high ratio of bars throughout Spain attests to the presence of communal spaces, frequented in most urban *barrios* by local people, which offer possibilities for joint participation in constructing a sense of localized identity. Private and public realms fuse here, the deterritorializing attractions of television and other media competing with more conventional ways of constructing identity at local levels through community interaction.

Equally important in such endeavours is the role played by municipal councils in many of the regional autonomies to foment a sense of responsibility to place. The locality of Lavapiés in Madrid is one of the most multicultural and multi-ethnic communities in Madrid, as will be seen in the third chapter. However, local residents, often recently arrived immigrants from diverse parts of the Third World, are urged to believe that 'Lavapiés es nuestro', as proclaimed by a banner displayed by the council in a square and several streets near the Rastro (April 2000). The incitement to residents is to develop a sense of attachment to place, further discernible in the urban drive, prevalent, for example, in Barcelona, towards establishing neighbourhood associations or communities of residents who are proactive in directing the uses and appearance of local spaces. In Gidden's terms, the postmodern context thereby presents the drive to re-embed as much as it disembeds people from places. Also relevant here are celebrations of community, such as those of the Comunidad de Madrid on the second of May every year. As reminders of community identity, these celebrations aim to construct and affirm communal belonging within urban settings. The updated web-sites of regional communities, such as this one, ensure that even those members of the community who are not physically present there can maintain contact and up-to-date knowledge of the events, extending community beyond geographical boundaries. Equally, however, it is worth noting that an increasing number of urban residents avail of the long weekend or *puente* resulting from such festivities to travel abroad or to other parts of Spain, clearly revealing their disengagement from such practices of community.

These examples indicate that the contemporary ambivalence towards community can surely be traced not just to the fragmentations of time and space brought on by modernity but also to the absence of a binding morality or shared system of values. Instead, the construction of community becomes a symbolic act, contingent and situational in such a way as to indicate membership of a social milieu. Written into contemporary community identities, therefore, is a refigured notion of citizenship functioning at multiple levels. To quote Rapport and Overing,

Hence the notion of community encapsulates both closeness and sameness, *and* distance and difference; and it is here that gradations of sociality, more and less close social associations, have their abiding effects. For, members of a community are related by their perception of commonalities (but not tied by them or ineluctably defined by them as are kinsmen), and equally, differentiated from other communities and their members by these relations and the sociation they amount to. (2000: 63)

Ironically, such relatively loose communal ties can be layered on to more essentialist forms of communal identity, serving to reinforce the latter. This, for example, is the case as regards urban expansion in some Andalusian towns under the Socialist government of the 1980s: in Jerez de la Frontera, new prefabricated housing developments on the town's outskirts sprung up in that decade in a move to provide improved housing for gypsies. The result is that the outlying geographical position of these *barrios* combines with their almost entirely gypsy population to construct a strong sense of community based on ethnicity, location, and, inevitably a stratification in terms of social class and status.

Spain's geographical position at the edge of Europe, its colonial history in Latin America and North Africa together with its on-going impassioned participation in Europeanization have made it an attractive point of arrival for immigrants from various parts of the world. The result, over the last two decades, has been the growing visibility of ethnic, religious, and racial diversity. Precisely as a result, therefore, of the modern project of advancement via capitalism, the cultural environment of Spain is becoming ever more diverse and complex. Despite a time lag in comparison to other former colonial powers in Western Europe such as the United Kingdom or France, Spain is coming to experience the daily resurgence of its otherwise forgotten colonial histories.

Thus the struggle of the postcolonial subject to stake a claim in European prosperity makes its day-to-day presence all too obvious. The plural imaginations of identity and the plural discourses of regionalized politics are now stretched to include a space for the articulation of such racial, cultural, religious, and economic difference. In particular, and in the wake of the events of 11 September 2001 in New York, the visibility of Islam in Spain is historically, culturally, and politically problematic. While extensive discourses of multiculturalism both seek to apparently accommodate difference whilst also containing them in safe 'spaces', it is at specifically communal level, understood in the sense of community as lived practice, that problems tend to arise. *El moro*, relegated to history as Spain's all too familiar 'other', makes a return in the here and now.[9] Thus, the construction of mosques in various parts of the country has met with objection from locals who, on the one hand, are happy to benefit from the economic gain resulting from the cheaper labour on hand from immigrant presence, whilst also objecting to any sign of their cultural relocation, which is no doubt indicative that the Muslims are here to stay. In this case, the alterity presented by the practice of Islam is perceived by the locals as pitting their own sense of 'community' against another construction of the same. In this spatial contestation, a politics of community comes to the fore, throwing up important historical and economic constellations which speak of postcolonial struggle and the violence of historical opposition. Once again, community is imagined as reified, unchangeable, and frozen despite, or even specifically because of, the proximity and historical familiarity of difference.

The persistence of ritualized community identities can also be witnessed, though in a very different light, in the many traditional celebrations that take place at particular points in the calendar in various parts of Spain. Examples of these abound: *San Fermines*, or the running of the bulls in Pamplona, the *Fallas* of Valencia, the many *romerías* that take place around Easter in Southern Spain, the *feria* in Seville. Rooted in place and cyclical in time, such festivities provide reassurance against the uncertainties of postmodern fluidity. Whilst these events can be considered sporadic resurgences of essentialized community identity in the midst of more dispersed sociality, equally it could be argued that precisely these dates in the year girdle a sense of continuous localized identity that withstands the sweep of postmodern fragmentation.

Rapport and Overing conclude their section on community by aptly stating that in spite of the impossibility of defining community, 'it is perhaps sufficient to say, in sum, that however diverse its definition, community ubiquitously represents a "hurray" term' (2000: 65). This positive connotation attached to the concept and its imagined practices is clearly why the latter abounds in political rhetoric. The emotive force conjured up by the concept of community without doubt dwells in a common imaginary that assigns it holistic desirability. Located within the larger history of modernity's liquidization of unities, Spain's history in the twentieth century of divisiveness, the forced amnesia surrounding Francoism's *anti-España* and persisting shadows of cleavage make community all the more appealing: it strikes a note of wholeness, of historical depth and spatial security. Precisely because of these imaginations and precisely because of the absence of such guarantees, in Spain as in the rest of the modern world, community eludes a single, concrete definition.

1. See Leo Strauss, 'The Three Waves of Modernity' in Leo Strauss (1975).
2. Of relevance in this context is Stephanie Sieburth's book, *Inventing High and Low: Literature, Mass Culture and Uneven Modernity in Spain* (1994), where she argues that the high-low division in culture acted as a means of reinforcing other social and gender separations that were in the interest of the elite in Spain, but which were under threat from the uneven advance of modernity.
3. As will be discussed shortly, Amitai Etzioni's theories of communities are an example of the 'organic' community.
4. In this context, it is no doubt important to point out that this definition of globalization is not without its measure of generalization. McDonald's, for example, are eager to boast of the alterations they make to their products according to local tastes: an example of this are the *masala burgers* they sell in India, which are flavoured with locally popular spices. Whilst remaining a burger, it is thereby adapted to local tastes. This marketing strategy clearly underlines globalization as a two-way process where hybridity is at play, not as uniform across spatial terrains, but presenting localized variants. This phenomenon is also sometimes known as 'glocalization'.
5. Debates around globalization and its definitions inevitably boil down to 'positions' which view this process favourably or unfavourably. In the same way, the issue of whether or not globalization implies Western domination or imperialism is one that is contested. In contrast to Tomlinson, Frank J. Lechner and John Boli state in their introduction to *The Globalization Reader* that 'globalization is westernization by another name' (2000: 7)
6. See pp. 287–89 for an exploration of the ambivalence of community in the context of deterritorialization.
7. It is worth noting in this context that neo-republican notions of community were very much a part of both Clinton's electoral campaign of 1992 in the USA and of Tony Blair's electoral campaign of 1997 in the UK, where Blair stressed community as a way of everyone working together for a common good. Earlier Clinton had vowed to repair the breakdown of unities such as family and community.
8. This is one of many of Appadurai's works which argue that cultural hybridity has always been a norm.
9. For an impressive analysis of the historical course of the image of the Moor in Spain, see Eloy Martín Corrales (2002).

CHAPTER 2

THE AESTHETICS OF MEMORY: COMMUNITY, TEMPORALITY, AND HISTORY IN THE WORK OF JULIO LLAMAZARES

Issues concerning the concept of community in the context of modernity which were presented in Chapter 1, will be explored in a more specific way in this chapter. My aim here is to problematize community identity by focusing upon key aspects of Julio Llamazares's prose narratives, attending particularly to *La lluvia amarilla* (1988), *Luna de lobos* (1985), and *El río del olvido* (1990). Where relevant, I shall also draw upon some of Llamazares's other works, namely *Escenas de cine mudo* (1994) and his earlier poetry, *La lentitud de los bueyes* (1979) and *Memoria de la nieve* (1982). My particular focus throughout is on narratives of memory and the attempt by these to remember, imagine, and produce discourses of community identities.[1] In line with Redfield's definition of the term (1960), the concept of community has conventionally borne connotations of shared spatial and temporal experiences which emerge from a single geographical location and a cohesive cultural memory constructed from collectively circulated narratives. Such stability of identity as is offered by this unified and 'organic' experience of space and time has been disturbed in the course of modernity, as is made clear in Llamazares's work, by the increasing prevalence of displacement and travel; equally the myth of such stable communal identity continues to fuel the modern imagination. A contradiction or tension — one that underlies much of Llamazares's writing — then ensues in terms of the notion of community: on the one hand, memory attempts to re-enact the remembered, or perhaps imagined, unity of community; on the other, the narrative attempt to articulate memory cohesively is itself confronted by the latter's fragments and gaps foregrounded by modernity's temporal and spatial displacements.

This chapter, therefore, will focus specifically on the attempt to construct narratives of memory within an overall cultural context of modernity. In particular, it is worth recalling the mobilizing drives of modernity, whose normalizing discourses sought to contain and make sense of the cultural experience of maelstrom, dislocation, and passage. An understanding of modernity as paradox, driven forward by the urge to seek progress, yet desiring of stability and embedding, is central to the analysis of community in this chapter and elsewhere in this thesis. Most importantly, modernity's liquidization of unities of time and space foregrounds the fragility of identity, presenting the future in terms of fragmentation and scattering.

Llamazares's work offers literature as a form of rescue from such oblivion, but the narrative act is repeatedly confronted by its own inadequacies and incompleteness. His creative work is thus forged from questions of time, memory, and narration, the very issues which have traditionally provided the foundations for the construction of community identity.[2] Equally his work offers a problematization of these issues through its focus on forgetting as a key aspect of memory, thereby highlighting the ambivalence of community. This focus on traditional concerns comes somewhat as a surprise when one considers that he belongs to the generation of young writers who came to the fore in the first decades of democracy in Spain.[3] It is important to note that while Llamazares's work belongs to the generation of new narrative that emerged in the post-Transition Spain of the 1980s, his work nevertheless centers on the socio-cultural experiences of Francoism from the 1960s onwards, a period which coincides with Llamazares' own childhood. The centralized state apparatus that was part of Francoist modernization (see Richards 1995) resulted in the breakdown of local communities, as attested by Llamazares's work. His exploration of temporality can be categorized as part of a larger contemporary preoccupation with temporal fragmentation, emerging from the modern experience of identity as fragmented, migratory, and unstable, but nevertheless desiring of and invoking stability. Llamazares's creative prose thus amounts to a modernist examination of the breakdown of community that accompanies the process of modernization, an examination which is clearly expressed in his many prose explorations of this issue. It can also be surmised that he sets out to offer in his literary output a forum, based on the imagination of a shared history of social ruptures, for the construction or imagination of communal identity through collective participation in his narratives. The relative linearity of narrative then can be viewed as expressive of an attempt to gather scattered memories and construct cohesion, be it through memory or imagination. What becomes clear, in fact, is the incompleteness of memory and the silence that covers much of the past. As we shall see, Llamazares's work presents a reiterated sentiment of loss which can perhaps be read as a desire to refigure a prior way of being. Such evocations of the past are, on the one hand, the basis upon which collective memory is constructed and extended and, on the other, themselves a statement of the temporal instability of memory.

The theoretical framework for my analysis will be drawn from the reworking and development of Heidegger's early ontological quest made respectively by Adorno and Ricoeur.[4] All three of these philosophers were concerned with the threat posed to 'true' or 'authentic' existence by a growing modernity. The increasing mechanization of modern life, together with its emphasis on the exchange of capital, was one of the causes for this preoccupation with the alienation of man from a 'true' life, which led to diremption or a profound wound. In this context, the notion of 'true' or 'authentic' life clearly refers to the awareness of mortality as an overriding temporal reference for living life. Adorno responds to Heidegger's apparent negativity by focusing on the value of art as aesthetic experience which contains a cognitive 'truth content'. Adorno therefore draws the aesthetic into the realm of social and collective experience by placing it in an immediate historical context and explores its potential to engender new understandings upon which to build subjectivities through the attempt to trace the past. Heidegger's concept of *Dasein* or 'authentic' being in the face of mortality is lifted out of its inherent anxiety by Ricoeur's emphasis on the cohesive power of narrativity. Loss, or the intimation of it, lies at the core of Heidegger's philosophy, whereby 'authentic' existence can only come about by living with and against time. Thus Heideggger viewed 'authentic Being' as the resolute anticipation or awareness of one's own death, in other words, as life lived in the face of death. Heidegger's concept of Dasein, however, leaves the individual isolated and insufficiently involved or implicated in relation to others. Ricoeur counter-acts the ego-centricity of such a view by developing a hermeneutics of narration as an ethical component of authenticity which, while being rooted in a coherent train of conceptual systems, is nevertheless indefinitely open-ended. Thus individuals contribute through narratives to the collective treasury of 'authentic' experience. Narratives of the past implement the concept of community by providing a tapestry of shared narratives and, hence, the reassurance of shared history. I wish to place these two theorists alongside one another when examining Llamazares's work, in order to gain a fuller appreciation of the latter when considered within his own social and historical contexts.

A triangular tract of land of approximately fifty kilometres near the basin of the Sabero river is the source of inspiration for much of Llamazares's literary work. The way of life of local village communities came under threat from the faster pace of modernization taking place in Spain in the 1960s as, with the rise of industrialization in other parts of Spain and an emerging national economy, an increasing number of the younger generation have left the villages for more money and more opportunities. In the words of the narrator of *La lluvia amarilla*, who is left as the last surviving inhabitant of a deserted mountain village:

La marcha de los de casa Juan Francisco fue el comienzo tan solo de una larga e interminable despedida, el inicio de un éxodo imparable que, dentro de muy poco, mi propia muerte convertirá en definitivo. Lentamente, al principio, y luego ya, prácticamente en desbandada los vecinos de Ainielle — como los de tantos otros pueblos [. . .] — cargaron en sus carros las cosas que pudieron, cerraron para siempre las puertas de sus casas y se alejaron en silencio por los senderos y caminos que van a tierra baja. Parecía como si un extraño viento hubiese atravesado de repente estas montañas. (1988: 76–77)

Clearly Llamazares's work serves to give voice to the unseen aspects of an increasingly urbanized and cosmopolitan Spain: the slow but steady demise of rural life and values, the irrevocable severance of man from a 'natural' habitat, the gradual but ruthless displacement of links with land and community. Llamazares's writing, which is firmly located in the socio-cultural context of a rapidly advancing modernity, therefore explores the links between time and its consequences, memory, and oblivion, which arise from the loss of the past. In this context, community identities, whether these be of the author or of his characters, are displaced and scattered through time and across space, as the very concept of community is uprooted and stripped of a stable spatial field.

The major premise of Llamazares's work is the experience of loss and the question of whether recovery of any kind is indeed possible. Although he gives no clear-cut answer to this question, Llamazares's repeated stress on oblivion is clearly an attempt to fight the engulfing force of the latter. The sleeves of his many books published by Seix Barral insist that he '[. . .] nació en el desaparecido pueblo de Vegamián', referring to the fact that Vegamián was flooded by a damn as part of Francoist modernization of regions of Asturias. This phrase clearly invites metaphoric readings. It would appear that, like the characters in his stories, Llamazares's 'true' origins have disappeared in the mists of time. Furthermore, this piece of information initiates the reader into a particular attitude or frame of mind of mourning when receiving his work. The disappearance of Llamazares's birthplace functions, therefore, as a metaphor for loss, as well as for the oblivion that engulfs the past and from which memory struggles to articulate its narratives. As Heidegger has stated, death provides a temporal border which frames authentic experience as life is lived in a state of care. In this context, however, Ricoeur's critique of Heidegger's concept of Dasein centers around concern with the self, as opposed to the self–other relation. The narration of collective loss provides, for Ricoeur, the grounds from which the self-other relation can exist, thereby allowing for communal bonds that arise in the imaginary through the engagement with fiction.

Paul Ricoeur's critique of Heidegger revolves around what he sees as a fundamental ego-centricity in the latter's concern with 'authentic' Being. Thus 'care' in Ricoeur's interpretation of Heidegger amounts to 'care for the self' since the concept of *Dasein* takes no account of the self's relation with those who are around it. What is lacking then in Heidegger's work, according to Ricoeur, are the ethical concerns which arise from relation with the other, without which ontology would be deprived of any ethical validity. Dasein's concern with solely the self fails to include a focus on the self–other relation, which for Ricoeur is in many ways the basis for the construction of the self. Ricoeur's emphasis on ethics requires a self whose relation to others, through the act of narrating, is in some way prior to the recognition of the self. In this sense, community is that from which a self begins. In a two-way process, the self is constructed from the narratives emerging from communal contexts and community, too, is thereby maintained. Ricoeur argues that the making of a story, the process he refers to as 'emplotment', is one which integrates readers with writer and past with present and future. It is also the common basis upon which history and fiction are founded. What matters is also that the narrative act provides a space for the formulation of identity: as Mark Wallace states in his introduction to the English translation of Ricoeur's *Figuring the Sacred*:

In scripting a life-story as one's own, a *self* is born in possession of a refigured identity. (1995: 13).

Thus identity or self-hood for Ricoeur is 'ipse-identity' or the struggle by a subject to constantly refigure itself through the narratives that it takes as its own. In Wallace's words:

The self, as neither a fixed entity, cultural cipher, nor biochemical remainder cobbles together its identity by constructing a life-story that uses the resources of various narrative fragments. In the narrative interpretation of a life, both history and fiction are borrowed from; and since the references of both genres crisscross the plane of human historicity, a life mediated by stories is a 'fictive history, or if one prefers, an historic fiction'. (1995: 13).

Ricoeur states that all stories could be told in myriad ways, all memories which are recounted fail to include aspects which have been forgotten. Forgetting or 'oubli' is stitched into the fabric of memory and the attempt at recovery is an act of imagination. This has obvious repercussions in our understanding of truth as of fiction. Ricoeur corroborates this point in his three-part work *Time and Narrative* (1984, 1985), where he also stresses the need to acknowledge the plural nature of history as that which has been made and that which has yet to be made, that which has been told and could still be re-told. He further explores the links between 'history' and 'fiction', whereby distinctions between the two are blurred by their mutual reliance on the basic historicity of human experience and the fact that the term 'history' itself blurs what really happened with how it is told. Ricoeur also stresses that the past should not be considered as finished time, but rather as a continuing dialectic which allows orientation for the present and future. Thus stories of the 'past' offer channels through which collectives and individuals can orient themselves into the future. Indeed, Ricoeur warns of the dangers of not examining past experience, whether individual or collective, when negotiating the present and future, for without this there would be no sense of orientation. Remembering the past and recounting it to the collective is then an ethical obligation for the refiguring of self-identity for both narrator and receivers of the narratives when it comes to navigating through time. Narration as history orients us towards the present and directs us towards futurity and is therefore integral to ethical action. Human experiences thereby become stories which have yet to be told and life itself awaits narration. Most importantly, narration allows the self to be refigured in terms of community. Narrativity, therefore, has an eminently mimetic function which serves not to distance it from 'reality' but, on the contrary, to uncover 'history' in the same way as the latter must be viewed fundamentally as a 'literary artefact' (1981: 289): the world of fiction leads us to the heart of the real world of action (1981: 296). Memory, therefore, may give rise to narratives, but is itself a vehicle for the alteration of temporal experiences which then has an effect on the present. The veracity of memory narrated, its link with the 'truth', is thus not of great consequence. Rather, what matters is memory's function as that which gives rise to (hi)stories.

Narration then becomes foregrounded in its role in the construction of contemporary identity via narrative approximations to the past, which themselves are complicated by the modernity's migratory impulses. Llamazares contextualizes his writing within the abrupt heightening of modernity in Spain, stating in his interview with José María Marco of the magazine *Quimera* (1988, 80: 22–29) that his work is reflects on the sudden cultural shifts and cracks experienced in Spain as a result of rapid modernization. Regarded in terms of Ricoeur's thought, it should be borne in mind that the latter's reiteration of the cohesiveness of narrativity is offered in terms of a hermeneutics which sees itself as an alternative to the slippage and deferral of deconstruction. For Ricoeur, history is viewed within the framework of the formulation of identity and so must shift with the subjects concerned. His work does not mention the position of a hermeneutics of narrativity within a fragmented and shifting environment, save to emphasize its importance as a means of counteracting the isolation of such fragmentation. The migrancy and fragmentation so evident in modern contexts undermine or threaten the unbroken line attempted by such an effort at continuity. While Llamazares's work is clearly a struggle for cohesiveness and temporal connections, its retrospective account of forgotten histories also reveal the complications of cultural memory in the course of modernity's drifts. As Llamazares states in the foreword to *La lluvia amarilla*:

Ainielle existe. . .
Todos los personajes de este libro, sin embargo, son pura fantasía de su autor, aunque (sin él saberlo) bien pudieran ser los verdaderos. (1988: 7)

The text allows for the author's imaginations based on memory to give voice to a landscape that has fallen silent in the course of modernization. In this sense, narratives arise not merely from memory, but also from gaps in memory, whereby they are simultaneously acts of imagination.

Llamazares clearly states that the enjoyment of writing lies in 'el placer de mentir'.[5] Thus his transposition of memory into narratives is not so much an act of recuperation as it is of offering his readership the means with which to (re)construct identity through the imagination of the past. Here, as Ricoeur states, the imagination is central to the construction of both fiction and history. Llamazares's work is of particular importance within the context of post-Francoist Spain, where identity has become problematic for a variety of reasons. By highlighting the struggles of memory over oblivion as human inevitabilities, Llamazares underlines the constructed nature of history, thereby placing the politically-imposed historical amnesia that was part of the Francoist regime (and of the regime's own essentialist and supposedly 'authentic' rendering of history) in a larger historical context of narrative instabilities. His provision of voices for the silenced history of Spain further allows for connections across time. The historical potential of fiction is thus foregrounded. Llamazares's act of recuperation and reconstruction, therefore, is one of placing spotlights on traces that can be gathered from the past.

Llamazares's creative work should also be examined in order to understand the impact of the undoubtedly intense aesthetic experience that it provides. In a personal interview/conversation with me (at a hotel in Sloane Square, London on 25 October 1997), Llamazares stressed the time and effort he puts into achieving the right rhythms and movements in his writing. He said that he would sometimes spend days working on a single phrase or passage. The importance he gives to this was previously mentioned during his lecture when he compared writing to painting or music, stating that 'el cómo, no el qué, se escribe' was what 'nos cambia la manera de ver el mundo'. Fictional writing, he stated to me, was no more than 'una mentira', but one which could provide moments of epiphany for those in contact with it. Llamazares's repeated preoccupation with the past ensures that such epiphanies act as flashes of memory into the past which illuminate the present. The coincidence of narratives of memory and aesthetic endeavour which reconfigures the present underlines Llamazares's exploration of temporality, opening up a connection through his work between the theories expounded by Ricoeur as laid out above and Adorno's development of aesthetic theory.

Adorno's view of modernity as crisis leads to an emphasis on moments of epiphany or, to use his terminology, the potential of aesthetic experience to provide 'truth contents', which lies at the core of his aesthetic theory. While there are many aspects of Adorno's philosophical project which coincide with Heidegger's, they diverge on issues of the *a priori* nature of historicity, as a discourse whose production is marked by contingency (i.e. the construction of historical narratives based on what is available or in view), as opposed to history, understood as a totalizing discourse. In this context, Simon Jarvis states that 'for Adorno, on the other hand, there can be no history of Being without a history of beings' (1998: 202). In developing a historicized approach to philosophy, Adorno engaged with Marxist traditions, arguing that it was false to endorse a universal totality of history. Thus Adorno employs Marxist concepts, but rejects the essentialism of such an ideology. Indeed, much of Adorno's work was linked to providing a critique of the real and conceptual obstacles to absolute truths of any kind, which formed the basis for his development of his work *Negative Dialectics* (1990). Implicit in his arguments is the formulation of *immanent critique* which came to characterize his practice of philosophy as a form of interpretation of particulars as opposed to the traditional 'transcendent' critiques more habitual to the discipline. For Adorno, immanent critique brings together not just a series of individual arguments, but also their place within a larger philosophical context. Thus Adorno insisted that the 'truth content' revealed by such analysis would amount to more than the sum of their parts, resulting in what he called 'constellations' of concepts. In particular, immanent critique made it possible to examine and understand the inherent contradictions within a body of work and to view them within the social and cultural contexts in which it was produced. Immanent critique was thus directly linked to actual social experience, contextualized locally and historically. In considering Adorno's work, it is important to bear in mind that it stemmed from his contention that there was a crisis in modernity. He understood this crisis in terms of a diremption, or profound wound, manifest in the gap that he perceived most obviously between the language of science and that of art, whereby the cognitive contribution of art was denied a validity that it merited. Similarly, he maintained that classificatory cognition disowned the mimetic element of language, relegating this latter to art. The ensuing cultural crisis, provoked as he saw it by 'science' and manifest through the pre-eminence in modernity of technology and capital, resulted in a crisis of subjectivity. The principle focus of Adorno's philosophical enquiry has been on the ensuing phenomena of disenchantment and diremption, which have led to a collapse of experience itself, whereby subjects are unable to experience their own diremption. In *Negative Dialectics* (1990), Adorno cites the trauma of Auschwitz as the projection of a world so fractured that it is without access to possibility. It amounts, he states, to the failure of culture, in a world where only culture could provide the means to overcome loss. Hence his insistence in his *Aesthetic Theory* (1984) on the importance of the 'truth content' of works of art and the focus on the historical constellations inherent to aesthetic experience. For Adorno, the cognitive content of art, whereby the artistic object supersedes either its creator or receivers, is linked intimately to the society from which it emerges, not because it accurately represents that society, but because it re-arranges and organizes aspects of the society into constellations bearing within them their particular historical experience.

Adorno's focus on the immediate or immanent clearly arises from his alarm at the diremption ensuing from a growing modernity. Llamazares has repeatedly echoed such fears in his creative work; in particular he is concerned with the effects of man's alienation from the 'natural':

Yo vengo de una raza de pastores que perdió su libertad cuando
                    perdió sus ganados y sus pastos
Durante mucho tiempo mis antepasados cuidaron sus rebaños en la
                    región donde se espesan el silencio y la retama
Y no tuvieron otro dios que su existencia ni otra memoria que el olvido [. . .]
Pero el momento llegó de no volver a la nada cuando los bueyes más
mansos emprendieron la huída y una cosecha de soledad y hierba reventó
                    sus redes
Ahora pacientan ganados de viento en la región del olvido y algo muy
                    hondo nos separa de ellos
Algo tan hondo y desolado como una
                    zanja abierta en la mitad del corazón. (1985: 16–17).

In his interview with José María Marco of the literary magazine *Quimera*, Llamazares rejects claims that he is a writer of rural novels, stating that he could perhaps be classified as a romantic writer because what he writes about is at the essence of romanticism, 'la escisión'. What matters therefore is the 'zanja abierta', the fissure from which he writes. The trauma that acts as a spur for his writing is the abrupt thrust experienced in Spain from one way of life to another, from the security of a set of constants to the choices and contradictions of pluralities, to quote his statement in *Quimera*: 'De repente parece que hemos pasado del neolítico a la posmodernidad sin haber sido nunca modernos.' (1988: 25). Despite the insistence here on premodernity in Spain, it should be remembered that Llamazares himself was born in 1955, when modernity was already well in place. Nevertheless, it can be inferred from the above quote that the uneven spread of modernity in Spain, together with the abrupt heightening of its pace from the 1970s onwards, leads to definitions of postmodernity as the awkward juxtaposition of local traditions and modernity (an example of this theory is to be found in Canclini [1995] in terms of his development of the concept of hybridity). For Llamazares, the impositions of modernity cause gaps in the cultural fabric. In *La lluvia amarilla*, nature absorbs those who have not been able to follow the rapid shifts and ruptures of society. The narrator of *La lluvia amarilla* can only look ahead to the time when his grave will be overgrown with weeds. In all of Llamazares's work, the imminence of death and the onslaught of oblivion are inevitabilities; nevertheless, his stories, as voices of the past, express the struggle to reach a contemporary audience as a last measure of survival. The temporal durability of the prospect of death is contrasted with the evanescent nature of life and its many voices, an evanescence which translates into the temporal instability of fixed 'truth', when he states later in a collection of journalistic articles entitled *Nadie escucha*: 'Y la mentira, mal que les pese a muchos, es lo único que queda cuando las verdades pasan' (1995: 82). Here 'mentira', of course, refers to the narrative act.

Antonio Sánchez aptly points out that Llamazares distinguishes himself from the modernist writer's focus on the individual and the postmodern tendency to deconstruct identity by insisting upon the importance of family and community in the formulation of subjectivity. Sánchez further explores the solitude of the modern writer as described by Benjamin and compares this to the solitary characters who reminisce in Llamazares's stories. For the solitary reader of Llamazares's prose (as opposed to the communal reception of orally transmitted narratives), his evocation of past temporal experiences leads to the construction of a communal imaginary even where there had not been one before, just as it paves the way for an identification with what is for the reader a fictitious or imagined, though historicized, past. The experience in Llamazares's lifetime of the progressive weakening of communal ties linked to land is what motivates him to forge meaningful narrative links between different historical temporalities, without attempting to produce any absolute temporal or historical totality. At the same time, his experience of loss has created a certain degree of alarm at the process of 'social progress' and, no doubt, also accounts for the awareness of the ruptures in temporal and historical experience that form the basis of his writing. In this he can be likened to Adorno, whose endeavour was to draw philosophy into the realm of the 'actual' (or real and contemporary). Philosophical interpretation for Adorno consisted in revealing historical truths. Much work has been done in recent years to link Adorno's thought with current poststructuralist theory and several affinities have been remarked upon. In his introduction to *The Actuality of Adorno* Pensky states that 'Adorno and poststructuralist theory generally are united in the essentially ethical-political motivation behind their complex rejection of the model of enlightenment rationality' (1997: 6). Pensky cites Frederic Jameson as emphasizing the relevance of Adorno to the postmodern age. In particular he focuses on Jameson's statement that this relevance of Adorno's work lies in its complication of temporality in order to better engage with history: thus Jameson focuses on Adorno's 'attention to temporality as a mode of grasping history, the use of existential time protentions and retentions as an instrument for grasping the dynamics of an external collective history otherwise available only in the 'facts' and 'faites diverses' (1997: 9). In this context, Pensky states that for Adorno,

natural history evoked more than just the graphic spectacle of historical processes displayed as fields of dead, abandoned and forgotten things. It also carried the strategic insight that, conceived as ruin, historical objects were not just dead but also liberated from a totalizing historical reason, and, as liberated, presented themselves to the attention of the critic as material for the construction of constellations. (1997: 9)

Thus Llamazares's work should be considered for even more than the loss which lends it authority or the continuity which it struggles to forge through the transmission of narratives: it should also be considered for its ability to historicize and temporally locate the very modern cultural contexts from which it arises. By tracing out the past and highlighting the ruins left behind, the present is contextualized and clarified. Adorno is quoted as having said 'Only in traces and ruins is reason prepared to hope that it will ever come across correct and just reality' (Pensky 1997: 2). The objects of aesthetic production must be seen as that which offer evanescent glimpses of such correctness. In defiance of the confused and confusing synchronicities that crowd the present, Llamazares's creative work provides a 'constellation' of temporal arrangements which, when considered in the midst of the cultural conditions in which they have emerged, produce a vision of history not as frozen in past time but as a fluctuating and complex process, dependent for its expression on narrativity and yet altered by the acts of narration.

Just as the narratives can be said to emerge from the writer's memory, so on a second level, the narratives themselves are reliant to varying extent upon the internal recollections of the characters themselves. At both levels, memory struggles to speak through the fog of oblivion. Death or loss, therefore, functions as a central theme in Llamazares's work, referring both to individual and communal contexts. His use of particular and repeated imagery, such as that of snow or yellow as the colour of death (no doubt the yellowing of age as in the title of *La lluvia amarilla* and in the photographs of *Escenas de cine mudo* or Juana's yellow head scarf in *Luna de lobos*), has a symbolic function in signalling to the reader the prevalence of mortality. *Escenas de cine mudo* is dedicated to the memory of his mother with the words: 'A mi madre, que ya es nieve' (1994). Like snow which is seasonal, people's lives are temporally bound. In all his mentioned works, nature's endurance contrasts with the fragility of communities which crumble 'como una estatua de sal' (1985: 27). For Llamazares, mortality as the temporal horizon of life is made all the more prominent by the modern abandonment of rural areas and the subsequent fragmentation of local communities. The following textual analysis, therefore, specifically seeks to consider Llamazares's work against this backdrop of death or oblivion, whereby both Ricoeur's emphasis on narration as a means of orientation through time and Adorno's historicized view of art become significant. In particular, Llamazares's focus on the lost traces of history will be considered in the light of Adorno's questioning of modernity's utopian ideals, since it is precisely the notion of social progress — modernity's central project — that comes under scrutiny in Llamazares's work.

In *La lluvia amarilla*, the nameless narrator–protagonist re-lives the last years of his life in its many instances. Therefore, through the act of narrating, this character looks backwards at his life and constructs meaning for himself via the attempt at reformulating the past. Almost dead in body, his existence is now fuelled by the painful exercise of memory, which remains as the sole provider of any purpose in a world that is devoid of future. Projections by the narrator into the future result in his imagining what will happen after his own death, this latter being the horizon that has closed in on him. Heidegger's insistence on the authority of death in the course of life is exemplified here. In contrast to the predominantly urban cultural contexts of modernized Spain, Llamazares offers a tale of the futility of a life without localized community. The book begins with Andrés imagining men from the near-by town discovering his body by the time it has already putrefied. Successive chapters work their way down into the past from this projected future and trace the unfolding of memories turned into narrative, as the story emerges in retrospect. The death of those close to him and the imminence of his own mortality are the only grounds for the narrative and it is this finality that lends authority to his increasingly incoherent narrative. In this sense, Heidegger's concept of living against time is in evidence in this work, which brings to light the solitary plight of an individual who has lost his entire community and thereby, the sense that time extends before him. The importance of communal belonging is underlined in *La lluvia amarilla* through its absence. Without community, the narrator's existence becomes a living death:

Pero, desde que murió Sabina, desde que en Ainielle quedé ya completamente solo, olvidado de todos, condenado a roer mi memoria y mis huesos igual que un perro loco al que la gente tiene miedo de acercarse, nadie ha vuelto a aventurarse por aquí [. . .] Y, aunque de tarde en tarde, hayan seguido viendo el pueblo desde lejos — cuando suben al monte por leña o, en el verano, con los rebaños — , en la distancia nadie habrá podido imaginar las terribles dentelladas que el olvido le ha asestado a este cadáver insepulto. (1988: 12)

The inference is that once he is devoid of communal belonging, the individual's life is stripped of meaning. Having been forgotten by those who have left him behind, the narrator must both remember his past in order to survive and at the same time accept that he lives in a double oblivion, both that of being forgotten by others and that within himself which engulfs his memories.:

Como un río encarchado, de repente el curso de mi vida se había detenido y, ahora, ante mí, ya sólo se extendía el inmenso paisaje desolado de la muerte y el otoño infinito donde habitan los hombres y los árboles sin sangre y la lluvia amarilla del olvido. (1988: 40)

The presence of community further served to protect the narrator from death, as if individual deaths within the community could be mitigated by a communal living force. Andrés explains that although deaths were common in Ainielle, nevertheless, a community could form a human chain that was able to deflect death:

Mientras hubo vecinos en Ainielle, la muerte nunca estuvo vagando por más de un día por el pueblo. Cuando alguien moría, la noticia pasaba, de vecino en vecino, hasta el final del pueblo y el último en saberlo salía hasta el camino para contárselo a una piedra. Era el único modo de liberarse de la muerte. La única esperanza, cuando menos, de que, un día, andando el tiempo, su flujo inagotable pasara a algún viajero que, al cruzar por el camino, cogiera, sin saberlo, aquella piedra. (1988: 116)

An interesting contrast is established here between the rootedness (and hence life-force) of a community that can push death away from its boundaries as opposed to the vulnerability of the 'viajero' or passer-by who unwittingly picks up a deadly stone. Without community, the solitary migrant, like the narrator, is vulnerable to oblivion. Furthermore, in line with Ricoeur's views on narrative and identity, the story of a particular death travels through the community, forming a life-preserving bond that will safeguard their collective navigation through time. When the narrator's wife dies, he goes to an apple tree planted by his father when he himself was born ('para ver cómo los dos crecíamos al tiempo' (1988: 116)), and tells it of her death. Like him, the tree is old and gnarled. The analogy between himself and the tree is such that, in fact, his actions amount to his lodging of death in himself. The action heralds his own end and marks his isolation, in that he is now both at the beginning and at the end of what would have been a communal narrative and a communal chain. Furthermore, Andrés indicates that the solitude he suffers forces him to split himself into a multiple self that can form its own community, as if the unified identity of individuals were itself dependent upon the tangible presence of a larger group. Thus he is at once the person who remembers his younger days and the person who shuts the memories up in search of the relative calm of oblivion:

La soledad, es cierto, me ha obligado a enfrentarme cara a cara conmigo mismo. Pero, también como respuesta, a construir sobre recuerdos las pesadas paredes del olvido. Nada produce a un hombre tanto miedo como otro hombre — sobre todo si los dos son uno mismo — y ésa era la única manera que tenía de sobrevivir entre tanta ruina y tanta muerte. (1988: 40)

Although a binary contrast is established here between memory and oblivion, nevertheless they are at once separate and entwined, since the efforts to remember and the efforts to forget take place within the same human being. Both the oblivion arising from the loss of community that surrounds Andrés and the memories he finds himself recounting are markers of death ('Yo me dí cuenta de que mi corazón ya estaba muerto el día que se fueron los últimos vecinos' (1998: 107)). This coincidence of opposites is stressed when he states that

[. . .] y, ahora, ante mí, ya sólo se extendía el inmenso paisaje desolado de la muerte y el otoño infinito donde habitan los hombres y los árboles sin sangre y la lluvia amarilla del olvido.
A partir de ése día, la memoria fue ya la única razón y el único paisaje de mi vida. (1998: 40)

In *La lluvia amarilla*, as in much of Llamazares's work, landscape is explored as a trope for timelessness or death. As the last human in his deserted village,

Andrés blends in with the landscape and seeks an ultimate refuge there by digging his own grave. Yet this too is a last and desperate attempt at reconstructing links with the closest members of his lost community, his own family:

Cuando la vean — si pasa mucho tiempo, quizá llena de nuevo de ortigas y de agua — , más de uno pensará que, como se decía, Andrés, de Casa Sosas, el último de Ainielle, ciertamente estaba loco [. . .] Si he cavado mi tumba, ha sido simplemente para evitar ser enterrado lejos de mi mujer y de mi hija. (1988: 131)

Landscape, like memory and its narratives, therefore, is both the resting-place of death and the affirmation of communal bonds that cross the temporal boundaries of individual lives. The deserted landscape presents a view not merely of what is in the presence, but also projects the past in terms of absence.

Death or oblivion is once again foregrounded in *Luna de lobos*. Again, here, the landscape offers a panorama of loss and acts as a silent witness to the tenacious approach of death. The imagination of community, despite — and also, precisely because of — the physical and emotional ostracism that is imposed by the prevailing political conditions of early Francoism, acts as life-blood for the four maquis in *Luna de lobos*. Memory, in this narrative, is an ambivalent source of torment for the men: on the one hand, it is the memory of a once unified community that sustains them in their isolation; on the other, they are faced constantly with the knowledge that they will soon be effaced from the cultural memory of their village. Once they cease to be remembered by those they love, they know that death, in the sense of a blanket of amnesia, will be upon them. The struggle to live is also the struggle to remember and be remembered. It is, in fact, the struggle to fight the temporal dispersal of unities, foregrounded in this context by the overwhelming political and social changes brought on by the Civil War and the relentless and violent grip of the Francoist State.

The four men return to their native village after the Republican front in Asturias has fallen and eke out an animal-like existence in the surrounding mountains in fear of persecution from the Civil Guard. The physical proximity of their families fuels the small and increasingly faint hope that they sustain of reuniting with them. Gildo, for example, draws solitary comfort from being in the area, as from the mountains he can at least see the roof-top of his house, where his wife and new-born son live:

La casa de Gildo es la última de Candamo. Se alza sobre los tejados de las demás, ya en al falda del monte, al borde del camino del cementerio [. . .]
Y ahora es ella, muertos los padres de Gildo y huido él al monte, la única que habita, con el niño, la vieja casa de corredor sombrío y chimenea de teja que se alza como un faro perdido en la noche de julio. Como tantas y tantas noches, Gildo has de resignarse a mirarla de lejos — y a recordar la soledad de su mujer y su hijo — [. . .]
(1985: 75)

Yet the very dehumanizing experiences of both the war and the struggle to survive its aftermath isolate the men further from re-entering their community, as social and family bonds are disrupted by the increasing opposition between communal life and their solitary existence. What is more, the villagers learn to reformulate their lives under the new political conditions which affect their daily contexts and which involve dissociation, at least on a surface level, from the maquis. At the same time, the four of them together form their own small community, bonded together by fear, by the love for a common birth-place and by the shared experiences of the war and its ensuing isolation. Furthermore, and most importantly, they are united by the common experience of living daily under the shadow of death or, at best, of a forced oblivion. The maquis' fight for survival against all odds is a desperate and obsessive acknowledgement of the immediacy of their own mortality and the social rupture resulting from the events of the Civil War. Thus Ángel looks at Ramiro and barely recognizes in him the boy he shared his childhood with. The strongest bond between the men, therefore, does not derive from a shared lifetime's experience, but from the projection of mortality that the future commonly holds for them. As the men die one by one, so the group's distancing from community is heightened and Ángel, as the last survivor, finds his existence reduced to that of a nocturnal animal. For Ángel, the occasional encounters with his girlfriend only serve to underline his exclusion from human society:[6]

María se aprieta suavemente, de espaldas, contra mí. — Hueles a monte — me dice — . Hueles como los lobos. — ¿Y qué soy? (1995: 57)

By being compared to a wolf, traditionally the enemy of 'settled' agrarian communities whose livestock are thus threatened, Ángel is marked in the course of time, not just as outside of social borders, but as a presence which has become intrusive and threatening. Implicit here is the contrast between the solitary individual as 'wolf' to be hounded and the community as a herd of 'sheep'. In *Luna de lobos*, family ties are once again seen to be vulnerable in the face of temporal and political change. This is brought home most poignantly when Ángel visits his dying father's bedside: the villagers present, including his sister, freeze at the sight of him, as if he were a frightening apparition. Repeatedly, Ángel's sister Juana tells him

— Tienes que marcharte, Ángel [. . .]
— Tienes que marcharte de aquí. (1995: 150)

to which he replies

— ¿A dónde, Juana? ¿A dónde? (1995:150)

The gulf that has grown between them, she as a member of the village community that is managing, despite severe hardships, to survive the war and he, in her eyes (and in the eyes of the others in the community), as no more than a ghost of a former self and a former time, is increasingly apparent towards the end of the book:

Los dos estamos ahora frente a frente, separados por el hueco de la fosa y la tibia penumbra de la corte. Juana inmóvil y distante, como una sombra más entre las sombras de las cabras, y yo, a sus ojos, blanco de muerte al contraluz pálido y gris de la ventana. (1995: 150)

Likewise the surrounding landscape, which in Llamazares's work bears the imprint of history, marks both the isolation and the oblivion imposed upon the men. Although Ángel has no option but to seek protection from the cavities of the earth or in the caves and deserted farmhouses on mountain-sides, he increasingly begins to experience his own existence as a living death. Like the memory of those whose community he was a member of, the landscape is ruthless in its abandonment of these forgotten people:

En torno a mí, un paisaje irreal y desolado marca las extensiones infinitas del silencio. Hay una luz metálica, como sobrevenida. Y, en el confín de las montañas que ahora me rodean, la línea del horizonte ha desaparecido otra vez borrada por la niebla. (1995: 142)

Ángel states repeatedly in the course of the book that 'Esta tierra no tiene perdón'. At the end, when he boards a train to France, Ángel, like Llamazares, becomes a 'viajero', his mobile status as a traveller the result of rupture and the confirmation of the spatial and temporal instability of identity, both communal and individual, in the face of impending mortality.

Oblivion is again the central theme of *El río del olvido*. Based on a seven-day walk along the river of his childhood, the Curueño, this book chronicles Llamazares's own encounter with the landscape of his early years. Here too, landscape forms a permanent and immutable backdrop to the movement and changes of the communities and villages of this mountainous region. The narrative arises from the confrontation of the author's own memory with reality. The steadfastness of the landscape through the years serves to emphasize to him his own growth and change and distance: his impermanence as a visitor contrasts with what endures:

El paisaje es memoria. Más allá de sus límites, el paisaje sostiene las huellas del pasado, reconstruye recuerdos, proyecta en la mirada las sombras de otro tiempo que sólo existe ya como reflejo de sí mismo en la memoria del viajero o del que, simplemente, sigue fiel a ese paisaje. (1990: 7).

The history of the region is imprinted in the landscape which, like memory, projects a silent narrative upon those who visit. Nevertheless, the history which is offered by the landscape is not monolithic and unified, but different according to when it is viewed. Llamazares states in his prologue to the work that while landscapes are unchanging, nevertheless the gaze of the viewer or 'viajero' never stays the same. In this context, the viewer is clearly the author/narrator himself, very much a drifting, modern subject for whom any 'return to origins' is an impossibility. Therefore, the memories that are reformulated by the landscape also alter in accordance with the viewer's current contexts. Memory in this way also becomes migratory and ambivalent. For Llamazares, his passage through the region of his childhood only serves to underline the migrancy of identities, as memories coincide with imagination, turning recollections of localized community into ghosts or spectres:

La memoria y el tiempo, mientras yo recordaba, se habían mutuamente destruido — como cuando dos ríos se unen- convirtiendo mis recuerdos en fantasmas y confirmando una vez más aquella vieja queja del viajero de que de nada sirve regresar a los orígenes porque, aunque los paisajes permanezcan inmutables, una mirada jamás se repite. (1990: 8)

As a 'viajero', Llamazares builds a contrast between himself and the communities of the villages that he passes through. The walk confirms his own distancing from community and the solitary condition of the migrant, whose mobility defies the confinement of borders of identity. The effacement of former communal bonds is emphasized by the futility of an attempted return to origins:

Memoria de un paisaje que un buen día volví a ver con la sospecha de haber regresado a un río y a un mundo desconcocidos y memoria de un camino que recorrí con la convicción cada vez más asentada de que los caminos más desconocidos son los que más cerca tenemos del corazón. (1990: 8)

Relevant here is the erosion caused by time, whereby memory becomes synonymous with death. This parallel is highlighted by the readers' knowledge, gleaned from the covers of his books, that the writer's own birthplace has become submerged under a dam. In this case, not even the landscape has survived to project narratives of history about those who lived in the village. The rapid encroachement of modernity has flooded Llamazares's 'original' landscape, together with any traces of the community that peopled it, and driven it into oblivion. Once again, however, memory and oblivion coincide as the silence of the former gives shape to the narratives of the latter, the narratives emerging in this case from the solitary voice of the author.

All three of the above texts delineate the struggle to articulate lived experience in the face of oblivion. Furthermore, the memories are clearly contextualized in terms of community, whereby individual lives gain meaning from shared communal bonds which have been eroded through the years. In his creative prose, Llamazares takes pains to emphasize his role as a writer who is propelled, not so much by a concern with history for its own sake, but by the irrevocable experience of social and temporal rupture, as can be witnessed in the repeated narrative attempts to grasp lost experience. He further stresses the role of imagination in any recuperative effort of memory, thereby underlining the alterability of historical perceptions. He emphasizes throughout *El río del olvido* that an experience is not the same as the memory of that experience, a gaze is not the same as a backward gaze, for in looking backwards, we are no longer who we were when we first looked nor can we be sure that the object of our memory was as we remember it to have been. Moreover, the way we regard the object of memory will have altered irrevocably from the way we first regarded it, Llamazares states in his introduction to *El río del olvido*. Similarly, in *La lluvia amarilla,* the protagonist re-tells the story of his life along the course of his recollections and yet, doubts the veracity of his memories:

[. . .] si mi memoria no mentía. ¿Y qué es acaso la memoria sino una gran mentira?. . .¿No lo habré quizá soñado o imaginado todo para llenar con sueños y recuerdos inventados un tiempo abandonado y ya vacío? ¿No habré estado, en realidad, durante todo este tiempo, mintiéndome a mí mismo? (1988: 35).

In *Escenas de cine mudo*, Llamazares once again wonders whether the discovery of the photo album caused him to remember the years of his childhood or to invent them. Clearly in recollection and narration, the line between 'true experience' and fiction is blurred. This is also obviously exempified by the narrative of *Luna de lobos*, which, as Llamazares stated in his talk at the Instituto Cervantes is a work of fiction based on 'true' accounts of the maquis' efforts to survive in hiding from the Civil Guard. What seems important then, is the creation of the narrative itself and its power to release different temporal experiences in the imaginary of those who receive it. History or a supposedly 'truthful' narrative of experience and fiction therefore serve the same purpose with regard to temporality. As Ricoeur states in *Hermeneutics and the Human Sciences* (1981: 274–96), the impetus to write history and to tell stories is rooted in a shared temporal structure, whereby orientation of the future draws its cues from our capacity to recall and gather the past.

Narrativity is thereby a process of temporal mediation upon which any cohesiveness of human experience is reliant, because it serves as the sole weapon to battle the ruptures and oblivion imposed by time. It is, therefore, as Ricoeur states, a matter of ethical primacy. The ethical importance of narrative acts lies not just in the temporal cohesiveness that narration offers to the narrator, but, more importantly, in the role of narratives as threads which weave communal affiliations through the collective engagement of imagination and, hence, collective memory. Equally, in terms of Adorno's theories, Llamazares's work shows the reconfiguration of the present through historical imaginations. Memory's prime role, then, is not to recapture the past as it was, for this is clearly an impossibility, but rather to cast narrative traces which make modernity's shifts and movements more coherent. In this sense, narratives, whether these be of memory or of forgetting, provide meaningful contexts across time and space for the displaced subjects of modernity.

The reference to film as a major modern form of narrative in *Escenas de cine mudo* makes this point most obviously. Film is clearly a fluid, evanescent form of expression. Experience remembered as shifting 'scenes' from a silent movie, which can be edited at will, cut and rejoined, underlines the contingency of identities. Here, memories take shape from the photographic album that chronicles and freezes forgotten moments in the author's childhood. The narrative emerges from the gradual, albeit partial, recollections that the photographs give rise to in the writer's mind. The photographs halt the moment in time, and in later years, when Llamazares discovers the album after his mother's death, the far-away existence that they represent is rekindled — but with a certain nostalgia and even surprise at the realization of how much distance has been covered. A contrast thereby is established between the temporally stagnant photographs and the author's own movement through time. In a deliberate paradox, this narrative of remembering then becomes a statement of temporal rupture. While in *El río del olvido*, Llamazares repeatedly refers to himself as 'el viajero', here his mobile subject-position is made graphic through the narrative effort of reaching back into the past. Indeed, the reminiscences which arise from the photographs would be devoid of meaning without distancing in time and space. The stillness of the photographs as opposed to Llamazares's own mobility as 'viajero' throws the latter into relief. If *Escenas de cine mudo* is a work of archaeology into the past, then it is also a testament to the migration and temporal instability of identity. Indeed the book's title makes this point clear: the memories flit across the writer's mind like scenes from a silent movie, leaving a lasting impression of movement and loss. However, Llamazares makes it clear that he himself is not still as he recalls; rather, the memories appear blurred and unfocused due to the speed at which he himself is travelling through time and space:

Cuando uno viaja en coche por una carretera, no ve pasar en dirección contraria coches idénticos al suyo, sino manchas de color tan hermosas y veloces como efímeras [. . .]
Lo mismo ocurre, seguramente, cuando uno va viajando sin pararse por la vida. Las referencias se alejan como los árboles a los costados del coche que va corriendo por la autopista y, sin que nos demos cuenta, la velocidad del tiempo se acelera y aumenta de manera paralela a la de nuestra propia vida. Pero un día nos paramos, como el viajero que se detiene a contemplar el paisaje al borde de la autopista, y entonces nos damos cuenta del trayecto que hemos hecho y de las cosas que hemos perdido y nos invade de golpe todo ese vértigo que, mientras nosotros también corríamos, no habíamos advertido: el vértigo del tiempo y del paisaje, que huyen. (1994: 53–54)

The speed of travel serves, most significantly, to distance the writer from the community of his childhood. The implication is not just that he himself has moved and changed from those times, but also that those who made up his world as a child have also disappeared or altered. In the final chapter of *Escenas de cine mudo*, Llamazares refers to the now non-existent 'colmena' (1994: 219) or community of his early years: like the snow which melts away, the 'colmena' too no longer exists. Nevertheless, and despite his awareness of movement, he persists in recalling the other members of his 'beehive' as immobile and enduring, as the photographs would suggest:

Es el último (retrato) del álbum y el último también que conservo de Olleros: ese montón de hombres anónimos, como mis padres que sigue inmóvil en mi memoria, pero del que yo ya me estaba yendo. Como la nieve. (1994: 219)

Two key points emerge from this: firstly, the transcience of communal groupings and their eventual dispersal is emphasized. Furthermore, communal bonds appear irrelevant or meaningless in time, so that even the writer's parents become 'hombres anónimos' and lose their individuality by being blurred into a 'montón'. The threat made clear here is not just, therefore, to communal links but also to ties of blood. Family, as the most essential and 'natural' of communities, is rendered vulnerable and defenceless by time. Secondly, individual memories mythify and decontextualize community by freezing it in time and place. On the one hand, narratives such as in this book offer a certain continuity or survival to communal bonds; on the other, while they each evoke a stable and essentialized notion of community, the overall narratives are filled with gaps, locked as they are within the spatial and temporal frames of particular recollections. The construction of plural, and perhaps even contradictory, histories, therefore, arises from the juxtaposition of such narrative traces as the past becomes refigured in a constantly evolving present.

Also worth noting is the medium that Llamazares uses in *Escenas de cine mudo* to arouse memories. The photographs in his family album gain meaning not only from the images and contexts they frame, but also from his own present perspective. In this sense, and as will be explored more thoroughly in the analysis of photographs by Andreú of immigrants in Spain, photography becomes expressive. By exceeding their frames, Llamazares's childhood photographs are refigured in the present, just as they provide narrative traces from which to reconstruct lived histories. Viewed in the light of the shifting and mobile contexts of late modernity that the author now inhabits, the narrative logic of the photographs as arranged in the album offers a vision of cohesive community, rendered all the more unified by the distant perspective from which they are now viewed. As such, what holds the different chapters — and hence photographs — of *Escenas de cine mudo* together is precisely this imagined stability of community, one which, no doubt, given modernity's drives towards displacement, amounts to no more than a myth.

Memory thus acts as a vehicle for temporal experience, bringing forth past events, not as they were, but themselves altered from what they used to be by contact with the present. Not only does Llamazares mediate across temporal shifts and ruptures in this way, but he also positions himself between two very different, and traditionally opposed, narrative forms, the oral and the literary.

His transfer of the 'storytelling' that marked his childhood to polished literary narrative nevertheless conserves the enchanting qualities of the former, since memory confers on the stories the mythical aura of stories from 'afar' — in time if not in distance. This quality is enhanced by repeated descriptions of nature, which shows its strength in contrast with the brittle lives of men. The landscape, and hence the past, is mythified as unruffled by the social ruptures it silently witnesses. As a stable backdrop to the narratives of change, landscape provides Llamazares with the temporal border from which to highlight the sweep of oblivion and to mediate death. The resilience of nature, however, also derives from its holes and cavities, which absorb those who, like the protagonists of *Luna de lobos* or Andrés in *La lluvia amarilla*, have been expelled from community in the course of social change. In this way, nature, like these characters, is rendered legendary as the narrative attempts to conserve memories through the mythification of these characters. Thus, the epic and mythic nature of Llamazares's narratives permit him to maintain a link with the communities which have ceased to exist; they also provide a metaphoric platform whereby they can serve to reformulate communal identity through imagination. In so doing, they invite the readers to experience past temporalities.

The form or style of his prose speaks clearly of this attempt, since the very preoccupations present in his poetry are re-presented in a narrativity which evokes the poetic mood. Key images and metaphors, such as snow or silence, repeat themselves in his work, forming definite patterns. Thus *La lluvia amarilla* bears considerable similarity in terms of content with the following, earlier poem:

Mi memoria es la memoria de la nieve. Mi corazón está blanco
                                como un campo de urces.
En labios amarillos la negación florece. Pero existe un nogal
                                donde habita el invierno.
Un lejano nogal, doblado sobre el agua, a donde acuden los guerreros
                                más viejos.
En un mismo exterior se deshacen los días y la desolación corroe
                                los signos del suicidio;
globos entre las ramas del silencio y un animal sin nombre que se
                                espesa en mi rostro. (1985: 45).

The image of snow evoked in the first line is recalled in both *La lluvia amarilla* and *Luna de lobos*, which ends with a reference to snow in the heart of the last survivor — clearly a metaphoric death. The link between snow and death is evident here and made more explicit later, in *El río del olvido*, which he dedicates to his mother 'que ya es nieve', as previously mentioned. The 'lejano nogal' recalls the tree planted by Andrés in *La lluvia amarilla*, as does the reference to suicide. In this context, it is important to bear in mind Llamazares's own movement in his literary career from poetry to prose. 'Yo soy un poeta metido a novelista' he says in his interview with Marco (1988: 27), thereby indicating his primary calling as poetic, but he stresses the intrinsic connection between the two genres for him by also stating 'Yo pienso que todo lo que he escrito y todo lo que voy a escribir en mi vida es el primer verso de mi primer libro de poesía' (1988: 24):

Nuestra quietud es dulce y azul y torturada en esa hora
Todo es tan lento como el pasar de un buey sobre la nieve [. . .] (1985: 11).

Thus his output in prose amounts to ways of reworking an original poetic preoccupation, divergent only in form rather than in content. His first publication, *La lentitud de los bueyes* (1979) was followed by *Memoria de la nieve* (1982), which won him the Premio Jorge Guillén. Despite this success, he has not published poetry since then, but the prose of his literary works is infused with an undeniably poetic cadence together with the rural and often mythic and haunting imagery of his verse. Once again, the presentation in prose of concerns first expressed through poetry must therefore be viewed as a terrain of negotiation, a compromise of genres that has its own logic. In addition, it should be considered in conjunction with the mediation he undertakes in the area of temporality as well as in the transfer from oral to literary narratives. What emerges is literature which attempts to bridge the gaps and ruptures caused by social change through its efforts to weave communal links across splintered time and distance.

The reformulation of Llamazares's poetic concerns in prose inserts the preoccupations into a tangible, historicized frame by providing a socio-cultural contextualization. In so doing, Llamazares 'up-dates' his narrative calling to match the receptivity of a present, predominantly urban, readership whose awareness of Spain's rural past, of his past, is perhaps somewhat sketchy. Furthermore, this contextualization in prose maintains the veiled poetic nature of his original expression in verse through the movement of sound in his writings. Walter Ong, in his *Orality and* Literacy,[7] stresses the dynamics of sound in oral narration, a quality that is clearly present in Llamazares's prose and which, no doubt, relates to his poetic inception into literary engagement. Ong also emphasizes the mnemonic base of orally transmitted, sonoric narratives, stating that 'you know what you can recall' (1982: 33). Llamazares's reformulation from memory of these narratives (a typical feature of oral storytelling) at the same time establishes rhythms, which combine with the content in the form of repeated phrases to evoke a lost temporality and landscape, characteristic of Llamazares's literary style:

He corrido con todas mis fuerzas. He corrido con rabia, como un perro herido, conteniendo el dolor. Monte abajo, sobre los matorrales, rompiendo la niebla, he corrido con todas mis fuerzas hasta caer reventado en el fondo del valle, a la orilla del río, entre la espesura vegetal y fría de la que brotan ya los primeros destellos del amanecer. (1985: 141).

In writing *Luna de lobos*, Angel's attempts to survive in the mountains are based on oral accounts of the lives of maquis during and after the Civil War. During his 1997 talk at the Instituto Cervantes, Llamazares mentioned these whispered stories heard when he was a boy of disappeared uncles and other men from the local community.[8] The hushed circumstances in which these stories were told, the fear they generated amongst those who, having heard them, became custodians of forbidden knowledge, elevated them to a mythical status, whereby what mattered was not whether they were true or untrue but, rather, the temporal depth, the mystery and the unity from knowing that they conferred on the group. The narrative of *Luna de lobos* further coincides with the encounter described in *El río del olvido* between Llamazares and an elderly man he met in the village of La Mata, Eufemiano Díaz González:

Mi padre tenía miedo de que, en uno de esos registros, me encontraran, y una noche, poco tiempo después de que yo llegara, cavamos una fosa en una esquina de la cuadra para esconderme allí hasta ver qué pasaba con la guerra y si las cosas se calmaban. Era una fosa estrecha y larga. Como una sepultura, para que se imagine [. . .] Yo me metía allí y mi padre o mi hermano me tapaban con un tablero desde arriba. Después, esparcían el abono de las vacas por encima y aquello quedaba perfectamente camuflado [. . .] Pero era muy jodido. Hay que vivirlo, ¿sabe usted? Hay que vivirlo para saber lo que es estar diez años enterrado [. . .] (1990: 35)

Clearly, *Luna de lobos* is a patchwork of the writer's imagination, his memories of orally transmitted stories and his own encounters with war veterans. Yet, at the same time, this fictional narrative provides today's Spain with a powerful account of the stifled history of 'la otra España' of Francoism. In this endeavour, Llamazares takes an important lead in the pressing Spanish task of historical recuperation.

Beyond the loss of a birthplace and the abandonment of a way of life, Llamazares's work therefore also marks the loss of a living oral story-telling culture in Spain,[9] one that coincides with the break-up of localized, rural communities. Much has been said about the influence in his writing of 'los cuentos con los que me durmieron' (to quote Llamazares from the talk he gave at the Instituto Cervantes in 1997).[10] In his interview with Marco, he reiterates that he comes from a popular tradition based on orality, which makes him 'un escritor profundamente español' (1988: 25) for Spain, he insists, is today 'una sociedad urbana con una memoria rural' (1988: 25). Thus Llamazares emphasizes the collective loss of oral narrativity and with this, the loss of direct communal participation in the dissemination and reception of stories suffered by Spaniards in their movement towards urban living. Contemporary readers are urged through his writing to evoke, perhaps for the first time, what must have been the lifestyles and experiences of their parents and grandparents. The finality of that way of life lends an aura of pre-eminence to his writing. Llamazares's creative work can thus be considered to gain its authority/

'authenticity' (in Heidegger's terms) from its direct engagement with Spain's buried rural memory and, on a more abstract level, its engagement with the experience of loss, both past and imminent. In this way, the present too is altered (more recently, this refiguring of the past is evident in the film *Flores de otro mundo* [Icíar Bollaín, 1999], which was co-scripted by Llamazares). Over and again, the narrative traces that Llamazares calls forth from a forgotten past problematize Spain's modernity, questioning the rush for progress and high-lighting the hidden costs of the latter.[11]

When considering the past that is alluded to in Llamazares's work, it is important to stress that his writing is not an elegy to a lost but idyllic rural environment, despite the many references to peasant communities: instead, his exploration of memory (*Escenas de cine mudo, El río del olvido*) chronicles the earlier (and slower-paced) modernity of Spain in the 1960s whereby the exploitation of nature and landscape for the sake of capital gain was already in place. His recollections of mining villages (where miners' families also engaged in agricultural activities) emphasize the cost of such industries both in terms of the ransacking of the surrounding landscape and also in terms of human lives. The subsequent submergence of some of these villages under dams was, therefore, merely a new dimension to the already existing practices of industrial exploitation. In this sense, the 'denaturalization' of communities, with the pace and timing of communal and individual lives organized around shift-work and its requirements, precedes the 'deterritorialization' that accompanies our contemporary late modernity. Furthermore, Llamazares's own literary discourse is formed out of the images and vocabulary that accompany the experience of mining. In this sense, Llamazares's use of language is clearly developed from the social practices of modernity. Most obvious in this sense is his description of memory as a mine and of recollection as a kind of 'unearthing'. In *Escenas de cine mudo*, Llamazares states that

Las minas deben de tener memoria. O, mejor: la memoria es una mina oculta en nuestro cerebro. Una mina profunda, insondable y oscura, llena de sombras y galerías, que se va abriendo ante nuestros ojos a medida que avanzamos dentro de ella; una mina tan profunda como los hundimientos de muestros sueños. Así, a medida que yo avanzaba en ella, en mi memoria se iba encendiendo una luz (una luz roja, difusa, como las de las linternas y los focos de mis dos acompañanates) que alumbraba cada vez con más intensidad la mina de mis recuerdos. (1994: 107)

Literature as recollection for Llamazares thereby becomes a process of mining, an exploratory venture into buried temporality that reveals unexpected and long-forgotten experiences. In this context, the construction of literature becomes an archaeology of time. Furthermore, Llamazares indicates that the route into memory is uncharted and throws up surprising findings, some of which may have been real and others imagined. Equally, no investigation of memory is complete as the act of remembering is at once an affirmation of oblivion:

Entre cada recuerdo -como entre cada fotografía — , quedan siempre una zonas en sombra bajo las que se nos ocultan trozos de nuestra propia vida; trozos de vida a veces tan importantes, o tan significativos, como los que viviremos todavía. (1994: 59)

Memories, like archaeological findings amongst ruins, are symbolic of a larger scheme of life that can only be imagined in retrospect. As disconnected findings, they can be assembled in many ways to produce different narratives of the past. The gaps in memory are therefore as important as the memories themselves. The incompleteness of memory leads to the multiple narratives and plural 'truths' from which identity is constructed. Llamazares's insistence on the many possibilities and movements of memory shows identity to be fluid and incomplete, a challenge to the modern notion that narratives must necessarily follow a causal, linear sequence. No master narrative therefore can bind identity at a communal level. Within such a context of inconsistency, the imagination of community can at best be partially expressed and experienced kaleidoscopically. Yet, without the incomplete efforts of narratives of memory, the imagination of community would cease to be at all possible.

The narrative act that Llamazares undertakes as a writer can be viewed, therefore, as an attempt to counter the finality of death or oblivion. Recalling Berman's much quoted borrowing from Marx that 'all that is solid melts into air', oblivion in Llamazares's work is a defining condition of modernity. Equally, it is this very temporal horizon which confers authority to his writing. However, the very loss that propels the narratives also allows a kind of refiguring, since the authority that mortality confers upon them feeds and affirms the story-telling process. The emphasis here is clearly on narration as a means of transcending the finality of death through the offering of experience turned into narrative to larger, though dispersed, collectives. Equally important, however, is the point that the shared narratives attempt to re-figure former experiences of community identity in the present by offering a tapestry of collective memory; the narratives provide a shared landscape as a backdrop to a communal imaginary, in the same way as they affirm the demise of localized, rural communities through modernization. Hence, Ricoeur's statement that fiction and history are both legitimate means of accounting for lost time and are necessary devices for the orientation of a 'self'. The imagination of communities thereby takes diverse forms, accompanied as it is by dispensability and temporal fragility. In line with Ricoeur's view of story-telling as a means of constructing communal identity through shared remembrances, Llamazares's work is a fictional or imagined evocation of often overlooked aspects of Spain's socio-cultural history. Equally important here is Adorno's insistence that aesthetic endeavour rearranges history through new constellations which lead to new understandings. In Llamazares's case, the spotlight he throws on the forgotten or silenced aspects of Spanish history contests the primacy of social progress as modernity's central project. By foregrounding death and oblivion, the story-telling act is rendered urgent, yet forever incomplete and open to revision. The spatial and temporal scatterings of modernity may, on the one hand, undermine cohesive narration and, hence, unified communities, making a single mnemonic landscape problematic or even impossible. On the other hand, and precisely because of spatial dislocations and temporal fragmentation, communal identifications can be constructed and experienced in myriad ways: the emphasis here falls not on one unbroken and all-encompassing narrative of the past, but on the open-ended narratives upon which the imagination of community identities can hang. Such narratives draw upon the memories and the oblivion of the past to further construct historical understandings, whether these be from 'true' or 'imagined' experience. While Llamazares evokes past experiences, he also underlines the impossibility of grasping or regaining the past, except through memory/ imagination, as is made clear in *La lluvia amarilla*. Llamazares's mnemonic narratives, thereby, are equally an expression of the deterritorialization of community in the course of modernity, as they are an attempt to rescue traces of lived histories and gather them into meaningful constellations.

1. A considerable corpus of publications already exists on Llamazares's writing. In particular, Robert Baah (1996 and 1997), Agustín Otero (1996 and 1997), Sonja Herpoel (1997), and the doctoral dissertation of Caridad Ravenet Kenna (1997) explore key issues of memory, history, narration, landscape, silence, and death — all central to an understanding of community in Llamazares's work.
2. Rowe and Schelling (1992) have produced a seminal text on the complications of memory in the context of modernity. While their work examines Latin America, nevertheless, numerous issues they raise are relevant in other cultures as well.
3. See Graham and Labanyi (1995: 398–99) for a discussion of postmodernism in Spain that has led to a profusion of cultural texts resulting from the 'experience of history as synchronicity' (398).
4. Krell (1992) outlines key aspects of Heidegger's philosophy. Similarly, Richard Kearney (1996) explores Ricoeur's move away from ego-centricity through his emphasis on narration. Valdés (1991) is also useful in this respect.
5. Title of Llamazares's talk at the Cervantes Institute, London, 21 October   1997.
6. Bullón de Mendoza and de Diego (2000: 83–100) collate stories of the ruptures suffered by family and sexual relationships during the Civil War, focusing particularly on the experiences of women, like María in *Luna de lobos*, whose husbands or boyfriends had either died or gone missing.
7. Ong also underlines the improvisatory, context-bound fluctuations in narrative renderings of memory, which again points to history as imagined construction.
8. Fraser (1979) provides detailed accounts of similar oral narratives of Civil War experiences. In this context, Perks and Thompson (1998) cover numerous issues concerning oral history in their reader.
9. John Macklin (1995: 31–48) links Llamazares to Unamuno in terms of a timeless wold created through memory as a refuge from modernity.
10. Sánchez's article (1995) is a case in point; so also José Carlón's book (1996).
11. Llamazares's alarm at the price paid for being modern is made explicit in his article 'Pueblos abandonados', in *El País Semanal* (30 April 2000: 66–71), where he states 'lo

acabaremos pagando. Cuando gran parte del país sea un auténtico cementerio, alguien querrá ponerle remedio. . .Y entonces querrá saber. . .qué sintieron sus últimos habitantes al ir quedándose solos, y porque ocurrió todo eso. . .Pero los únicos que le responderán son el silencio y el viento' (71).

CHAPTER 3

TEMPORAL MOSAICS: JUGGLING COMMUNITY, NARRATIVE FRAGMENTS, AND POSTMODERNITY IN THE WORK OF BERNARDO ATXAGA

This chapter will examine two works by the Basque writer Bernardo Atxaga, *Obabakoak* (1988) and *El hombre solo* (1995), in order to assess their treatment of contemporary Spanish experiences of history and temporality and the subsequent effects on community identity. The previous chapter probed these issues in Llamazares's work in the context of modernity. My aim here is to intensify the problematization of community in modernity presented in the first chapter through an analysis of Atxaga's focus on identity in the more recent contexts of post-Francoist Spain. Underlying the key issues which arise in this chapter, therefore, is the postmodern incompletion of modernity that was explored in the first chapter. In particular, this disjuncture need to be considered in terms of Spain's uneven modernization and sudden, jolting thrust into the transnational, globalized, and capital-driven networks which abruptly altered notions of unified identity, following the transition to democracy (1978–82). The ensuing complications to conventional practices of community that paradoxically coincided with mounting discourses of community identities based on imagined unities of time and space are diversely explored in Atxaga's work.

It is therefore worth recalling at this point the complexities and unevenness of the Spanish experiences of modernity in the late twentieth century. Bearing in mind Delanty's view (outlined in the introduction) that postmodernity marks a shift in the modern prioritization of Self over Other (2000) as well as a heightening of reflexivity, then the notion of community as 'rooting' or 'home' becomes all the more poignant in the context of postmodernity's rapid and multi-dimensional cultural shifts. Add to this the steep acceleration of modernization in the post-Francoist years together with the reflexive emphasis on plural identities at regional, national and European levels. It then becomes evident that a cleavage arises in the notion of community: its appeal, on the one hand, derives from the myth of stability and anchoring that is attached to it; its practices, on the other, reveal fragmentation, mobility, and ambivalence. Community, thus, as group belonging, both offers notions of stability to the collective imaginary and undermines the latter through its own implications in the fluid dynamics of postmodernity.

Equally important to a reading of Atxaga's work is an understanding of the shifts in Basque nationalism in the twentieth century.[1] Clearly, as autonomous 'community' and as 'nación histórica', contemporary political discourses in Spain blur nation with community in the Basque (and other) context(s), infusing the former notion with the localized, unified, and secure identity traditionally implicit in the latter. Indeed, this emphasis upon regional community can be viewed as a reversal of the Francoist stress on State unification. It also provides the basis for new nationalisms, as in the Basque case. However, closer scrutiny of this contemporary discourse reveals the shifts and fragmentations of Basque nationalism. As of the late nineteenth century, Sabino de Arana, generally hailed as the father of Basque nationalism, stressed the racial uniqueness of the Basques, allying the latter with the Catholic Church and thereby merging Catholicism with nationalism (Juaristi 2000: 24–27). Following the Nationalist victory and the forced assimilation of Basque identity, a split occurred in the Church, officially allied with the State but sympathetic at some local levels to the Basque predicament. Simultaneously, increased immigrant presence in the Basque Country together with accelerated industrialization saw a rise in trade unions and workers' organizations. As Sullivan (1988) points out, the development of ETA in the late 1950s was an essentialist attempt to foreground Basque identity in the face of Francoist assimilation. Like Carlos in *El hombre solo*, Marxism served for many young nationalists in the 1960s and 70s as the ideology harnessing activism, the result, in part, of the Church's failure to back Basque identity. The essentialism attached to nationalism, its supposed indivisibility from notions of racial and religious 'purity', thus belies the shifts and movements inherent to it as process rather than as an essentialized form of identity. In more recent times, further splits have appeared in nationalist discourses in the Basque Country; so also major splinters within ETA. As Antonio Elorza points out, contemporary discourses of plurality both balance tensions between regional and central identities and exacerbate nationalist factions wishing to splinter off from Spain. In this sense, discourses of Basque identity have shifted and altered with contexts, but nevertheless continue to be essentialist. It is small wonder, then, that this tension persists as a preoccupation in the work of many of the more prominent Basque intellectuals, such as Atxaga (another, very different, example being the work of the film-maker Julio Medem), whereby cultural texts attempt to articulate the indeterminacy resulting from the myth of essentialism lingering, paradoxically, in the midst of postmodern pluralities.

Both *Obabakoak* and *El hombre solo* grapple with this paradox, though in different ways. Whilst *Obabakoak* presents a reworking of Basque traditions of oral narratives[2] into a chain of partially-connected tales, *El hombre solo* problematizes the question of coherent identity and purpose in postmodernity.

Both works, therefore, struggle with the fragmentation of identity within contemporary cultural contexts, an issue that is itself closely linked to the processes of globalization and overriding capitalism that are associated with postmodernity. Atxaga's works, thus, reveal the dilemmas relating to communal identity which have grown since the fall of socialism witnessed in Europe after 1989, a historical moment which, in his view, marked the displacement of any given belief[3] as a motivating force providing unity and coherence of identity. The diverse stories of *Obabakoak* and the multiple voices of *El hombre solo* attempt to narrate the history of lived experience, but are constantly challenged by the impossibility of a stable rendering. What emerges, then, is the question of whether fragmented narratives can render history and so maintain and construct social cohesion in the form of community identity. Another question which arises is whether the concept of community identity is being refigured by such fragmented narratives which force the latter to be viewed, not in terms of cohesion, but in terms of mobility and passage.

This chapter will begin with an outline of key aspects of Atxaga's work and the cultural and political climates from which it ensues. I shall then lay out first Laclau and Mouffe's and then Jameson's reworking of Marxism, so as to clarify the theoretical framework for my analysis. This is drawn from an alignment of the theories developed by Ernesto Laclau and Chantal Mouffe in their work entitled *Hegemony and Socialist Strategy, Towards a Radical Democratic Politics* (1985) with Fredric Jameson's critique of postmodernity developed in his *Postmodernism, or, the Cultural Logic of Late Capitalism* (1991), which marks the collapse of temporality into spatiality, with an ensuing loss of critical distance and aesthetic depth. Jameson further insists that all narratives should be placed within the greater historical narrative of Marxism, for the cultural changes brought on by the giddy shifts and flows of globalized, transnational capital themselves force a kind of stasis deriving from the spatial fragmentation of the subject and the loss of historical consciousness. I shall then proceed to analyse firstly *Obabakoak* and then *El hombre solo* in the light of these theories. In this context, it should be borne in mind that while the concept of hegemony, central to Laclau and Mouffe's theories, will be particularly relevant to *El hombre solo*, it is less so to *Obabakoak* where the play of power is not so much in evidence.

Laclau and Mouffe as well as Jameson draw on Marxism for the formulation of their theoretical positions with regard to postmodernism. These theorists therefore engage with postmodernism in order to reconstruct radical politics. In this regard, Best and Kellner state that, as dialectical thinkers, Laclau and Mouffe view postmodern discourse as:

a borderline discourse between the modern and the postmodern that allows a creative restructuring of modern theory and politics. (1985: 181)

Jameson views postmodernism not as a rupture with history, but as a stage in the development of the latter. Postmodernism, therefore, is for Jameson the cultural expression of globalized, accelerated capitalism. The relevance of Jameson's theories to Atxaga's work was made evident to me in my interview with Atxaga (London, April 1999), when he stated that he followed Jameson's work with keen interest, considering him to be an insightful analyst of contemporary culture. This focus can be tied to Atxaga's own former Marxist position and his current ambivalence regarding postmodernity's cultural consequences (personal interview, London, April 1999). While Jameson and Laclau and Mouffe develop their ideas from a tradition of Marxism and are equally engaged in efforts to write a new radical politics within the current post-structuralist theoretical climate that is marked by plurality and deconstruction, it is nevertheless important to bear in mind what it is that makes their work quite different. Jameson asserts the supremacy of Marxism over other social theories; Laclau and Mouffe, on the other hand, have shifted their focus towards an attempt to refigure Marxism in terms of postmodern theory in order to formulate a reworking of the Gramscian concept of hegemony that allows for a 'radical plural democracy'. In this context, Jameson states in his *Postmodernism, or, the Cultural Logic of Late Capitalism* that

the foundational description and the 'working ideology' of the new politics, as it is found in Chantal Mouffe and Ernesto Laclau's *Hegemony and Socialist Strategy*, is overtly postmodern and must be studied in the larger context we have proposed for this term. (1991: 319)

For Jameson, this 'larger context' is clearly that of the postmodern loss of an ability to 'map cognitively', i.e. to orient a stable self in relation to temporal and spatial boundaries, a loss which itself must be accorded a historical location.

The plural and diverse affirmations of cultural identities expressed simultaneously at regional, national, and European levels in Spain following the transition to democracy came to the fore in literary circles when, in 1989, Bernardo Atxaga received the Premio Nacional de la Literatura, the Premio de la Crítica and the Premio Euskadi for his novel in Basque, *Obabakoak* (1988).[4] The book also reached the round of finalists for the European Literary Award in Glasgow in 1990. The award of the National Prize for Literature for a novel in Basque blew away any last, lingering cobwebs of Francoist suppression of cultural difference; it also raised important questions about writing in a language with a fragile literary tradition and under a surrounding socio-political imperative of promoting regional identity. Emerging as it did in the period of transition to democracy, Atxaga's work at once expresses his Basque origins as well as his membership of a larger intellectual community of diverse and interconnected textualities. Writing within the multi-referential veins of postmodernism, Atxaga brings together a variety of narrative practices which invite questions around concepts of community identity, history, and temporality in the context of postmodernity. Evident in his work is his familiarity with important aspects of European literature, philosophy, and politics. Like other Basque writers who are faced with the relatively recent emergence of Basque literature and the lack of translations into Basque of the canon of Western literature, he uses the Basque context as a spring-board for re-working the conceptual paradigms borrowed from other cultural contexts. This in turn leads to a kind of writing which is experimental and exploratory. Thus, whilst Atxaga has undoubtedly put Basque literature on the world map, his narrative strategies nevertheless reveal the former to be a hybrid site of inter-connections.

The challenge that Atxaga takes up, willingly or not, is thus to probe any assumptions on the part of the reader of a unified and rooted Basque identity and nationalism. Atxaga's status as a Basque writer with a worldwide readership is inevitably juxtaposed with the socio-cultural implications of the Basque Country's fervent nationalism and, more particularly, decades of media focus on ETA's terrorist activities.[5] In the course of his writing, Atxaga pulls at the loose threads of essentialist rhetorics of identity through intertextual references that underline the migrancy of cultural identity and the insufficiency of discourses of cultural authority. At the same time, he explores the driving need to believe in essential 'truths', upon which fixed notions of identity rest. The problem he struggles with as a result is that of juggling the simultaneous, competing, and fragmented narratives of lived experience in tandem with the apparent need to believe in a single authoritative version which would allow for a simple, linear, and unified rendering of history. The multiple narrative strands in his books come up against the same issue of ruptured temporality, whereby questions surrounding the cohesiveness of community identity and shared history are raised. In an interview with *Cambio 16* (6 Nov. 1995: 14–15), Atxaga states that despite his international success as a writer, he remains a son of Asteasu, a small Basque village. Clearly, the issue at hand in his work is that of the stability of identity when threatened or fragmented by the acceleration of late modernity. The connections made possible by modernity and accelerated by postmodernity open up the supposedly tight units of identity maintained in earlier times through shared narratives within enclosed spaces. Atxaga's evident use of postmodern narrative techniques (the use of multiple narratorial voices, co-existing and contradictory identities, the closing-in of temporal horizons, etc. being examples of these) problematize essential perceptions of localized identity. As myths, legends, narratives, and experiences cross paths at many levels in *Obabakoak*, for example, Atxaga states that:

no hay, hoy en día, nada que sea estrictamente en particular. El mundo está en todas partes y Euskal Herria, ya no es solamente Euskal Herria, sino [. . .] *el lugar donde el mundo toma el nombre de Euskal Herria.* (1993: 493)

For Atxaga's characters, the deconstruction of cultural identity leads to a crisis of belief, as the apparently solid pillars of community identity give way to a series of indefinite connections, experienced diversely from different angles. As identity becomes 'spaced out', there is at the same time the problem of having to slice time up, leading to splintered and disjointed narratives. The problem of such multiplicity is explored in different ways in his *Obabakoak* (1988) and later in *El hombre solo* (1993).

My juxtaposition of the theories of Laclau and Mouffe with those of Jameson is a deliberate attempt on my part to engage with this ambivalence developed in Atxaga's work and shown to lead to a sense of crisis. Laclau and Mouffe describe their stance as post-Marxist and rooted in anti-essentialism, with an emphasis on a plurality of forms of struggle and on the relations which these forms establish amongst themselves. For Laclau and Mouffe, therefore, unities are symbolic and, in practical terms, composed of antagonisms or differences which constantly enter into play with one another and evolve into ever-changing new patterns. They insist that the socialist project has had to abandon the essentialist logic of class which formed its basis due to what they call 'historical mutations', as can be witnessed by the many socio-political movements (such as feminism, the protest movements of racial and other minorities, etc.) that have arisen in recent years. They therefore view traditional Marxism as reductionist, in that human concerns are perceived solely through an essentialist logic of class. Furthermore, they reject the Marxist objective of universal homogeneity as limiting rather than liberating. Laclau and Mouffe argue for a 'radical democracy' which is based on discourses of pluralities which enable multiple and pluriform struggles to be played out. Only this postmodern vision of politics, they argue, will allow the projects of modernity to be fulfilled.

Central to Laclau and Mouffe's argument is their understanding of subjectivity. Points of contact between antagonisms and different forms of struggle create 'subject-positions' which are always partially in a state of flux within an overall system of differences. Thus identity is necessarily kaleidoscopic and never set. Mouffe explains their conception of identity in an essay entitled 'Democratic Politics and the Question of Identity' in the following way:

It [ie. the social agent] is constructed by a diversity of discourses, among which there is no necessary relation but a constant movement of overdetermination and displacement. The 'identity' of such a multiple and contradictory subject is therefore always contingent and precarious, temporarily fixed at the intersections of those subject positions and dependant on specific forms of identification. This plurality, however, does not involve the 'co-existence', one by one, of a plurality of subject-positions but the constant subversion and overdetermination of one by the others, which makes possible the generation of 'totalizing effects' within a field characterised by open and determinate frontiers. (Laclau and Mouffe 1985: 33–34)

Any attempt to articulate identity can therefore only be partially fulfilled. Arising from this understanding of subject-positions is their development of the term hegemony. Laclau and Mouffe have extended the traditional understanding of this term from the Gramscian concept of the organization of consent between social classes to denote a fixed terrain of floating elements operating in diverse and opposing camps.[6] To quote:

Thus, the two conditions of hegemonic articulation are the presence of antagonistic forces and the instability of the frontiers which separate them [. . .] Without equivalence and without frontiers, it is impossible to speak strictly of hegemony. (1985: 136)

Thus hegemony for Laclau and Mouffe is the process of negotiation between diverse and opposing factors which themselves are in a state of partial flux. It is therefore an on-going process of relation that takes place within an 'open, non-sutured social'. Best and Kellner describe Laclau and Mouffe's concept of hegemony in the following way:

[. . .] Laclau and Mouffe see hegemony as the crucial category whereby, once freed from an essentialist logic, one can comprehend the nature of social reality as plural, complex and overdetermined, grasp the new social movements as autonomous from class struggles, and appropriate their historical possibilities for constructing the conditions for radical democracy. (1991: 195)

Hegemony arises not from what there *is* in any category, but in fact from what there *isn't*, i.e., it arises from a lack. Openness is hence a vital condition for hegemony, since it allows for the mutations that strive constantly towards a wholeness that cannot be achieved and the lack of which is its very source of definition. Furthermore, for Laclau and Mouffe, a hegemonic situation allows for a limitless range of possibilities and as such is in turn flexible and open by nature.

Laclau and Mouffe and Jameson walk the ground where modernity blurs into postmodernity in their reworkings of Marxism. They deal differently with the problem of juggling Marxism's totalizing structural emphasis with postmodern fragmented subjectivity. My juxtaposition of their respective theories and their critiques is aimed at highlighting the dilemmas that mark Atxaga's work. In turn, perhaps an examination of Atxaga's writing sheds light on the problems faced by these theorists in abstracting the shifting, ambivalent contours of late modernity.

The divergence between Jameson, on the one hand, and Laclau and Mouffe, on the other, however, lies in their understandings of social structure and historical agency. A postmodern rewriting of Marxism is by definition problematic. The master narrative of Marxism is at variance with postmodernity's stress on the demise of grand narratives. Laclau and Mouffe, as seen earlier, deal with this problem by adopting the concept of an 'open non-sutured social'[7] and focusing on the question of hegemony through antagonisms between multiple positions. Jameson's critique of Laclau and Mouffe points to an inferred totality in terms of their concept of the 'open social' (1991: 331–40). It could be argued that the metaphor of containment is present in their language of openness, since 'open' can only be understood in relation and in contrast to 'closed'. He states, thus, that their eschewal of the term 'society' in favour of the 'social' stigmatizes the former in an effort to evade totality (1990: 231). Furthermore, it could be stated that by abandoning the framing historical narrative of Marxism, Laclau and Mouffe can no longer address the temporal parameters of social experience. The antagonisms they describe between the multiple subject-positions lack temporal definition through having no recourse to historical narratives.

Jameson, thus, develops the notion of the interpretive act within the framework of Marxism. Even prior to the collapse of communism in Europe, i.e. prior to what Atxaga has termed the end of ideology, Jameson had stressed in his *Political Unconscious* that history is encoded in narrative form:

(past events) can recover their original urgency for us only if they are told within the unity of a single great collective story; only if, in however disguised and symbolic a form, they are seen as sharing a single fundamental theme [. . .] only if they are grasped as the vital episodes in a single vast unfinished plot. (1981: 19–20)

Jameson's stress on form should be especially noted, since he views it not as separate from content, but rather as bearing content. This is a view that is reiterated in his more recent work *Postmodernism, or, the Cultural Logic of Late Capitalism* (1991). Narratives must be viewed within an overall historical structure because, according to him, they arise as a means of 'managing' the contradictions of particular historical conjunctures. Jameson's work on post-modernity, most notably his major work cited above, is a plea for retaining a conception of history in order to better apprehend the universalizing logic of late capitalism. As Homer states when writing about Jameson, 'he contends that postmodernism represents a significant decline in our sense of history, narrative and memory, and simultaneously of aesthetic depth and critical distance' (1998: 130). What Jameson thereby underlines is the loss in postmodernity of temporal dimensions. Cultural artefacts thus arise from alienation and estrangement and history can be apprehended through them. Jameson's efforts, therefore, are to reassess culture within the context of late capitalism and its ensuing postmodern collapse of temporal parameters into spatial ones:

The crisis in historicity now dictates a return, in a new way, to the question of temporal organization in general in the postmodern force field and, indeed, to the problem of the form that time, temporality and the syntagmatic will be able to take in a culture increasingly dominated by space and spatial logic. (1991: 25)

The loss of temporal dimensions clearly translates into a loss of coherence of experience, rendering the latter into merely 'heaps of fragments' (1991: 25).

For Jameson, the dynamic of historical/narrative forms takes place within what he calls the Real, a term he borrows from Lacan to signify that which is beyond representation. In this sense, Jameson describes history as the Real. If the Real as a limit can therefore be equated with the confrontation with mortality and is at the same time synonymous with history, then cultural and literary narratives become artefacts of death. Such texts therefore both reveal shadows of lived experiences and fail to apprehend them. Textual representation affirms death and emerges from it. Thus, according to Jameson, narratives, regardless of how spatially dispersed they may be, must eventually encounter the temporal finality of death/history. Narratives therefore can be considered to arise as a means of managing history.

The weakness of postmodern narratives can thus be understood in Jameson's terms as a failure to address the inexorable Real through a collapse of the temporal into the spatial. Thus Jamesons states 'the postmodern period [. . .] eschews temporality for space and has generally grown skeptical about deep phenomenological experience in general' (1991: 134.). In Atxaga's work, the spatially scattered narratives eventually run up against their own temporal finality. Interestingly, it would seem that his preoccupation with finding the last word through endlessly related tales or despite them — at once an expression of the impossibility of such a quest — is closely linked to his own socio-cultural experiences. In the hour-long interview that I had with him,[8] Atxaga said that he was perturbed by the apparent loss of ideology in contemporary Spain (see footnote 2 of this chapter) which led, he said, to fear, an emotion which transforms people. Atxaga stated that fear gives rise to voices, stories, madness. Interestingly, he said that in the course of his own life, he had encountered several people who had slipped into 'madness' or schizophrenia. He was obviously inferring a link between the 'voices' they heard and the postmodern context they inhabit. The fear he alludes to can similarly be understood to be the expression of temporal confusion and impending mortality, an existential panic which ensues from the breakdown of traditional social structures and the cultural chaos of globalization. Atxaga's work can be read, therefore, as a statement that, despite the apparent loss of such 'confining' or 'shaping' structures, there are limitations to the freedom offered by plurality, as the latter is itself contingent upon historical circumstances. Here, Atxaga's writing avails of the Basque context in order to illustrate postmodernity's own historical contingency that is applicable to more widespread global contexts.

The implications of the above to conventional concepts and practices of community are evident: on the one hand, as what is 'Basque' becomes increasingly indeterminate and interconnected to other forms of identity, community is deterritorialized and temporal depths are lost. On the other hand, the nostalgia for community colours the imaginary, so that, as Jameson states in *Postmodernism, or, the Cultural Logic of Late Capitalism* when writing of the video as the archetypal postmodern art form:

these films can be read as dual symptoms: they show a collective unconscious in the process of trying to identify its own present at the same time that they illuminate the failure of this attempt, which seems to reduce itself to the recombination of various stereotypes of the past. (1991: 296)

For Jameson, the prevalent mood of postmodernity is nostalgia, an aimless hankering after an imagined, holistic past stripped of historical definition, significant of the collapse of temporality in the present.

As is made explicit in both *Obabakoak* and *El hombre solo,* the issue of unified community identity is particularly poignant within the Basque context. The post-Franco politics of plurality which, since the Basque Autonomy Statute of 1980, has allowed a great deal of autonomy to the Basque region, also throws into disarray the prior ideological struggle for independence. Spain's hurried efforts to accelerate its economy in order to align itself with Europe has led to a fragmentation of traditional social links. This in turn has led to broken narratives of community identity, struggling for coherence but unable to maintain linear cohesion due to the coexistence of plural and competing time frames and spatial displacement. However, Atxaga does not view the socio-cultural changes in the Basque region merely within the context of an overall national politics of plurality. Rather, as his above quote on the indeterminacy of local identities suggests, Atxaga's choice of a Basque setting speaks of the indeterminacy of local and national identities, caught up in the larger, global sweep of late modernity.

Obabakoak blurs the genres of short story and novel through a kaleidoscopic interweaving of separate narratives which spring from a single imaginary location of Obaba, although several of them traverse the globe in the course of their telling. Thus a rural Basque village in the author's imagination serves as a point of departure for the crossings of orality, postmodernity, and multi-layered and exchangeable identities. The book is divided into three main parts, each of which is a further composite of inter-related narratives. Atxaga combines the Basque traditions of oral narratives with reworkings of literary tales from other parts of the world. Through such inter-relation, the reader is invited to connect the different parts of the book, although it is not always certain that these connections do exist. Furthermore, the stories weave webs of connections across temporal frames and geographical locations.

A reading of *Obabakoak* is suggestive of the shifts and ambivalences of identity in postmodernity. Equally, the title, which can be translated into English as 'The People and Things of Obaba', evokes community in its most basic form, i.e. in terms of social group or family and, more specifically, of unified spatial parameters. Generally considered a novel, the work defies the coherence and continuity of plot of such a genre. Despite the brief narratives that compose the volume, *Obabakoak* can neither be considered an anthology of short stories because of the suggestive inter-relation of content and possibly narrator between

several of the stories. Nevertheless, a question mark hangs in the air as to the
certainty of these relations. Furthermore, one is never sure whether the narrator
of the three parts is the same person, two different people, or even three. What
holds the book together are the diverse and pluriform glimpses of Obaba and its
inhabitants, as well as the repeated surfacing of a preoccupation with identity as
'role play', disguise, and transfer. Furthermore, the very construction of a
mythical Obaba through narratives of supposed experience privileges textuality
as the sole means of approximating 'reality', even as the latter is thereby
distanced.

'Infancias', the first section of *Obabakoak*, opens with a story entitled 'Esteban
Werfell'. Immediately, the reader is struck by the hybridity of the name, as an
inhabitant of the remote village bears a Germanic surname. The presence of
Esteban's German father in Obaba serves to open the latter to the outside world
and thereby make possible the feigned correspondence set up by Esteban's
father between the boy and an imaginary German girl. While Esteban persists in
believing that Maria Vockel was his first girlfriend, he also is aware that the
relationship, though real at the time for him, was nevertheless contrived by his
father's imagination and fear and was, therefore, no more than a myth. What is
more, this myth arises from the overlapping of Esteban's father's fear of cultural
difference with the equally narrow-minded community of Obaba. What Werfell
fails to recognize is that his own presence in Obaba stretches the latter's
horizons. Therefore, in Laclau and Mouffe's words, Werfell's 'antagonisms'
with his immediate social context lead to imaginary subject-positions for him
and for his son, in the same way as they 'construct' the person of Maria Vockel.
In later years, as Esteban struggles to write his story, he comes face to face with
the insufficiencies of writing about specific conjunctures in his life: 'Es posible
que la vida sólo pueda ser juzgada en su totalidad [. . .] y no a trozos, no
separando los años como las piezas de un rompecabezas. . .' (1989: 36). This
view of history coincides with Jameson's stress on the need for totalizing
horizons within which to form relations. Nevertheless, Esteban is frustrated by
the limitations of thought and the inability to capture history:

Nuestro pensamiento es arena, y cuando intentamos recoger un puñado de ese
pensamiento, la mayor parte de los granos se nos escurren entre los dedos. (1989:
35)

The instability of thought and recollection must inevitably lead not just to the
imaginary constructions of historical narratives but also to an equation between
history and loss.

The second story once again explores the overlaps of myth and reality through
the fragmented letter left by Canónigo Lizardi. His illegitimate paternity of
Javier becomes evident through his account of the boy's transformation into a
wild boar, hunted by the villagers in revenge for his attacks on those who

maltreated him when he was a human. Emblematic of the major features of *Obabakoak*, this story underlines the relationship between texts through the letter within a story, in the same way as in the former story, Esteban's memoirs give rise to the account of the correspondence. In the last section of the book, Atxaga includes various snippets of dialogue in English: perhaps Lizardi's name is an early indication of this through the possible connection it suggests with the 'lagarto' that is central to the final section and to the principle preoccupations of the book and whose picture appears on most, if not all, editions of *Obabakoak*.[9] In this context, the connotations of the lizard or 'lagarto' in terms of Basque nationalism should be underlined. As Jon Juaristi points out in his introduction to *El bucle meláncolico* (1997: 34), the Basque poet José María Aguirre, better known as *Lizardi*, made a significant contribution through his work to the construction of nationalist discourse in the Basque Country. Atxaga's multiple ways of playing with his pseudonym in the course of *Obabakoak* underline the preoccupation with nationalism that ties much of his work and which, by extension, leads on to a questioning of fundamentalist notions of identity.

Canon Lizardi conducts his life through the mask allotted to him by his social and religious role. All the same, he is clearly tormented by the 'natural' feelings of paternal concerns, but has no direct means of expressing them. The parallel with the Basque situation under Francoism (the alliance of State and Church here leading to the stifling of 'natural' identity) whereby there is no outlet for patriotic or nationalist sentiments thus becomes obvious, particularly if this is considered in the light of conventional links — as can be deduced from the etymology of the two terms — between patriarchy and patriotism.[10] The text of his letter, of which only fragments have survived the ravages of time, expresses the myth of Javier turned 'jabalí' in order to demarcate, not merely Javier's isolation, but also his own torn and isolated subjectivity. Other members of the community of Obaba are also shown as isolated, fractured both in themselves and in their social roles. In an interesting reversal of Esteban's imaginary relationship, the schoolteacher in a later story misjudges postal delays as signs of no interest from her boyfriend in her hometown. Once again, the imagined unleashes a series of actions and thoughts that serve to isolate and fragment the individuals concerned. The passage of the train through Obaba at night, the shrill sound of its whistle, arouses the imagination to evoke what might be. Its associations differ according to who hears it and when it is heard:

El tren reduce velocidad al atrevasar el puente, y ése es el momento más importante de la noche. Es entonces cuando enciendo el cigarro que suelo tener guardado en la mesilla; y es entonces cuando me pongo a imaginar. (1989: 140)

or, for example,

Y de los railes no es lo único que te da miedo cuando viajas en tren, porque de pronto caes en la cuenta de que otro tren podría surgir de la oscuridad, en dirección contraria, quiero decir, y chocar de frente contra ti. (1989: 141)

Strange connections and disconnections arise from such imagination and association, as the characters of these stories are discovered to move within shifting webs of social and imaginary networks.

The second section of *Obabakoak*, 'Nueve palabras en honor del pueblo de Villamediana', shifts location to a small village in Castile. The 'nueve palabras' consist of vignettes of village life and the narrator's friendship with various local characters. Thus, in this section, the narrator becomes an active participant in the events that are narrated, as much an actor as a storyteller. His incentive to recount, however, stems from the first story where he initially encounters a man who remembers everything and later, a man who can remember nothing. Memory, the source of orally transmitted narratives that serve to maintain communal identity, is thus either in excess or absent:

Entonces, ¿cuánto hay que recordar?, le pregunté. . . — Ni poco ni mucho — Pero por ejemplo, ¿cuántas palabras? — Nueve palabras, dijo riéndose. (1989: 160)

The result in both cases, and for the two characters concerned, is entry into madness with its attendant social confinement. The link between unbalanced memory and madness also points to uneven temporal experiences, a kind of schizophrenia or split self whereby the characters behave in 'abnormal', i.e. plural and contradictory ways. The storytelling that is projected by such experiences is therefore coloured by the threat of madness or socially disabled mental faculties, a current that runs strongly through the third and perhaps most thought-provoking section of *Obabakoak*. At the same time, stories also clearly emerge from the experience of madness. Here it is worth recalling Atxaga's statement to me that postmodernity led to a kind of madness — one, presumably, which also paves the way for narratives such as his own works. The vignettes of life in Villamediana further present the narrator's odd friendship with the dwarf poet, Enrique de Tassis. Again Atxaga plays with identity as disguise or mask, as this character hides his own real name and work as a fairly well-known poet. The child-like presence of the dwarf living in isolation from the community of Villamediana, his fondness for exploring language, his intense but unexpressed emotionality and the location of the narrator's encounters with him in the woods all contribute towards a mythical, or 'unreal', vision of him. This is contrasted by the acquaintances made in the village by the narrator (also an outsider to the village community), as they meet in the bar to discuss matters such as hunting and so share a social life. Nevertheless, the village characters are not devoid of schisms: there is rivalry between the bars as to who frequents which one, indicting rifts in the community. The narrator's neighbour gifts him a clock, so that the ticking may keep him company, thus expressing both a preoccupation with temporality and his own deep isolation which is also evident in his resentment when the narrator accepts firewood from other neighbours. The nine vignettes end with the narrator's decision to leave Villamediana, although we are not told where he will be going to. Instead, the last vignette focuses on the night before his departure. In an earlier section, the narrator had discussed with Tassis a poem about dusk. On that occasion, Tassis had become emotionally agitated over the poem (written by himself, although he would not say so). Dusk, he had said, was a moment of both joy and sadness, of death and life. The narrator had answered that it was 'la hora espectral' (1989: 217), whilst thinking to himself that spectres do not move (the use of the word 'espectral' here cannot but recall Walter Benjamin's repeated emphasis (e.g. 1985: 316) on ruin or death as a feature of modernity, spectres being the shadows of past temporality that linger in the present, refiguring the past in the present). Nevertheless, in his last evening in Villamediana, the suggestion in the ninth vignette is that spectres do indeed move at dusk. As he looks from the hilltop at the stars, the narrator's friend Daniel states 'Ya vienen los reyes magos' (1989: 232) — a reminder that remote, unknown places have long had unexpected visitors, real or imaginary, from afar. The myth of the three kings arises only with the closing down of day, which is also 'la hora espectral'. Thereby a connection can be drawn between death, implicit in the temporal horizons suggested by the close of day, and the need to narrate stories in order to negotiate the finality of the latter. What matters is not where the narrator goes next but rather that he has reached the end of his narrative. Viewed in the light of Laclau and Mouffe's theories, death appears as an ultimate 'essential' which delimits the open-ended social that they focus upon. Despite slippery frontiers between subject-positions, therefore, temporal finality provides a frame or boundary. In this sense, the novel implies a disagreement with Laclau and Mouffe's notion of indefinite openness through its eventual focus on temporal limits.

The final section of *Obabakoak* makes explicit, as its name suggests, the book's efforts to go in search of the last word. The narrator's stories — and here we are not sure whether he is the same as or different from the previous narrators — begin in Obaba and evolve from an overall narrative concerning a childhood incident whilst a schoolboy and a warning from grown-ups never to sleep on the grass in case a lizard crawls into your head through your ears. The framed stories, however, travel beyond Obaba and Spain to different parts of Asia, Africa and Europe and to diverse historical moments. Again, a link begs to be drawn between the lizard and a possible play by Atxaga on the multi-lingual connotations of the Basque nationalist poet *Lizardi*, mentioned earlier in this chapter. The narrator's obsessive determination to investigate any possible connection between Albino Maria's idiocy and the lizard which escaped from Ismael's hand at the moment of having a school photograph taken takes a surprising twist at the end of a winding road of narratives. Spatial connections are emphasized as the narrator's uncle from Montevideo hosts the reading session of stories which span the globe. In his search for the 'truth', the narrator moves from tale to tale, but ignores any temporal contextualization of the stories. Thus the stories are considered in terms of context and displacement, not any historical contingency. The result is a seemingly limitless deferral of meaning onto yet more stories, in line with Laclau and Mouffe's emphasis on multiple discourses and subject-positions. Once again, mental 'illness', this time in the form of idiocy, is connected to the lack of a stable identity or origin. The lizard, if it is to be understood in terms of nationalism as would be suggested by the possible play on the poet Lizardi's name, points to the mobility and ambivalence of supposedly stable notions, such as national or communal identity. In conversation with his uncle, the narrator is at last made aware of the need to historicize narratives in order to interpret them effectively. In the course of their literary discussion, the uncle stresses the spatial and temporal dimensions of language and cultural concepts, thus urging his guests to look beyond immediate meanings for connections, borrowings, metaphors and hidden references which have shifted according to their particular historical moment. The uncle also stresses the need to contextualize concepts or ideas historically in order to interpret them effectively. In particular, he stresses the need to understand the dizzying socio-cultural effects of modernity, which he locates as having begun in the nineteenth century, most notably through the image of the arrival of the train:

El ferrocarril llegó aquí a mediados del siglo diecinueve y supuso un cambio enorme [. . .] a la gente le daba miedo [. . .] miraba por la ventana y no veían el paisaje o lo veían completamente borroso [. . .]. (1989: 472)

Nevertheless, the narrator's obsession with uncovering the link between Albino María's idiocy and Ismael's fondness for lizards ends surprisingly with his unexpected enclosure in the lizard house and his own ensuing idiocy/madness. In other words, the quest to find the meaning in what defies interpretation leads to loss of meaning. Despite his uncle's explanation of the historically and spatially harnessed chain of linguistic and cultural referents, the narrator's impatient search for the last word, his obsession with reaching the bottom of things, challenges the assumptions of a 'truth' which underlies his efforts, relaying them into yet more tales:

Pasaban los días y no adelantaba nada. La última palabra no aparecía por ninguna parte. Y me decía a mí mismo: hoy no ha aparecido, pero puede que aparezca mañana. [. . .] En lugar de preocuparte ¿porqué no redactas el cuento de Bagdad? Y eso hacía. (1989: 484)

The lack of a final rendering thus gives rise to the narrative shifts and overlaps of *Obabakoak*. What, however, seems clear at the end of this section is that the mortality of the narrator shifts to the foreground, thereby framing postmodern narrativity within the context of history. In this sense, narratives of community identity, i.e. the narratives of Obaba, are shown to be temporally vulnerable, incomplete, and open to re-tellings across time. Most of all, they lead not to an affirmation of Obaba's clear-cut identity but to indeterminacy and ambivalence.

The author's afterword, 'A modo de autobiografía', problematizes two facets of his writing. Firstly, he connects his own efforts to write in Basque with the intertextuality that marks his work. Secondly, he locates narrativity in the context of mortality through reference to La Gran Madre Oca. With regard to the first point, Atxaga states that the problem for him and other Basque writers is the lack of antecedence with regard to Basque writing. Atxaga stresses that in this sense he is not referring to merely an absence of Basque writing. Writers today, he says in an interview with Annabel Martín, avail themselves of a global tradition of literature, whereby they have access to writing from different ages and places (2000: 193). He indicates that it is the lack of translation of such texts into Basque that makes the Basque writer's task so difficult. Thus, he states: 'Pulgarcito no había pasado por nuestro camino; imposible buscar las migas de pan que habrían de llevarnos a casa' (1989: 494). *Obabakoak* can thus be viewed as an attempt to fill this lack by providing diverse intertextual, spatial, and temporal connections between the oral narrative traditions of Basque and the larger outlying circles of world narrative. This attempt to update or 'modernize' Basque can be considered comparable to the uncle's description of the arrival of the train to Obaba in the nineteenth century: 'A la gente le daba miedo y había muchísimos que no se atrevían a montar en él' (1989: 472). Like the first trains of the nineteenth century, *Obabakoak* can be considered as a vehicle of narratives moving speedily across spatial and temporal fields, crossing tracks with other stories and with many stops but with no final destination. In the course of this journey, any attempt to articulate the identity of the 'people and things of Obaba' (the title's significance in Basque) comes up against other articulations of cultural identity within an overall 'social' and global textuality. This problematization of textuality can be read beyond the surface level to open onto the second point.

Atxaga's reference to the 'juego de la Oca' — and perhaps it is worth noting the word 'juego' or 'play' here as indicative of the performance of identity within discursive structures — compares the narrative movements in life to the playing out of a board game until the 'la Gran Oca Madre' is reached. He clearly expresses here the uncertainties and apprehensions of writing in a global context. These include not just the increased risks that chance affords him when writing in a global context, such as the dangers and fears of moving into unfamiliar narrative terrains, where nothing is any longer particular. In this context, Atxaga states in his interview with Martín:

... postmodernism — as a framework, ideology or paradigm — is more favourable to a writer in Basque [. . .] Zulaika argued that, with globalization, Basque reality suddenly acquires added value because the emphasis is now on markers of difference [. . .] there are two different things here that often get confused [. . .] It's a socially more favourable situation because no-one will say to you today, 'Ah, so you write in the local language. . .' [. . .] On the other hand, I can't say I am different because I write in Basque. I know a lot of people who write in Basque, and there is nothing different about them . . . quite the opposite' (2000: 197)

The postmodern 'celebration' of cultural difference, therefore, is not altogether a positive development: the juxtapositions of difference also can be viewed as superficial pastiche, whereby historical dimensions are lost. Postmodernism, in *Obabakoak*, thus includes possible threats to narrative continuity, should the narrator/writer fall accidently into the 'cárcel' or the 'calavera' of the boardgame: 'Nada es peor, en cambio, que caer en viñetas como. . .la del laberinto o . . .la de la cárcel o. . .en la que lleva la calavera' (1989: 492). Within postmodernity, the narrator's position as conferrer and agent of meaning is undermined by the socio-cultural contexts in which the narratives arise as well as by the problem of narrative style as enactment.

The book's deliberate blurring of myth, legend, and history further questions the frontiers of identity. Narrative constructions of experience, which accommodate social and communal dislocation, place in question the notion of historical certainty through fragmentation and inconclusiveness. The collage of stories, no doubt a play on the postmodern predilection for pastiche, both constructs a narrative of Obaba and deconstructs notions of enclosed and essential community identity. Temporal experience is shown to be multiple and synchronic, simultaneously real and imagined. Thus, in a clever inversion (or subversion?) of post-structuralist concepts of reality as imagined, some of Ataxga's characters are seen to play with the possibility of wandering from the imagined into reality, itself no more than an allegorical reference for death as the inescapable reality, but one which is also perplexing and indeterminate. The stories that arise from the pursuit of the 'truth' about the lizard act as a metaphor for the author/narrator's search for the final word. The danger is that such a quest is in itself misguided and can only open on to the confused narratives of (in)sanity, which are themselves marked by the finality of death. Mortality therefore draws a temporal and spatial circle around the possible travels of narrative structures. As in his later book, *El hombre solo* (1995), the question of finality becomes paramount. When confronted with the frontiers of mortality, narratives of postmodernity which are marked by and play with temporal ruptures and spatial displacement are silenced. Mortality further provides the ground from which history, in the form of new narratives, can arise. As suggested by the title of the final section 'En busca de la última palabra' (1989: 233–490) and confirmed in the author's afterword at the end of the work, as also by the very format of the book, there appears to be no other final word on life, only an endless slippage and deferral of meaning through networks of discourses and overlapping, interconnected structures. The play of slippage enters history when it is marked by death, the borders of time thus acting as the end of such stories and the beginning of (hi)stories. This, as will be demonstrated below, links Atxaga's work to Jameson's theories.

The narratives of *Obabakoak* sustain a textual performance where the identity of the narrator/s remains obscure. The only certainty in the 'Juego de la Oca' is the ultimate destination of the la Gran Oca Madre. Living day by day by the gameboard, today's narrator, according to Atxaga, navigates his narrative treck according to chance. The last move in the game is the confrontation with mortality, which delimits the freedom of narration to wander spatially and temporally. In a global context, where the particular is by definition contingent and variable and where essential 'truths' are no more than an imaginary construct, the narrative act is predominantly sustained by chance encounters. Death acts as the final chance encounter, refiguring narrative in the context of history. The absence throughout *Obabakoak* of a sustained community prefigures the final ambiguity where death hovers and the fate of narration remains in question. The question of community is posed in the absence of cohesive community, just as the question of narration is posed by the lack of either a sustained narrative or a recognizable narrator.

This is precisely Jameson's view, the weakening of historicity leading, in his opinion, to a culture of simulacrum. To turn to Laclau and Mouffe, in such a context, it is questionable whether hegemony, as the negotiations and tousles for power between different subject-positions, can at all function. This is underlined in *Obabakoak* by the absence of obvious power struggles. It could be said, therefore, that Jameson is a more relevant theorist to an analysis of *Obabakoak*, in particular because the book's exploration of nostalgia coincides with the loss of particularity and definition. It is important to bear in mind Jameson's insistence that, while postmodernity can be characterized as the loss of any organic consciousness of history, nevertheless even such non-historical postmodern texts articulate history as the 'Real'. Similarly, the indefinite meanderings of tales around Obaba also construct a place for Obaba within the historical conjuncture of postmodernity.

Nostalgia for a lost homeland is also a key sentiment in *El hombre solo*, as is the exploration of synchronic identities which compete with one another. On the surface, however, the novel adheres to the traditional format of the thriller. As such, it sits comfortably within the post 70s vogue in Spain for suspense fiction, a literary feature of democracy transposed from mass-consumed Anglo-Saxon fiction. That *El hombre solo* should in fact deal with the life of a former ETA activist whose predicament, though fictitious, is credible in its portrayal of current dilemmas, comes as no great surprise, given that the suspense genre has in recent years become particularly popular in Spain as a means of conveying matters of historical and political concern. Literary critics and scholars have often explored the link between this genre of fiction and politics in latter-day Spain, which they attribute to the fact that it aptly expresses the political realities of contemporary living and offers a platform where the reader can come to terms with these realities. Together with science fiction, the thriller has come to be one of the more prominent voices of the new Spain; no doubt the urgency and uncertainty inherent to the form give expression to the angst felt by members of the younger generation in terms of their own identity and orientation. The mortality of one or other main character that is implicit from the start of any thriller mirrors to some extent the postmodern sense of running out of time. Likewise, the parallel events that are a crucial part of suspense fiction echo the pluralities and contradictions of contemporary living. In the case of Atxaga's novel, the urgency of the thriller form successfully draws the reader into sharing not just the tension experienced by the protagonist, but also that which ensues from all the issues that the novel raises, thus making the experience all too 'real' for comfort. Paradoxically, therefore, what is often regarded as an escapist form of fiction runs a parallel course to recent events in the cultural history of Spain.

Ostensibly, the story of *El hombre solo* centres around Carlos, former activist turned hotel owner, who has turned a new leaf in Catalonia and yet, despite his best interests, agrees to hide two wanted ETA terrorists. Carlos, together with three other former ETA colleagues, has sought to start life 'afresh' in Catalonia, where his past can remain an unmentioned secret. The narrative follows him for five days as he struggles to maintain an appearance of normality while secretly attempting to move the terrorists on to the next stage in their escape away from the authorities. From the very start of the book, the reader is made aware that not only are the two terrorists hidden from view, but so is Carlos's true identity: the opening lines, 'El hombre al que todos llamaban Carlos. . .' (1995: 9), implies the question 'who *is* Carlos?'. The suspense therefore is two-fold, since as the reader searches for an understanding of Carlos, so Carlos searches for a way-out of his situation. A reading of *El hombre solo* throws into question the intrinsically linked concepts of the self, community and nation. It reveals the plural and fragmentary nature of each of these categories and defies pre-conceived expectations of essential unities. Furthermore, the novel emphasizes the need in human beings to continue seeking meaningful cohesiveness in a world which belies any unity or essential truth.

In *El hombre solo*, Atxaga portrays hegemonic spaces that fall in line with Laclau and Mouffe's definition of the term at the three levels of national, community, and individual identity. Each of these levels is seen in the course of the novel to be a forum for the struggle between diverse and often opposing articulations: that is, strains and tendencies that are at variance with one another with each seeking predominance over the others. Thus, in keeping with Laclau and Mouffe's argument, notions such as nation, community, and individual which have traditionally been regarded as essential categories and basic markers of human existence are stripped to reveal their fragmentary and multi-stranded composition, open to reversals and unstable hegemonies. However, the very openness and instability of such a plural system of elements leave open the possibility of an undermining of hegemonies. Atxaga further extends his portrayal of hegemonic situations to reveal their inherent weaknesses, a point which has been overlooked by Laclau and Mouffe in their campaign for radical democracy based on a politics of difference. In their separate critiques of Laclau and Mouffe, Hans Bertens (1994), and Best and Kellner (1991) point out the possible pitfalls in their line of argument. In particular, Bertens points out that such a pluralist democracy depends on a common ground of a politics of difference for all the participants in the hegemonic state. In other words, in practice, the 'open' hegemonies they refer to could well be confronted with an opposing camp of a fundamentalist or essentialist nature. Such a confrontation would throw up a problematic that cannot be resolved within a democratic framework, since there is no provision within the latter for apprehending it. Bertens expresses his concerns regarding Laclau and Mouffe's argument in the following way:

On closer inspection, the politics of difference always turns out to be a new version of what might somewhat paradoxically be called the history of (western) uniformity. In order to function — or even to survive — the politics of difference must exclude those who are *really* different, such as Iranian fundamentalists or staunch defenders of apartheid, that is, those who don't include themselves in their idea of difference, for whom it is only the others who are always different. . .One can understand why [. . .] Laclau and Mouffe [. . .] are reluctant to confront the fundamental otherness of refusing to participate in difference, in the universal agreement to be free. Such a refusal, which puts an end to the politics of difference, can only be confronted through the exercise of power, if not the use of force. (1994: 192)

I wish as a basis for this analysis to pay particular attention to Bertens's statement that the politics of difference collapses if one group insists on an essentialist position that refuses to accept the difference of others. In particular, *El hombre solo* typifies the problematic of a pluralism which is born out of an essentialist background. Indeed, this is the very basis for the emergence of Laclau and Mouffe's theories, since they have set themselves the task of rethinking the essentialist Marxist tradition, from Marx to Gramsci and Althusser, along pluralist and democratic lines. Their failure to mention the problem of conjoining a politics of pluralism with a fundamentalism that refuses to join with difference is perhaps indicative of the impossibility of the effort. Yet it is all too probable that there are lingering essentialisms which continue to make themselves felt in the present in one form or another. As *El hombre solo* shows, the politics of pluralism is undermined by the closed, essentialist terrain that it springs from. With this in mind, my examination of the hegemonic spaces portrayed in Atxaga's work seeks not just to explore their multifarious nature, but also to search out the areas of irreconcilable confrontation with essentialism.

The question of national identity runs as a vibrant chord through the novel. The acknowledgement of plural nationalisms and regionalisms in Spain, with

Catalonia and the Basque Country receiving the greatest degree of autonomy due to their status as 'naciones históricas', forms an important backdrop to the novel. The Spain of *El hombre solo* has moved on from the unified, essentialist entity of Francoist conception to a community of autonomous regions. Yet it is precisely this high degree of autonomy that gives rise to the splits explored in *El hombre solo*. Paul Heywood states in his work entitled *Government and Politics of Spain* (1995) that by the 1980s, clear generational divisions were apparent within ETA, as older members, who had lived through the years of Francoist repression, came to question the efficacy of violence within a larger context that was increasingly flexible and accommodating. The newer members, represented in *El hombre solo* by the characters of Jone and Jon, had themselves no direct memory of the Franco years and reacted by adopting a more radical stance, relying on explosives manuals for learning the tactics of terror. For them, it would appear that membership of ETA provides an outlet for the frustrations of unemployment and lack of purpose prevalent in their current socio-economic contexts. The novel revolves around the hunt by the security forces for two ETA terrorists; the very plot therefore is indicative of the lingering presence of fundamentalist elements — in this case, seen both in the armed activists hiding in the basement and the armed representatives of the central state in the form of the Civil Guard — within a pluralist democracy. Indeed, the tension of the story line is derived from the threat of a violent encounter between the terrorists and the authorities, an encounter that would have an inevitable impact on the protagonist Carlos and his small community of co-hotel owners. It is clear to the reader from the start that, for the sake of national security, fundamentalists would have to be dealt with in a radical way. In a conversation with Jone, the female terrorist, Carlos makes clear that he does not back ETA's persistence in armed action in present times: he says 'Yo creo que vuestra lucha actual es absurda' (1995: 45), thereby indicating that while at one time ETA's struggle might have been well-founded, the advent of democracy and the establishment of autonomous regions has removed its validity. Nevertheless, he continues to harbour her and her male colleague despite the risk that this puts on the new life that he has built for himself since leaving the organization. I shall return to this point later in order to explain this ambivalence.

The novel charts the course of transition as the former activists adapt from a closed totalitarian environment to an open, pluralist Spain. The four Basques, Ugarte, Guiomar and Carlos, and Laura who own the hotel — no doubt an emblem of a new global postmodern Spain based on post-industrial late consumer capitalism — outside Barcelona are bound together by their prior involvement with ETA and their underground activities in the 70s for a free Basque nation. Following their release from prison, they further collaborated in forcing the institutionalization of Carlos's brother Kropotky on false grounds of insanity in order to gain illegal access to funds that they then used to jointly purchase the hotel in Catalonia. This action is later defended by Ugarte as morally acceptable, since he viewed this money as a sort of repayment for the years and effort they gave to Basque nationalism. Thus, from a present capitalist stance, Ugarte rationalises a deviant action and considers the ill-gotten money to be just reward for his former sacrifice to ideology. Nevertheless, Carlos alone carries the burden of guilt with regard to his brother's fate. At the same time, all four members of the group are united in their capitalist endeavour to start life 'afresh' in Catalonia, where their past can remain a buried secret. Though Atxaga makes no direct statement on the matter, clearly, Catalonia, with its own sense of nationalism, offers the ex-terrorists the chance of a new and peaceful beginning that would be unacceptable had it been in 'Spain'. In Catalonia, the group seek to merge with the general material prosperity of the Catalan social environment, yet confine themselves territorially to their hotel and own surroundings. Their desire to integrate is rarely matched by any determined action. Thus, on several levels the scene of the hotel becomes a potential hegemonic space for the working out of national identity. Despite decisions to shed their native Basque identity and despite personal relationships between Carlos and Ugarte and female Catalan members of staff, they remain a foreign group in a Catalan space and are viewed as such by the Catalans around them. Integration is viewed by Guiomar and Carlos largely in terms of capital investment in Catalonia, primarily in the form of the hotel (of which the child Pascal is the 'hereu') and in the prospect of buying a flat in the city. Thus their Catalan citizenship derives its significance from material power. National identity is no longer an issue for risking life and limb as it was in the past, but rather associated with the gaining and investment of capital. They plan at some future time to learn the Catalan language. Nevertheless, all of them continue to enjoy and promote traditional Basque food, prepared by their Basque chef. At any given moment, the members of the group are only able to articulate or express an aspect of their plural national allegiances.

In fact, feelings of unified national identity can only be played out in the football field, as a series of matches receive plentiful press and television coverage. Sport benefits from its own platform that is sufficiently removed from every day life to allow a reversal of the pluralist hegemony of national identity into essentialist allegiance with a team or a nation. The Polish team, lodging in Carlos's hotel, represent their nation before millions as the sportsfield becomes a forum for the expression of national sentiment. While football undoubtedly upholds the image of a unified nation, what it fails to address is the question of what lies behind the symbol. The irony is explicit in the person of Danuta, whose bilingual skills speak of a 'forked tongue' or deceitfulness. As the interpreter of the Polish team, she, on the one hand, speaks in public for her team and her nation and, on the other hand, tells Carlos that what substance there is to her country is no more than an accumulation of contradictory popular symbols, external manifestations that are at variance with one another:

[. . .] a fin de cuentas los que van tras el espejismo no beben más agua que los que sólo ven arena. Y ahí tenemos el resultado: por un lado Boniek, por otro Walesa, y por encima de todos, el Papa con la Virgen de Chestozova en brazos. (1995: 242)[11]

Danuta makes it clear that the unity of Polish national identity is merely superficial and is in fact a composition of competing antagonisms. Further references to the failure of essentialist national fervour, not just in Spain but elsewhere as well, can be seen in the many references to Peter Kropotkin and Rosa Luxemburg. In the face of his antagonistic and multi-stranded present, Carlos thinks back to the revolutionary fervour of both of these figures. Kropotkin's anarchist theories in favour of expropriation or the abolition of private property were instrumental to Carlos's decision as a teenager to join ETA, in an effort to establish a new age of equality and brotherhood for the Basque people. If Carlos was inspired by Kropotkin's fervour, his actions in fact led not to the network of collectives that Kropotkin advocated but to the closed essentialism of nationalist ideology. Strong beliefs, whatever their focus, do not, however, withstand social and political ruptures: Kropotkin lived to be disillusioned by the revolution of his times, as did Rosa Luxemburg and indeed Carlos himself. Most importantly, the novel marks the sweeping effects of global capitalism, most visible in terms of the example of Poland given by Danuta's ego-centric hunger for material prosperity. In the count-down to the end of the novel, Carlos finds solace in reading the private letters of Rosa Luxemburg, who rejected national boundaries and national identity as markers of the political and cultural confines of the proletariat and believed that true revolution could only take place within the frame-work of a common humanity. Nevertheless, Luxemburg conceived of revolution solely in class terms (1972). Ironically, Danuta recommended this reading to Carlos, although her nostalgia for the revolutionary fervour of her youth merely cloaks her desire to acquire money and jewellery by giving a tip-off to the police about the whereabouts of the terrorists. Danuta's criticism of her compatriots therefore can be extended to herself. For Carlos, the parallel clearly exists between himself and Luxemburg as revolutionaries who had outlived their historical moment. Both lived to see the fragmentation of their revolutionary dreams in the face of historical alterations that they had not expected. The unexpected turns of history have made Carlos's nationalist commitment redundant and he finds that his own actions have displaced him from the land that he had unquestioningly considered to be his. Currently faced with plural national identities, being Basque, Catalan, and Spanish at the same time, and no longer greatly bothered by the issue, Carlos nevertheless has to contend with the problem of what to do with his previous essentialist nationalism.

Displacement therefore emerges in the novel as a consequence of material prosperity. Furthermore, it can be qualified in multiple ways, since the experience of it supersedes mere physical trajectories. Carlos, his friends and Danuta all suffer displacement through the fracturing of subjectivity brought about by the privileging of the material through Spain's post-Franco 'openness' in economic and political terms. However, they are without choice in the matter, since the material overlaps with the other socio-cultural features of Spain's new plurality. Pressurized by having to hide the terrorists and evade the Civil Guard, Carlos becomes aware of his impending mortality. As he writes his will, he thinks wildly of leaving his wealth to his old home town, Obaba.[12] At the same time, he is aware of the impossibility of soldering the rifts of time:

Pero no, todas esas posibilidades, aunque pudieran resultarle agradables en parte, aunque supusieran una oportunidad de sellar todas las grietas de su pasado, eran mentira. El nuevo Obaba de 1982 nada tenía que ver con el pueblo que él había conocido en su infancia [. . .].' (1995: 171)

By acknowledging the cracks in his relationship with his 'original' community, Carlos thus also points to the displacement suffered by the latter as well as by himself. The resulting crisis of existence is most evident in Carlos's multiple subjectivity experienced as temporally incoherent voices which offer splintered chronological depths and no unity. No longer able to narrate to himself a succinct imagination of community, Carlos runs up against the barriers of time. Plurality of national identity thus translates into plurality at levels of both community and individual.

Community identity, thus, becomes pluriform and complex in the novel. Any assumptions that Carlos's prior membership of ETA would have enabled the establishment of community between himself and his co-activists through shared historical and political experiences are quickly challenged. On the surface, however, the four Basques appear united and, to the knowledge of most of those who come to stay at the hotel, jobs are evenly shared, material investments are divided equally and everything runs smoothly. Furthermore, the spatial unity provided by the idyllic surroundings of the hotel, located on the outskirts of Barcelona, allows for the physical cohesion required for unified community. Yet, on closer inspection, the cracks within their tightly-knit group become apparent. Each member of the group is marked by different pulls and tendencies. Of all of them, Ugarte is the one who is most openly cynical about their unity as a group. The failure of his marriage to Laura and his relationship with Nuria offer him the potential to wander out of the given communal space at the end of the novel. Laura's obsessive and unquestioning belief in the values of Leninism and their historical relevance in the present deflects any self-reflection or awareness of the plural and contradictory nature of her own life and actions. She continues to hold on to her rigid beliefs despite benefiting materially from the possibilities that pluralist Spain and Catalonia in particular make available to her. Laura's renewed relationship with Guiomar inevitably marks a break with her husband, though it would seem that there never was a closeness between them. Whilst resuming a relationship with Guiomar, she nevertheless resents her husband's affair with Nuria. Guiomar, once he realizes that he is the father of Pascal, wishes urgently to found a home with his family and to take the child to visit his Basque relatives. Clearly, the fact of fatherhood raises in him a nostalgia for 'origins' whereby he seeks to regain a place in localized community. The weight of his native traditions suddenly weighs heavily on Guiomar and he desires only a safe and traditional life, albeit in Catalonia, far removed from his previous life-style as a freedom fighter.

The child, too, is closer to Guiomar (whom he thinks is a friend when he is in fact his father) than he is to the man he thinks is his father, i.e., Ugarte. Here Atxaga sets up a contradictory situation. The child's confusion at one level implies a critique of the rhetoric of early Basque nationalism, in particular Sabino de Arana's emphasis on the supremacy of blood ties as the basis of community, whilst also pointing to the fractures of family life in postmodernity. Pascal is also confused about who his grandmother is, since he is unable to distinguish her from Danuta. The indeterminacy of the child's blood relations shrouds issues pertinent to both community and national identities in ambivalence.

Carlos, in his role as resident baker, avails himself of a separate spatial territory in the form of the bakery, in the basement of which he hides the terrorists. This role also allows him to keep different hours from the group, since he has to bake the bread at dawn. Furthermore, he spends time walking his dogs and swimming at La Banyera, which makes him often unavailable to the rest of his group. Despite their apparent closeness, the other Basques have rarely set foot in the bakery and are aware that Carlos will only socialize with them up to a point. Still, they are bound together in the secrecy of their past and the hotel represents a new beginning for all of them. Yet the very presence of the terrorists in the bakery point to the open nature of the territory that the four Basques have outlined for themselves in that it is their new 'freedom' which allows the terrorists to be present; similarly, the overriding presence of Civil Guards in the hotel, ostensibly for the protection of the football team, reveals the vulnerability of Carlos's safe haven. The presence of the terrorists in the bakery can also be interpreted as a metaphor for the hidden, even buried, strands of essentialism in the underground recesses of Carlos's private sphere. When Stefano, the policeman disguised as a journalist, enters the bakery, it becomes clear that despite Carlos's intentions to the contrary, no frontier, however barred or closely guarded, is uncrossable. The hotel, together with all its residents, is thus a site of constant hegemonic antagonisms where the push and pull of different interests is played out. Like cells which split and divide, the interplay between the various characters in the novel could go on indefinitely were it not for the lurking presence of this essentialist element that signifies danger. The play of power that takes place in hegemonic negotiations is best encountered through this essentialist strand. More to the point, the existence of essentialist elements exceeds the presence of the terrorists hidden by Carlos. Not only is essentialism a facet of Carlos split psyche, as we shall see, Laura's contradictory personality or even Danuta's multi-layered persona, it is also present in the overall political context of Spain as a nation state, displayed in the pursuit, both overt and covert, of the activists by the police. Furthermore, the hunt for the terrorists by the authorities, and in particular, the antagonism displayed towards Carlos by the Civil Guard, Morros, clearly indicates the persistent power of the central state. Like ETA, the State represents rule by force. Thus, essentialism, linked once again to notions of the State, lingers not merely in opposition to pluralist Spain but also in conjunction with it.

Nor does essentialism always appear in expected spaces. Most obviously, the two terrorists appear to represent the presence of an unyielding essentialism in what would otherwise be a prosperous, multi-national hotel. Yet, this essentialism (Haywood, 1995) coincides with the fact that the unity experienced by Carlos and those of his generation has yielded to fracture and lack of cohesion. The disorganized staging of the terrorists protection from the authorities is indicative of such splits. Their presence in the hotel is threatening because it is unbeknown to everyone but Carlos. He has betrayed trust by agreeing to hide the terrorists with neither the consent nor the knowledge of the others. Nevertheless, the threat is not so much of 'essentialist' action on their part as of their potential to unleash 'essentialist' reactions in those around them, the hotel owners as well as the state authorities, should these learn of their whereabouts. Their confinement in the basement of the bakery gives physical expression to the underground layer of essentialism that lies beneath the 'open' ground upon which the pluralities of the hotel and its residents play themselves out. Nevertheless, it cannot be forgotten that their presence owes itself to Carlos, who could well have refused to help them out. It can then be deduced that if the two of them are in the premises of the hotel, then it must be because some allegiance to essentialism lingers on from his own past in Carlos.

From the start of the novel, the reader is anxious to discover why Carlos would agree to shelter the terrorists. Atxaga alerts the reader from the beginning to the fact that, while he interacts with those who form his present, Carlos's mind is in fact inhabited by several voices which defy distance and time, belonging to the principal figures of his past. Indeed, it is possible to state that Carlos's true community is made up of presences that are internal rather than external; the voices in his head prevent him on several occasions from recognizing aspects of his present, thereby trapping him in a temporal disjuncture. Even as he moves forward in time through the narrative, the voices delineate his past. Thus, Carlos's identity is a compound of the roles that he plays and the people of his past. The unity of his being is, therefore, purely symbolic and, to use Laclau and Mouffe's term, he is himself a composition of multiple and antagonistic subject-positions. Of the many voices that resound in his head, the three most prominent ones are those of Sabino[13] (the coincidence between Carlos's mentor's name and that of the leader of Basque nationalism, Sabino de Arana, is hard to overlook), his friend and mentor within ETA, his brother Kropotky and the mysterious Rata who pierces Carlos's faith in himself with his all too apt cynicism. Through the five days of the narrative, it is Sabino who inspires Carlos to plan the necessary stages for the safe exit of the terrorists. That Sabino in fact died in a shoot-out several years ago appears of no consequence. In an extreme postmodernist effacement of temporal depth, even death is seen to set no limits on Carlos. Sabino continues to provide Carlos with the steady, logical thought and planning that is crucial for any strategic effort. He aids Carlos in dealing with the policemen and the Civil Guard who watches him as he bathes in the waters of La Banyera. Past allegiances thus cross temporal barriers to aid in confronting present 'essentialisms'. Unlike Carlos, Sabino has no doubts about the validity of the activist's actions and Carlos relies on his resolve to carry his actions through. In opposition to that of Sabino, Carlos carries with him another voice, the voice of La Rata, who insidiously intervenes when Carlos thinks that he has secured small victories. It spares no effort in showing him the moral and legal flaws in his undertakings and takes pleasure in undermining his self-esteem. La Rata, as its name indicates, gnaws at Carlos's well-being and has done so since his time in prison. The reader is told that this voice emerged while he was there. Clearly, Sabino and La Rata are 'subject-positions' that are opposed to each other in every way. They each have a hold on Carlos and try to bend him in their opposing ways.

Yet another voice that rings in his ears is that of his brother Kropotky. Although Carlos has not seen his brother for a considerable period of time, the latter's words, once discarded as trite, now reveal themselves as prophetic. Furthermore, Carlos carries with him the burden of guilt, stemming from the fact that his present prosperity together with that of the other members of his group is based on the false declaration that his brother is insane and the latter's subsequent institutionalization in an asylum. Kropotky took his name from reading Kropotkin's *The Conquest of Bread* (1972), though, unlike Carlos who chose the path of the activist, he chose a spiritual path to freedom. Ironically, in later years, it is Carlos who makes bread for the hotel and who does so in a space and time apart as if it were an exercise in meditation. The 'conquest of bread', then, a central aspect of which for Kropotkin was the foregrounding of community, becomes Carlos's imaginary quest, one that he embarks upon even as his actions drive him further away from such a goal. The tie of blood — i.e., community in its most 'essential' manifestation — binds the two brothers together even as they fall apart (as in the case, of Pascal and Guiomar, Atxaga once again foregrounds the tie of blood over other social ties, thus foregrounding 'essential' links, yet reveals even such links to be weakened by a context of overriding capitalism) and Carlos's thoughts turn increasingly to his brother in his final days, despite having betrayed him so cruelly. Indeed, Carlos's act of betrayal implies a 'split' in himself arising from split allegiances. In a further twist, Kropotky's supposed madness endows him with visionary powers whereby his words ring true in Carlos's ears and Carlos, to all intents and purposes sane, descends into the madness of despair at the end of the novel. In line with Laclau and Mouffe's understanding of subjectivity, Carlos's predicament speaks boldly of the impossibility of a fixed, stable subject; at any given moment, he can only adopt subject-positions that find themselves in danger of being overthrown by others. He serves as the battle-ground for diverse struggles, whilst still having to remain open to new encounters and the new situations that he finds himself in. Atxaga's painstaking depiction of the self, therefore, shows itself to be not so much determined by the surrounding collective as it is a meeting point for a range of conflicting discourses drawn from a communal pool, spanning different time-frames and open to extensions.

Just as the voices in his head are of a plural nature, so Carlos's actions in the present are multiple and contradictory. Carlos feels a pull towards a life of simplicity and away from it. On the one hand he finds peace in the making of bread and in the open air life which he enjoys with his dogs; on the other, he remains unaware of his patently bourgeois tendencies, explicit in his insistence on expensive aftershave and designer shirts. The contradictions further play themselves out in his relationships with women. He juggles three liaisons in the five days and is only able to think seriously about his long-standing girl-friend María Teresa at the very end, in the face of extreme uncertainty and danger. Even then, the only commitment he can make her is to mention her in his will, in other words, to make her a commitment of money. He has a brief and hurried sexual encounter with Jone, the female terrorist he harbours and yet, at the moment of escape, he regards her more as a sister, a member of what at the moment of extreme danger he thinks of as his 'true' family made up not of friends and relatives, but of those who, like him and other activists, had experienced fear — shared experience, not blood ties, now being the basis for feelings of communal unity.

Thus, the character of Carlos is a hegemonic space for the struggle of opposing and multiple antagonisms. Inhabited as he is by discourses that are very different from one another, his actions stem from the overdetermination of particular subject-positions within himself. At times, he is led by Sabino, at others, by his brother or La Rata. Carlos's crisis, then, derives from the fact that his subjectivity is, despite the plurality of the elements that compose it, only partially an open and democratic hegemony. As evidenced by his repeated efforts to commune with the 'essentials' of nature in La Banyera and his final immersion in its deep whirlpool, his contradictory and multiple personality eventually confronts its limits. The repercussions are inevitable on those he leaves behind. Equally, it could be argued that the encounter with death in a whirlpool — rather than offering the security of a 'final' resting-place — is significant of shifting, fluid depths beyond life, pointing therefore to an existential indeterminacy that exceeds the socio-political contingencies of Carlos's life-time.

Although *El hombre solo* ends at this point, it does not take much to imagine the fate that must await the others. With Pascal's death and with the civil guard in pursuit, the stresses would be extreme on the three members left behind. With the future so dashed, time and space would inevitably close in on them. The explosion caused by the 'essentialism' that lurked in their midst would have its undeniable effects on their lives, although they may have believed that they had left 'essentialisms' behind. It was ironic that, by identifying himself with Peter Pan (who refused to grow up), Pascal unwittingly threw light on the fractured and disintegrating unity of his immediate circle — his disavowal of temporality translating into the unexpected finality of death, just at the moment when, by building himself a 'home' (in the same way as his parents had planned to set up a 'family unit'), he had sought the imagined security of a stable temporal and spatial basis whereby he would not have to face growing old.

In the figure of Carlos, Atxaga offers the reader a poignant portrait of a man who desperately tries to juggle dilemmas. Although Carlos manages to sustain his act before the police and all those around him, he nevertheless knows that he is faced with a problem that defies resolution. His decision to shelter the terrorists was taken on the spur of the moment, fired mostly by the desire to retain some worth in ETA's eyes:

Le preocupaba mucho lo que de él pudieran pensar Jone y los de la organización, no quería que le tomara por un flojo. Y quizás ahí residía la clave, en la servidumbre que aquella preocupación ponía de manifiesto, ya que de haber sido indiferente a aquellas opiniones jamás habría entrado en el juego. (1995: 331)

However, that action implied the assertion of a subject-position that he had carried within him for a long time, one that had been determined at a previous moment in history when the fundamentalism of the Franco regime dictated a fundamentalist response from the Basque people in the name of freedom. It was also a subject-position that he had relied upon in the past in order to formulate his sense of identity. This same subject-position, conceived in a necessarily essentialist frame-work, had steered the course of his life until he emerged from prison and went to live in Catalonia. It had led him, among other things, to prison for the kidnap and death of a businessman, as La Rata often reminds him. The emergence of the other dominant subject-positions in Carlos had coincided more or less with the birth of a plural and democratic Spain. They were more compatible with the liberal climate of the Spain of 1982. Their condition of being was also that he put his former source of identity away once and for all. However, the adoption of plural antagonisms within a flexible democratic framework, as Laclau and Mouffe describe, merely implied the temporary submersion of a more radical and essentialist thread within Carlos. When the latter finally re-asserted itself, Carlos was faced with a problem that could not be reconciled: one of his subject-positions stood on ground that was firmly essentialist while the other subject-positions in him stood on premises of anti-essentialism, in other words, they were committed to a politics of openness. The undermining of openness by the presence of an essentialist element was in fact a problem of historical and temporal disjuncture. Carlos believed that ETA's current struggle was absurd; yet their opinion of him still mattered enough for him to put so much at stake. He was unable to leave history behind and move on with the times; at the same time, his new open life-style was incompatible with a former way of being. Clearly it was not a problem that could be resolved. The discourses of plurality and the discourse of essentialism cannot dialogue because they stem from fundamentally different grounds. The only possibility is that of a violent encounter.

By the end of the novel, Carlos realizes that he has reached an impasse in time and history. The confrontation which is pointed out by Bertens in his critique of Laclau and Mouffe and, acted out visibly in the police hunt for the terrorists, takes place at a deeper level within Carlos as he faces an ethical quandary. Torn between past allegiances and present responsibilities, indeed, able to assert older essentialist leanings precisely because of the open and plural nature of the present, he is faced with a temporal and historical incoherence. It is not surprising, therefore, that in the final moment of his life, he should strip himself naked and seek death in the whirlpool of La Banyera. Nature, despite its treacherous depths, became for him the ultimate and most tangible of essentials where Carlos could hope to find refuge. Yet, as we have seen, it too could be unreliable, fluid, and dizzying. With the collapse of temporal barriers, as Jameson asserts, the vortex of postmodern uncertainties could well continue beyond death. The return 'home', be it to nature, Obaba, ETA, or elsewhere, i.e. the nostalgic quest for the security of origins, could yet again prove to be no more than a figment of the rootless postmodern imagination.

Jon Juaristi, in his critique of Basque nationalism, *El bucle melancólico*, underlines this sentiment of nostalgia or melancholia that accompanies national-ist fervour. The quote taken from Giorgio Agamben which appears at the start of the latest edition of his book refers back to Freud's work on melancholia, emphasizing the vagueness of both what causes the latter sentiment and what it is aimed at (2000: 11). Its significance to the contents of his book soon become clear: as Juarisiti states in his prologue, it is precisely the memory of the violent encounter between the Basque separatists and the Francoist state, and precisely his own involvement in that clash, which allows him to see through the discourses of nationalism. The aptness of the term melancholia for the prevalent mood of nationalism stems from its vagueness, because nationalist melancholia focuses upon what does not as yet exist:

[. . .] los nacionalistas no lloran una pérdida *real*. La nación no preexiste al nacionalismo. (2000: 47)

Furthermore, the justifications for such a mood are drawn from imagined memories, whereby the past, in this case the memory of Sabino Arana, is adorned with a pseudo-religious halo:

Los vascos de mi generación [. . .] hemos vivido una niñez y una adolescencia inmersas en el culto clandestino a la memoria del fundador, de *Sabin*. Pero no llegamos a saber gran cosa acerca de su vida. Arana-Goiri era, fundamentalmente, una teoría de imágenes [. . .] Era un culto visual. (2000: 160)

Juaristi states that this image was saintlike, firing the nationalist endeavour with passion. He emphasizes the parallels between religion and nationalistic fervour, a link that is also made consistently by Atxaga in *El hombre solo*.

The multiple voices and textual references of *El hombre solo* take place, interestingly, against a backdrop of imagery that is uniformly Biblical. It is impossible to disregard the parallels between the area of La Fontana and the Garden of Eden. Likewise, Carlos's occupation as a baker, his dedication to his job and the care with which he kneads and bakes this most 'essential' of substances recall the Christian belief that bread is the flesh of Christ and, as such, life-enhancing. Miquel too is associated with fish, another typically Christian image. Yet Miquel hides the terrorists in his van under the fish, thus raising a metaphorical or allegorical contradiction. Similarly, the dinner where Carlos recognizes Stefano to be a policeman in disguise is reminiscent of the Last Supper. Both occasions were outward expressions of trust and both took place in the shadow of betrayal. Carlos and Danuta speak of the passion with which in their youth they embraced revolutionary activity, also bringing to mind the passion of Christ. Like Carlos's repeated return to the whirlpool, the religious backdrop figures as a constant image of immutability. Carlos aptly keeps a poem by his prophetic brother in the bakery, indicative perhaps of his own contradictory position:

Arriba y abajo anda errante mi alma, implorando reposo: de esta manera huye el ciervo herido hacia los bosques . . . Pero el lecho de musgo ya no le ofrece deleite a su corazón, y se queja insomne sintiendo miedo de la flecha, e inútiles ya para ella el calor de la luz o la frescura de la noche, inútilmente también baña sus heridas en las aguas del río . . . (1995: 86)

The frantic movements of the wounded deer speak of a schizophrenia that is overwhelming and frightening, yet the deer knows its own situation and understands the futility of its desperate actions. Such fixed temporal and spatial parameters for plural, shifting antagonisms or subject-positions question the openness within which Laclau and Mouffe consider hegemony to take place in postmodernity. Nevertheless, the deer's frantic movements signal entrapment. Unable to find sufficient answers to the paradoxes of postmodernity or to step outside of its splintered subjectivity, the deer is merely delimited temporally. When Laclau and Mouffe's shifting antagonisms reach a temporal dead-end as here, it is perhaps useful to consider Jameson's views on postmodernity and Marxism, in particular his notion that postmodernism, with its attendant stress on indeterminacy, image, and space, is the cultural articulation of globalized politics and economics. In this sense, it is worth recalling Bertens's warning that Laclau and Mouffe's concept of hegemony depends upon an acceptance of plurality amongst all those concerned (there is in this assumption an evident 'totalizing' sweep of uniformity that is more usually associated with Jameson). Thus any encounter with a fundamentalist or 'essentialist' position would result in violence, in turn leading to mortality or the total collapse of the temporal.

El hombre solo 'vocalizes' the dilemma of 'essentialism' in postmodernity explicitly and darkly. The splits suffered by Carlos through his fragmented subjectivity lead to the ultimate finality of death. The backdrop of Biblical imagery and evocations of nature, bread, etc. serve to undermine the many possibilities for plurality, collage, and masked identities. Carlos shifts constantly between 'antagonistic' and irreconcilable temporal and socio-cultural positions and seeks the depths of La Banyera where he can 'submerge' himself and so quieten the noises in his head. The schizophrenia he suffers mounts through the count-down of the days and eventually crashes into the irretrievable collapse of self and community.

Although they differ greatly in form, both novels reflect remarkably similar concerns on the author's part. While *Obabakoak* appears to deal with the ruptures of modernity (it is worth noting the contrast established in some of the stories between contemporary Obaba and Obaba in the 1960s), nevertheless the narrative technique used in retelling the stories is one of collage and deferral, typical of postmodernist writing. *El hombre solo* can to some extent be viewed as linked to *Obabakoak* through the fact that Atxaga makes Obaba the protagonist's home town. When viewed side by side, they also appear as attempts by the author to tackle the same problems from different angles. The many stories in *Obabakoak* strangely evoke only the possibility of a complete narrative, but ultimately serve to open on to yet more stories. In this sense, the stories of Obaba reveal more about the open-endedness of a single location than they do of a coherent and unified community. The principal character of *El hombre solo* appears unified, but reveals himself to be a site of conflicting and competing discourses. While *Obabakoak* ends on an open note with the unravelling of intertextual possibilities and connections, *El hombre solo* closes with the character's immersion in the depths of nature in an end that is suggestive either of temporal finality in terms of death or of the giddy labyrinths of a whirlpool. While the many narrative discourses in Carlos sink ultimately into the reality of death, the stories of *Obabakoak* treat reality as the play of text. Haunting the surface voices that populate both works is the question of what, if anything, is real. The apparent absurdity of surface existences leads to a sense of nostalgia that marks both these works with the search for unity and coherence. Equally, this unity is located in the imaginary in terms of a lost wholeness in the past. Subjectivity in both of these books is decentred, a chance pastiche of collated voices or stories that turns history into imagined narratives. At the same time, such narratives provide the only glimpses into lived experiences and past fragments of time. The postmodern experience of fractured narratives renders any traditional separation of myth and history suspect.[14] As 'reality' spills over in Atxaga's work into the imagined or mythical, Atxaga can be placed within a group of 'third-world minority writers' whose uses of magical realism must, in Zamora and Faris's words, be understood as:

a mode suited to exploring — and transgressing — boundaries, whether the boundaries are ontological, political, geographical or generic. (1995: 5–6).

The result is that, in Atxaga, a dialectic emerges between myth and history, as the plural and imaginary constructions of the former negotiate the latter and attempt to fill in for the splintering of unified subjectivity.

Atxaga has spoken on several occasions of his fear of being classified as a 'Basque' writer. That, he says, would be akin to being cornered in the ring. The political, cultural, and historical intent of literature, therefore, exceeds the explicit demarcations of particular political allegiances. Critics of his work could point to a propensity for metafiction and a lack of direct engagement with specifically Basque issues. Others would view these very features as his strengths. Nevertheless, the intertextual and multi-vocal aspects of his work should be considered in terms of form as well as content, so that associations arise not just from what he writes, but from how he writes as well. In this context, it is important to stress that my alignment of the theories of Laclau and Mouffe and of Jameson in this discussion provides a metaphor for the problematization expressed in Atxaga's work through his exploration of deferral, multiplicity, and 'essential realities'. Thus the surfacing of 'essentials' in *El hombre solo* can be related to Jameson's overriding emphasis on postmodernity as a historical conjuncture of Marxism. Both *Obabakoak* and *El hombre solo* juggle with the confusing pluralities of the particular and their confrontation with temporality, as the sole meaningful overall framework within which they can be situated and understood. The two works explore this problem differently: *Obabakoak* through its attempt to construct an imagined community of Obaba via tales originating from a single location — an attempt which, however, results in travel and global cross-currents and ends with the metaphorical 'juego de la Oca' —

and *El hombre solo* through its dramatization of multiple identities, all of which dissolve into the vortex of mortality and temporal closure.

In his postscript to *Obabakoak*, Atxaga compares life to 'el Juego de la Oca'. The Gran Oca Madre serves in this instance to represent the final literary horizon which he seeks and so is the ultimate 'essential'. Yet, this goal is never reached and the game just goes on. The many stories of *Obabakoak* merely serve to pass the time whilst travelling to meet her. The diverse tales in the book travel down long, winding roads that supposedly lead to a temporal and spatial finality which defies articulation in the present. However, as Atxaga says, for Basque writing, the journey has just begun. Within this overall structure of the 'Juego de la Oca', *Obabakoak* is not just about the 'people and things of Obaba', as the title would indicate in Basque. It avails of metafiction and intertextuality to form a wide-reaching community of narratives, which make sense when viewed in relation and yet never provide a complete picture. Inter-relation, and not antagonism or opposition, holds the work together. Furthermore, *Obabakoak* when viewed thus locates the Basque language and culture at the particular historical conjuncture of plural democratic Spain caught up in a cultural project of what Jameson refers to as the globalization of the local as well as the 'localization' of the global. In this context, 'communities' of narratives, as well as the narratives of community, are composed of diverse spatial and temporal frames in their constructions of the historical conjuncture of postmodernity.

Jameson's critique of contemporary narrative focuses upon the loss of temporal referents through a heightened emphasis upon spatial dimensions. His critiques of literary narratives can also be applied to the discourse of theory. Thus cultural and literary failure to apprehend phenomenological experience is transferred to theory itself, as is seen in Jameson's own eschewal of the temporal marker implicit in the word 'death', evident in his preference for the more ambivalent term 'Real'.

Neither *Obabakoak* nor *El hombre solo* provide answers to the problem of juggling history, postmodernity, and community. Atxaga's problematization of these issues clearly highlights the complexity brought about by fractured temporality in terms of historical coherence. In an interview given to the magazine *Cambio 16* (6 November 1995), Atxaga blamed the fear which he identified in his interview with me as a by-product of the sudden and unexpected emergence from forty years of dictatorship into a climate of democratic plurality. In conversation with me, he stated that modernity had aroused the phobic in villages such as the imaginary Obaba. Spain's abrupt leap into plurality, he said, had accentuated this fear into a kind of schizophrenia. In this context, Atxaga contrasted Spain with England, saying that the time to absorb social changes had been dramatically foreshortened in Spain since the transition to democracy. Perhaps this can be understood when considered in the light of Carlos's experience of prison. Prison, like the 'enclosed' cultural and political space of

Francoist Spain, implies the tightening of space and the extension of time. The 'release' experienced by Carlos as well as by Spain upon Franco's death resulted, not in an even balance of spatial and temporal axes, but as an inverse experience of the postmodern collapse of time into space. Atxaga says that desperate actions often ensue from this experience of fear. In the above-cited interview with *Cambio 16*, he dismisses ETA as 'la última chispa del franquismo. Un grupo del pasado' and insists that the only way forward is through leaving aside revolutionary dreams. It is a matter now, he says, of maintaining dilemmas, not beliefs. Nevertheless, he admits to keeping a Bible at his bedside every night. Obviously, even if revolutionary dreams must be laid aside, one still needs the dream, if not the reality, of 'essentials' drawn from the belief conjured up by Biblical narratives. The imaginary, therefore, provides a temporal harness which can balance the slippery pull of spatial displacement. The referential framework provided by the finality of la Gran Oca Madre forces diverse narrative acts to confront history; at the same time, the splintered voices of incoherent temporalities undermine narrative cohesion.

Within such a context, the concept of community appears marked by ambivalence, both for the supposed inhabitants of Obaba and for its prodigal son Carlos. The attempt to enact community through narration turns the central characters into a site of displaced confusion. The babble of narrative voices stray from their 'origins' in the struggle for survival, only to be eventually silenced by the shut down of temporality. Community, whilst dispersed in terms of space, strives for temporal coherence and is therefore narrated in an attempt to defeat the fragmentation and dissolution of temporality. Yet this confrontation with the final 'essential' of death/history must also be considered, as Jameson points out, as the launching pad for the narrative discourses of imagined community. It is precisely the breakdown of narrative and communal cohesion and linearity in postmodernity that gives rise to the synchronic pluralities of postmodern narratives. When placed within the larger framework of temporal finality, the impetus to narrate community, however disjointed, splintered, or confused in its articulations, clearly becomes all the more pressing even as it is more endangered.

1. Surprisingly, relatively little scholarship exists on Atxaga's work. Of what there is, Basque scholars, both in the Basque country and abroad, have taken the lead in analysing Atxaga's work. Of those Basques and non-Basques working on Atxaga, perhaps the most notable name is that of Mari José Olizaregi (1998, 1999, 2000). Other scholars whose cited works I have consulted but not directly referred to in my chapter on Atxaga in recent years are Cristina Ortiz (1996), Martin Solares (1997), Alan Smith (interview, 1995–96), Ibon Izurieta (1994), and Miguel Riera (interview, 1989). The various literary stages of Atxaga's literary and intellectual development, myth, temporality, and orality are considered by these scholars.
2. For more details of the influence of Basque oral traditions on Atxaga's work, see the introduction to the cited edition of *Obabakoak*. Equally, Izurieta (1994) provides very useful details of this aspect of Atxaga's work. Mari José Olizaregi underlines the late

entry into modernity of Basque literature: 'Se ha afirmado que la Literatura Vasca entró tarde en la Modernidad, que no fue hasta finales de los años 50 cuando la literatura escrita en euskera se institucionalizó en el interior de la vida social como actividad cultural autónoma. Es a principios de la década de los 70 cuando Atxaga inicia su trayectoria literaria' (1999: 30).

3. In my personal interview with him (April 1999), Atxaga stated that, in his parents' generation, there had been belief in the Church; in his generation, there had been belief in Marxism; now, with the predominance of capitalism, the question of belief had ceased to be relevant. This point will be elaborated later in this chapter.

4. Translated by him into Castilian in 1989.

5. See Joseba Gabilondo's article (1998) on the Basque historical novel.

6. See Bottomore (1991) for definitions of this term.

7. Torfing defines their use of the term 'suture' (a Lacanian concept) as 'referring to the processes whereby the lack in the structure is healed' (1999: 307). However, he states that, for Laclau and Mouffe, social antagonisms prevent a fully sutured society.

8. Atxaga agreed to combine an interview with a walk around Bloomsbury in London on Thursday, 15 April 1999, when he came for the launch of the English translation of his novel *Esos cielos*. The interview was more of a conversation, as neither taping nor immediate note-taking were possible under the circumstances.

9. In this context, Atxaga told me that this idea of the 'inner lizard' came from a letter left by an old woman in his village when she died. She said that she was happy to die because she wished to be free of the serpent that hissed in her chest and stopped her from breathing freely. Although doctors affirmed that she suffered from a lung complaint, she always believed that a serpent had gotten into her chest. Atxaga used this as an example to demonstrate multiple understandings of 'reality' and possibilities for the same. Also evident in this example is the link between 'reality' and the imaginary.

10. Interestingly, Carrie Hamilton's work on women in Basque activism (2000) overturns such conventional patterns of association

11. Kaminski (1991) and Monticone (1986) are both useful for a fuller understanding of the socio-political changes in Poland since the 80s and the role of the Church in Polish politics.

12. Carlos's own imagination of an 'original' community emphasizes the role of the imagination in the construction of community identity. This imagination of community is also present in *Obabakoak*.

13. Interestingly, Sabino had been ousted from the organization because of a shift in ideology. He thus became an easy target for the authorities since he lacked protection. Carlos's continued allegiance to Sabino thus also marks his own rift with ETA, further emphasizing the splits and discontinuities in the latter.

14. Joseba Gabilondo's earlier cited article (1998) on the Basque historical novel further explores this issue.

CHAPTER 4

COMMUNITY, ETHNICITY, AND BORDER CROSSINGS IN *ALMA GITANA* (CHUS GUTIÉRREZ)

This chapter aims to examine concepts and narratives of community identities in relation to representations of ethnicity in the film *Alma gitana* (Chus Gutiérrez, 1995).[1] This film, which projects a love story between Lucía, a gitana, and Antonio, a *payo*,[2] problematizes ethnic and communal boundaries not just as borders which fence off identity, but also as possible points of crossing. The borders of ethnicity therefore fulfil the dual function of demarcating 'self' from 'other' whilst also being presented as bridges for the passage of cultural exchange. Ethnicity is simultaneously projected in the film, on the one hand, as fluid and adaptable through musical performance and, on the other, as bound by 'solid' and essentialist borders as portrayed through the *gitano* community.[3] Furthermore, this essentialized portrayal of the *gitano*s is viewed against the backdrop of a larger multi-cultural environment, so that the film furthermore presents spectators with an opportunity to reflect upon the possibilities and limitations of multiculturalism.

The concept of community, as bound by shared values and self-perceptions, is clearly central to multicultural articulations of identity, themselves attempts to preserve traditions and cultural difference in the face of modernity's migratory flows and movements. In this sense, the 'organic' myth of community as stable and unified is readily confronted with the modern inevitabilities of displacement and relocation. Central to the notion of multiculturalism is the juxtaposition of different communities, whereby the border or boundary acts both as dividing line and point of close contact. The border, thus, is both protection and threat. As stated in the introduction to this dissertation, the cultural complexities of globalization and postmodernity reify both the myth of community and its spatial dispersal and temporal breakdown in terms of practice. The problematiz-ation of community in postmodernity that was developed in the previous chapter will thus focus here on the dichotomy thrown up by border discourses and practices, at once fixed or impermeable and porous or flexible. My aim here is to explore the failure of the myth of community as closed and holistic within postmodernity, whilst also underlining the persistence of this myth in the postmodern imaginary.

The contradictory problematisation of ethnic identity within the postmodern cultural context of contemporary Madrid will be examined through an ethnographic analysis of the film's narrative, since the ambivalence of identity as represented here echoes on-going debates in ethnography. Traditional demarcations of the ethnographic field as 'other' to the ethnographer are being questioned since the late twentieth century as a result of post-structuralist dissatisfaction with the encapsulation of culture within defined spatial and temporal boundaries. Equally, this is an attempt to wrest ethnography from its ranking as a colonial and Western discourse of otherness, an endeavour which falls in line with a postcolonial and postmodern reassessment of the ethnographic task as an engagement 'en route'.[4] Nevertheless, much contemporary anthropological work continues to view culture as frozen within contained fields and has been unable to move beyond the discipline's conventional practices and discourse. Gutiérrez's portrayal of *gitanos* in *Alma gitana* complies in part with such otherized, ethnographic findings on a demarcated field of *gitano* identity, but departs from the latter in emphasizing the socio-cultural mobility of such groups. In this sense, the tension in the film's narrative between identity as fluid and identity as fixed acts as a metaphor for contemporary ethnography's struggle to engage with culture as a contingent process and not as an essential or unified state.

A link can therefore be drawn between the above tension and Atxaga's treatment of residual essentialism that was explored in Chapter 3. Both Atxaga and Gutiérrez emphasize in their respective 'texts' the persistence of essentialism in the midst of contemporary Spanish pluralities. Clearly, however, their treatment of this troublesome problem differs greatly: whilst Atxaga tackles the issue consciously, teasing out its many consequences, the problem surfaces in *Alma gitana* despite itself. Thus a clear difference emerges in terms of prevalent levels of reflexivity.

The parallel aimed at here between the film's contradictory perspectives of ethnographic borders and the current engagement in ethnography with the ambivalence of identity will serve to problematise the issue of community identity from the dual and partially overlapping perspectives of ethnography and cultural studies, the latter's emergence as a discipline coinciding with the above-mentioned questioning of ethnographic certainties. Since the 80s, ethnography has increasingly taken into account the shifting and fluid nature of the field under study. At the same time, a disciplinary overlap has resulted from the growing presence of cultural studies in academic circles. The subsequent renegotiation, and even blurring, of disciplinary boundaries forces a rethinking of culture in terms of travel and deferral of definitions. This indeterminacy can lead to the contrary attempt by competing discourses to maintain and enforce their specificity. While ethnography can be thought to situate itself in the everyday practices of people and communities, cultural studies may be more reliant on text; yet such a binary and opposed division of the two disciplines is highly debatable, particularly within a postmodern context where texts and practices in diverse fields are increasingly entangled and mutually reliant in constructions of cultural identity. Whilst an analysis of ethnicity in *Alma gitana* is derived from a fictitious, and hence textual, source, the narratives of identity that arise from ethnographic study traditionally have their source in lived practice. However, the film itself presents a fictional narrative mapped over a documentary-style portrayal of contemporary Madrid, members of a prominent *gitano* family and the current practices of fusion music. In this context, Penelope Harvey probes the disciplinary distinctions and overlaps between cultural studies and anthropology, arguing against a binary opposition between the analysis of text and of lived experience. Her view of cultural studies as compatible with 'auto-ethnography' or ethnography of the familiar (1996: 12–13) leads to the conclusion that

a consideration of the distinctions drawn between the representational and the embodied. . .is itself a consideration of social relations and the workings of creative and/or coercive power. What we often present as abstract theoretical concerns are simultaneously embedded in very social practices. (1996: 19)

Likewise, an examination of the issues of ethnic identity which arise in the film through the lens of theory might throw light back onto the latter. This may serve to bring into relief the theoretical nuances that would otherwise be lost to view. It is therefore also my aim to establish a dialogue between the narratives which arise from textual analysis and those which arise from ethnographic enquiry.

The theoretical framework for my analysis is drawn from the tension arising from two different ethnographic perspectives: firstly, the movement in Pierre Bourdieu's ethnographic work from what he called his early 'blissful structural-ist' analysis of the Kabyle house as a symbolic system based on binary oppositions to a later preoccupation with overcoming this reliance on dualistic concerns which inevitably freeze the object of study in time and space. Bourdieu's critique of much current ethnographic practice is based on his own shift from 'rules' to 'strategies', thereby allowing ethnic identity to be understood in terms of contextually defined spatial and temporal movement, rather than as a stagnant provider of definition. Central to this emphasis on strategies, for Bourdieu, are his concepts of habitus and field.

Secondly, I shall refer to two ethnographers who have focused extensively on *gitano* communities in Madrid, Teresa San Román of the Universidad Autón-oma de Barcelona and Paloma Gay y Blasco of the University of Dublin. San Román has established herself as an authority on subaltern groups in urban settings, in particular on *gitanos*. From a centralized *payo* perspective, San Román's several published works examine the attitudes and behaviour of an urban *gitano* underclass. Gay y Blasco focuses on the means through which *gitano* identity is maintained: binarily opposed gender behaviour which, she says, emerges from culturally contingent conceptions of sex and gender, serving to distinguish established sex roles within the community as well as to preserve *gitano* group identity as distinct from *payo*s. Her study reveals *gitano* identity in an overwhelmingly majority *payo* context to be maintained through adherence to a pre-determined code in the face of the constant threat of assimilation. Both San Román and Gay y Blasco demarcate the anthropological 'field' of *gitano* studies in order to clarify the focus of study. This in turn makes explicit their own *payo* perspective which is seen, not just as culturally distinct from the *gitano*s, but also as located centrally within the 'national' and disciplinary domains. This ethnographic position, together with the socio-economic limitations of the *gitano*s studied, establishes an implicit political hierarchy in terms of power relations, based on the authority of the ethnographers to construct and organize knowledge about *gitano*s. Ethnographers such as James Clifford and George Marcus are currently engaged in pursuing means of loosening these power structures which have been part of ethnographic practice since the colonial beginnings of the discipline. Bourdieu's emphasis on the spatial and temporal contingency of culture can equally be seen as an attempt to 'decolonize' or to dislodge ethnographic discourse and practice from a kind of structural stasis.

The 'organic' concept of community as a binding unit which establishes clear borders through discourse and practice is an implicit backbone to the film's narrative. Nevertheless, the single defining code of morality that binds the *gitano* community is challenged throughout by the female protagonist, who thereby risks alienation from her group. The love affair between the protagonists Antonio and Lucía (one a *payo* and the other a *gitana*) defies the policing of communal and ethnic identity and thereby carries the threat of destabilization. Equally, however, adherence to essentialist perceptions of ethnic identity is seen as central to the *gitano*s' survival as a distinct community in the face of assimilation. In a brief commentary on *Alma gitana*, Annie Brooksbank Jones states that

Schematically, the gypsy girl Lucía is marginalized in relation to outer (non-gypsy) social groups by her ethnicity, and in relation to inner (gypsy) groups by her gender. Both she and her '*payo*'. . .boyfriend cross the boundaries of traditionally acceptable behaviour within their groups, and are able to do so precisely because these boundaries are breaking down. (1997: 157)

Thus Lucía struggles to maintain her distinct ethnicity whilst venturing into a love affair that exacerbates the issue of cultural hybridity already thrown up by her participation in overlapping and culturally diverse social fields. The cultural cross-currents of a plural and postmodern Madrid constantly challenge the demarcations of fixed cultural identity; as Brooksbank Jones states,

The permeability of ethnic and gender boundaries in the film is linked, via its insistence that the 'other' is part of us, to the rapidly evolving multiculturalism of Madrid and many other large cities in Spain — a multiculturalism heteroglossically underlined in characters' regional Spanish, Latin American, African, US and other accents. (1997: 157–58)

This multiculturalism[5] is made visual by the film's location in Lavapiés, an ethnically diverse locality of Madrid. It is further emphasized in the film by its presentation of music, and more precisely, of flamenco, as an arena of cultural and ethnic encounters. Flamenco is dislodged from stereotypical or purist[6] views of it as an 'essential' expression of unbridled gypsy passion and is explored for its versatility and openness to other musical forms and ethnic groups. Music thereby provides a meeting ground for otherwise distinct ethnic groups, so that communities emerge mosaic-like from a shared musical forum out of fusion or the encounter with cultural difference, rather than from unified identity. The postmodern cultural context is thereby seen to destabilize traditional communities, but also to offer opportunities for constructing new experiences of community identities through fleeting cross-cultural and aesthetic contacts. Equally, however, the spatial and temporal fluidity of such communities with their subsequent scattering fails to satisfactorily erase the social persistence of conventional boundaries of ethnic distinctions and hierarchies. Community in postmodernity, as exemplified in this film, loses both its moral and political force and is converted instead into a 'mood' or a 'feeling', becoming, in other words, an emotionally arousing facet of the postmodern imaginary.

The question of community identity is tackled in the film, therefore, through the juxtaposition of apparently incompatible perspectives: on the one hand, as fixed binary opposition illustrated by conventional social behaviour; on the other hand, as fluidity and movement illustrated by music and love. The ambivalent ending leaves the issue unresolved but supposedly tilting towards the latter, as can be assumed from the positive note implied in the final scene. Equally the denial of a definite 'happily ever after' to the young couple leaves this point in some considerable doubt. Cinematic technique, whereby the camera cuts rapidly from scene to scene in the Sala Caracol and all those mileux where Antonio engages with multi-cultural friends, underlines fusion as fragmentation, rather than as cohesion. The multi-ethnic communities born of shared music, or of postmodern aesthetic encounters, clearly lack any real destabilizing force in the face of the socially divisive and hierarchical discourses and practices which they seek to oppose. Furthermore, the persistence of such normalizing structures can be seen not just in the course of the film, but also in the director's cinematic approach. This is made especially evident through the camerawork which inevitably centralizes *payo*s by offering visual perspectives of the *gitano*s and other ethnic groups as 'others'. As will be discussed later, the camera's repeated alliance with the male *payo* protagonist further implicitly aligns the spectators' vision with his. The construction of the film, therefore, repeatedly undermines the director's stated intentions to establish tolerance of diversity.

Structural ethnography has traditionally relied upon binary oppositions as a means of gaining information about ethnic groups. Ethnography in general has depended upon an internal view by an outsider of the culture being studied, with the ethnographer then returning to a more academic environment to draw theoretical conclusions from the experience of fieldwork, based on dualisms which emerge from the perspective upon which the study was based. Therefore, cultures have been conceptualized as enclosed fields, away from outside interferences. Borders which serve to demarcate the area of study thus allow the ethnographer to make contrasts and thereby to 'know'. The localized approach to the ethnographic task, however, cannot stand up in the face of increasing globalization, with the resulting accessibility of a plurality of cultural forms and voices. This view of culture as multiplicity is perhaps exemplified in the film by the easy movement of ethnic expressions which characterize 'world music' whereby the ethnically particular shifts to embrace and accommodate what is ethnically different.

Bourdieu's early analysis of the Kabyle house as a symbolic system proved to be of crucial importance to the development of his later epistemological concerns with regard to the study of culture. In this study, he established the Kabyle house to be a system of binary oppositions whereby a web of social relations is produced so as to give a pattern that exemplifies the social — and primarily gender based — relations existing in Kabyle culture. The series of binary oppositions extend from the division of space within the house for the use of humans and animals, men and women, to light and dry spaces as opposed to dark and damp ones. Such concrete oppositions lead to oppositions of concepts, such as male honour versus female honour, so the tangible and the concrete express an entire system of cultural values and ways of being. Meaning is derived here from opposition, the most basic or essential of which is perceived as gender opposition.

Despite this account of the Kabyle system, Bourdieu's subsequent development as an ethnographer and sociologist is the result of a clear dissatisfaction with the limitations of a structuralist approach. His analysis of the Kabyle does not take into account any temporal shifts in culture, thereby producing a set of 'rules' governing social practices. Nor in the course of this study had he overcome the subject–object dualism of the ethnographic task, leaving it unclear as to whether the system of binary oppositions is the result of the ethnographer's analysis or is something intrinsic to the culture under scrutiny. Bourdieu's development as a social scientist led, however, to an increasing awareness of an ethnographic approach whereby a systematic order is imposed on the culture under study as a result of the structuralist urge to establish coherence and order on human behaviour. The practice, or everyday behaviour, of the people about whom structuralist models were being constructed was often at variance with the rules that supposedly governed their conduct and that formed the foundations of such models. Thus an important source of Bourdieu's dissatisfaction was the means by which information is gathered in the social sciences. In particular, he problematizes the ethnographer's position as privileged observer, which gives rise to a hierarchical and binary relation between observer and observed.

In this critique of the structuralist project most clearly exemplified in French ethnography by Lévi-Strauss, Bourdieu's effort has been to find strategies for overcoming the binary opposition of such an approach. His stress has been, therefore, on an avoidance in social research of the objectification of the reality being studied. A key experience that marked Bourdieu's move away from structuralist methods was a final piece of 'hands-on' ethnography among the farming community of the Béarn in France where he himself had grown up. This experience of ethnographic enquiry amongst his 'own' people clearly overturned the traditional structural relation between subject and object and brought to the fore the epistemological concerns manifest in his own work. A gap became obvious here between the models constructed by a formal structuralist analysis and the reality of social practice. In particular, Bourdieu stressed the inadequacy of the term 'rule', which blurred the ethnographer's mode of explanation with principles adopted and observed by the social agents themselves. Hence Bourdieu's theoretical shift from 'rules' to 'strategies' as the means by which social practice defies structuralist attempts to encompass it within a mould. Social practice is viewed, instead, as an on-going scene of improvisation, reliant upon implicit, unspoken contextual knowledge and altering according to context. Social practice is therefore improvisatory and strategic. In order to grasp this emphasis on strategy, however, it is important to understand the dialectic that Bourdieu establishes between the concepts of habitus and field. Bourdieu's attempt is to incorporate a perspective of real-life agents within structuralist perceptions of culture. Practice then becomes the result of the dialectic between structure and agency or habitus and field.

Habitus, for Bourdieu, denotes the cognitive structures internalized by people through which the social world is apprehended. Bourdieu states that habitus results from the internalization of the structures of the social world and is therefore embodied. (1984: 468) As a collective phenomenon, habitus allows people to become members of communities formed from shared perceptions. Equally, variations in habitus according to social strata, income, or class lead to different positions within the social world. These positions result from distinct historical courses, turning habitus into a historical manifestation, at once the product of history and the bedrock of history. To quote Bourdieu:

The habitus, the product of history, produces individual and collective practices, and hence history, in accordance with the schemes engendered by history. (1977: 82)

Habitus therefore both mediates and is mediated by the social world and results from the dialectic between the internal and the external realities of individuals. While habitus positions individuals in the social field, and is thereby a system of structures, it nevertheless relies upon practice in order to manoeuvre through different fields. George Ritzer states that

The habitus merely "suggests" what people should think and what they should choose to do. People engage in a conscious deliberation of options, although this decision-making process reflects the operation of the habitus. The habitus provides the principles by which people make choices and choose the strategies that they will employ in the social world. (1996: 405)

This is an important point because it suggests that while habitus is a structure, it is nevertheless flexible and adaptable according to circumstance. Moreover, habitus is a relational concept since its significance only emerges in the context of two other principle concepts employed by Bourdieu, these being practice and field.

While habitus is the internalized scheme through which individuals assess the social world, fields emerge from the network of relations where power is contested. Bourdieu describes fields as 'strategic emplacements, fortresses to be defended and captured in a field of struggles' (1984: 244). This view of the field as an arena of competition emphasizes the political weight at stake in all fields, so that agents within any field employ strategies individually and/or collectively in order to maintain and improve their positions. Strategies emerge, not from calculation or premeditation, but from the contingencies of practice, differing according to the positions of actors within fields. Habitus and field are mutually implicated in a relationship which generates cultural practices. To quote Bourdieu from *Distinction*:

The dispositions constituting the cultivated *habitus* are only formed, only function and are only valid in a *field,* in the relationship with a field. (1984: 94)

Bourdieu's relational concepts of habitus, field, and practice offer a processual vision of cultural identity. Habitus as a regulating structure does not preclude flexibility, allowing for change as a result of spatial and temporal movements. Equally, the concept of field takes into account contestations for power that define the strategies of practice that agents employ. Such contestations inevitably imply negotiations and shifts in social and cultural positions and attitudes.

To turn now to two important ethnographers working currently on *gitano* identity, namely San Román and Gay y Blasco, the persistent marginality of *gitano*s in San Román's findings freezes their spatial location on the peripheries of the larger, and apparently unified, cultural context of *payo* Spain. While San Román makes a brief mention in her more recent book (1997) of the relation between *gitano*s as an ethnic minority and the relatively new presence of other ethnic minorities in Spain in the form of immigrant communities, her analysis is brief and cursory. Whilst her focus is on the *gitanos*, hence placing a 'spotlight' on them and bringing them into view, nevertheless, San Román's work is also interesting for the cultural assumptions of a unified Spanish, as opposed to *gitano*, identity that it reveals. The binaristic view of *gitanos* as a minority can only emerge from the general stereotype that she partakes of that *payos* — an apparently homogenous group — are essentially a powerful 'majority'.

The play of power presented by such a picture is somewhat disturbed in *Alma gitana* through a partial reversal of this stereotype. The central location of the *gitano* family in the film's narrative establishes their inequivocable cultural presence. *Payos* are not seen as a clear majority, just as the *gitano* family is not presented as 'marginal'. Interplay between the two ethnicities results, however, not in blurred or hybrid identities — with the exception of the protagonist Antonio, whose *payo* origins are surely questionable — but in the binaristic co-existence of apparently immiscible categories. Furthermore, the concept of unified ethnic community of *gitanos* only emerges in relation and in opposition to a larger social context of ethnic diversity. Implicit in the film is the idea that, if the national (i.e., *payo*) imaginary has long relied on the *gitano* for self-definition, then *gitanos* too rely on the received image of the *payo* in order to outline their own ethnic boundaries. Such a binary relation is complicated by the underlying stereotypical assumption that any given community is locked within its own boundaries in line with essentialist precepts, in spite of the easily accessible abundance of shifting and plural cultural discourses. As Paul Julian Smith points out,

The shop, like the gypsy home, church and sala de fiestas, is a proper place in both senses of the word: the bastion of a restrictive moral code that asserts autonomy only by enforcing exteriority. It is Antonio who is the nomadic outsider, roaming the metropolis on his motorbike . . . *Payo* promiscuity thus provokes and reinforces monogamy and endogamy. (2000: 172)[7]

Lucía and her family regard themselves as, and even pride themselves on being, traditional *gitanos*; yet her actions and practices challenge the established norms of 'good' *gitano* behaviour. This results in the inevitable breach, as pointed out by Bourdieu, between cultural notions or beliefs on the one hand and cultural practices on the other. Yet, Lucía is persistently otherized by her actions, both by her community and by the film-maker, whose portrayal of her as outside the norm is reinforced by the allocation of clichéd parts to *gitanos*, as well as to the other ethnic minorities and to the *payos* — despite the surface attempt to explore cultural diversity.

The reliance upon structuralist perceptions of identity is also apparent in the work of Paloma Gay y Blasco.[8] Despite her statement that her work is based upon an indeterminacy in terms of sex and gender, her analysis of *gitano* identity and practices depends upon the stability of the latter provided by a spatial and temporal enclosure. Gay y Blasco lays out the centrality of her own (fixed) identity as a woman and as a *paya* to the ethnographic work that she carried out in the course of researching her doctoral thesis during fifteen months of fieldwork in the largely *gitano* neighbourhood of Plata y Castañar on the outskirts of Madrid. Her gender and ethnic identity created an obstacle to the 'participant observation' that she believed necessary for ethnographic work. The *gitano*s, she states, resisted her entry into their midst due to their own convictions with regard to gender and ethnicity. The status of privileged observer, traditionally associated with anthropological studies (and generally considered by ethnographers working with gypsies in general very difficult, if not impossible, to achieve) became unfeasible. She states that she was only able to observe from the ethnic boundary separating *gitano*s from *payo*s once she *appeared* different through her dress and behaviour from the *gitano*s' preconceived notions about *payo*s and payas. She further states that, despite attempts to conform to *gitano* codes of dress and behaviour, she was never able to get 'inside' the community throughout her fieldwork. This is exemplified by the fact that for much of the period of her fieldwork, she had to live outside of the *gitano* community and only spend the day there. A binary divide leading to *gitano* mistrust of *payo* intentions therefore lies at the source of all her work and colours her findings. Implicit in Gay y Blasco's work is the assumption of hierarchical differences in the *gitano/payo* dualism. In line with San Román's findings, *gitano*s live as an enclosed and subaltern group within an overall *payo* nation. This unequal relation further plays itself out inside *gitano* circles where people slot into positions within the group in accordance with their gender, age, and behaviour. Central to Gay y Blasco's work is the discovery of a unified conception amongst *gitano*s of the overall group or community, individuals, their behaviour or actions and their bodies. Bodily 'purity', best exemplified by the virginity of unmarried women, in this sense translates into the moral integrity of an entire ethnic group. The maintenance of virginity amongst unmarried *gitanas* is hence the single, most important proclaimer of *gitano* ethnicity. It further provides the main ethnic marker that differentiates *gitano*s from *payo*s, since *gitano*s stereotype payas as morally loose and promiscuous owing to the absence in *payo* culture of an overt stress on virginity.

The interplay between Bourdieu's conceptions of habitus and field at once establishes certain guiding structures that determine cultural practice and allows for a degree of permeability in terms of cultural identity. His emphasis on the question of empowerment, whether in terms of economic capital or cultural capital, places the spotlight on culture as processsual, contingent, and politically driven. The spatial and temporal mobility that he attaches to cultural identity further removes the latter from any essential attributes. The results of the participant observation practised by Gay y Blasco involve adherence by her to apparently fixed social norms prevalent amongst *gitano*s. Despite her aim of slotting her work into Judith Butler's questioning of perceptions of sex and gender, her work is reliant upon essential attributes of *gitano* — and by deduction, *payo* — identity. In this context, Bourdieu' development of the key concepts of habitus, field, and practice problematize cultural identity to a much finer and more complex degree. His overcoming of the binary divide between the objective and the subjective through the employment of these concepts places the focus on culture as a process of engagement, thereby dispensing with the binary split wrought by notions of 'otherness'. My aim in bringing these two diverse ethnographic approaches to bear upon *Alma gitana* is to tease out both the aspirations of the film in its portrayal of cultural movements and contacts and its failure to do so owing to its reliance upon structuralist visions of identity. In order to do so, I shall rely upon the theoretical framework provided by Bourdieu's own shift away from structuralist analysis.

Alma gitana is inevitably viewed against the many Spanish (and other European) cultural texts which represent the gypsy as a threat to the dominant discourses and symbols of ethnically or racially conceived communal and national unity. The film apparently sets out to subvert romantic visions of the gypsy as primitive or exotic 'other' by weaving a fictitious Romeo and Juliet — style love story around a documentary-style portrayal of a *gitano* family in contemporary Madrid. *Gitano*s are seen here as central to the cultural life of the capital, in deliberate contrast to a general perception of gypsies as marginal. For Gutiérrez, as she states in her interview with Delgado, the film amounts to

una patada al folclore y los estereotipos de navajas, peleas, chabolas o venta ambulante, con los que el cine y la sociedad han identificado al calé. (1995: 84)

As Hancock, Dowd, and Djuric show in their compilation of gypsy history and poetry (*The Roads of the Roma*, 1998), persecution and marginalization have often led to more determined constructions of gypsy identity and communal adherence to the norms of the latter. In this sense, boundaries constructed to fence off distinct categories that are perceived as essential are also markers of the implication of 'self' with 'other', since the 'self' propagates itself through both relation with and difference from the 'other'. Dominant social discourses which locate the gypsy as a peripheral 'other' avail of the latter's marginal location to enhance their own position. Exoticized notions of gypsy identity serve, therefore, to reinforce and empower the normalizing discourses of European national and communal identities. Ironically, the threat of assimila-tion underlying such dominant discourses can, as Hancock points out, lead to similar discourses of fixed cultural identity on the part of the minority 'other'. Social discourse can in this sense diverge from social practice which may in reality involve subtle fields of negotiation between apparently empowered and disempowered cultural groups. While the film draws upon this generalised view of the *gitano* as 'other' and takes pains to display this attitude amongst the *payo*s, it nevertheless strays from the norm by presenting the *gitano*s as socially well-placed, particularly in terms of economic status. Indeed, its projection away from such perceptions relies upon the latter assumption as a launching pad. *Gitano*s are presented as central characters, alongside *payo*s. The film, in fact, goes so far as to reveal the prejudices held by *gitano*s as regards *payo*s, showing them to be perpetrators, and not merely victims, of ethnic intolerance. In an interview with *La Vanguardia*, Peret, who plays the role of the Evangelical pastor in the film, states that

el tema del racismo . . . va a aparecer en la película reflejado por ambas partes: no sólo el de los *payo*s, sino también de los *gitano*s, porque nosotros tambié somos racistas, es una manera de defenderse. (Diego Muñoz 1995: 54)

This is a view which coincides with Hancock's findings. However, if as Gutiérrez has stated in *Diario 16* (Noceda, 1996), her aim has been to establish recognition for *gitano*s ('he intentado demostrar que los *gitano*s son personas que viven como el resto de la gente'), then such an emphasis on ethnic exclusion serves mainly to reinforce and freeze ethnic boundaries. Not just does this result in the temporal stasis of ethnic identity, but it also negates the possibility of any negotiation of hegemony between the two groups.

It is highly debatable, therefore, whether any political benefits can be derived from such a portrayal, as a mere reversal of prejudices locks the two ethnic groups into a self-perpetuating battle which cannot redress the balance of social inequality. Gutiérrez's presentation of Madrid as a cultural, and in particular musical, melting pot fails to take into account the political unevenness and subalternity of the majority of *gitano*s or other ethnic minorities in Spain today. Furthermore, the affluence endowed upon the *gitano*s portrayed denies the film any possibility of engaging with the very issues of ethnic barriers and social discrimination affecting *gitano*s which are undoubtedly determined by the larger postmodern context of late capitalism. In this sense, the film lacks any real political engagement with the socio-cultural realities of *gitano*s.

Despite the documentary approach of *Alma gitana*'s cinematic technique, the film fails therefore to represent *gitano* realities. Tomás Calvo Buezas emphasizes the long history of persecution that has been experienced by *gitano*s in Spain:

as far as the gypsies themselves are concerned, their cultural reality is something quite different: during their five-hundred year residence in Spain, coexistence has been neither just, peaceful nor respectful of their cultural uniqueness. Wretched living conditions, prejudice and stereotyping have made a mockery of the democratic and egalitarian ideals formally set forth in all European countries and constitutions. (1998: 14)

Calvo Buezas stresses the gap between what he sees as the constitutional right to behave 'ethically' by respecting cultural difference and the reality of ethnophobia where a dominant *payo* majority ostracize *gitano*s and squeeze them into impossibly difficult economic situations. Drawn from a series of surveys, Calvo

Buezas expresses an extreme binary view of *gitano–payo* relations that also fails
to take into account any negotiating strategies on the *gitano*s' part. He coincides
with Gay y Blasco in delineating a distinct and fixed *gitano* identity and with San
Román in emphasizing the socio-economic minority status of *gitano*s. This view
is one that itself self-perpetuates the disadvantaged situation of *gitano*s. Equally,
it perhaps draws accurately upon the socio-economic contexts within which the
majority of *gitano*s still live in Spain today.

Despite her focus on the overlaps of community identities, Gutiérrez's
deliberate choice of one of Spain's most successful *gitano* families as the subjects
of her portrayal can be seen to undermine her stated intention of a 'realistic'
representation of *gitano*s. The actress Amara Carmona states in *Ya-Madrid* (Gil
1996) that 'en la película salimos como gente normal, que tiene un negocio, que
estudia, que están limpios y no salen niños descalzos, ni chabolas'. This view of
what is 'normal' or common for *gitano*s cannot but invite criticism, since
Carmona's membership of a privileged social class as part of Spain's leading
flamenco fusion family (Antonio Carmona of Ketama is her cousin) removes
her experience of *gitano* identity from that of the majority of *gitano*s. What is
usual for her may not be so for many other *gitano*s, so that the glossing over of
economic unevenness in the film actually works against its apparent intention of
addressing ethnic prejudice. In an article in *El País Semanal,* the writer Rosa
Montero states

Parece que el mundo del espectáculo acaba de redescubrir a la gente de bronce: se
han dado cuenta de que, además de gustar a las audiencias tradicionales, también
pueden gustar a los posmodernos. Puede que esta moda ayude a rebajar los
prejuicios de los *payo*s. Pero me fastidia que todo se quede ahí, en una gitanería que
resulta exótica y apreciable cuando se ve en una película, pero que la sociedad
repudia cuando es de carne y hueso, sudor y hojalata y marginación. (1996: 12)

It could, of course, be argued that films such as *Alma gitana* counter the
essentialist vision of unified Spanish identity previously projected by Francoist
ideology through their emphasis on the plural, synchronic, and fragmented
experiences of identity characteristic of postmodernity. The image projected by
Alma gitana of ethnic plurality is in keeping with these current trends in cinema.
Nevertheless, the film does depend largely on an essentialist view of *gitano*s as
exoticized or 'other' through their rigid attachment to moral and communal
codes of behaviour. In line with Montero's views, the *gitano*s in this film offer a
spectacle of 'otherness' that does little to mediate the social realities of *gitano*
communities in Spain[9] — despite the backing given to the film by *gitano*
audiences.[10]

A vision of collective groups or communities as mobile, and not fixed or
governed by set 'rules', is best exemplified in *Alma gitana* through its presentation
and use of music, both in terms of the film's narrative and in terms of the choice
of cast. In this sense, *Alma gitana* documents the tendencies and movements of

contemporary flamenco in its recent evolution towards the ranks of world music. With the exception of Pedro Alonso (in the part of Antonio) who had previously worked with the Catalan theatre group La Fura dels Baus, Gutiérrez's choice of actors has been from outside the acting profession. Amara Carmona, who plays Lucía, is from the well-known Carmona-Habichuela family of guitarists and singers (related to Antonio Carmona, lead singer of the fusion group Ketama, which also appears in the film) and is herself trained in flamenco dance. Jesús, her brother in the film, is played by Pepe Luis Carmona, her brother in real life, who previously was lead singer of the flamenco fusion group La Barbería del Sur. As a family, the Carmonas have been responsible for much of 'new' flamenco which seeks integration with world music. Darío is played by the once well-known singer Peret, whose real-life conversion to born-again Christianity is mirrored in the film. Peret is best known currently for his CDs which celebrate Jesus, yet another form of flamenco fusion that is also projected in the film's scenes of church celebrations. The choice of a high media-profile cast for the film immediately locates the narrative within the context of contemporary postmodern Spain. Personal involvements from cast members in a number of well-known cultural productions such as those by La Fura dels Baus and fusion music construct a series of postmodern 'narratives' around them which influence viewers' perspectives of the film itself and the issues it raises. The faces on the screen can be recognized from their participation in other cultural productions which are themselves known to run against the grain of fixed cultural identity. The film's projection of the spontaneous gatherings of different ethnic groups around the field of music, gains 'authenticity' from such a cast of experienced musicians who, in real life, seek to stretch the traditional in flamenco to merge with foreign influences. Yet, the adaptability of gypsy culture to foreign influences, its undeniable exploitation as a medium for projecting the 'new' Spain and its occupation of cultural spaces at national and international levels do not mitigate the gulf between culture as superficial, aesthetic enjoyment and culture as lived, social practice.

In a deliberate blurring of binary oppositions, Gutiérrez converges actors with real-life musicians, thereby attempting to project what is 'real' through 'fiction'. This characteristically postmodern overlapping of these supposedly distinct categories of actor and character may be seen to foreground the performative elements of identity and highlights its cultural mobility. For Spanish spectators, the inevitable recognition of the cast as belonging to the vibrant scenes of flamenco fusion, already in high profile in the media, links the concept of 'authenticity' with the necessary processes of experimentation and growth needed to keep any art form alive. Thus *Alma gitana* aims to challenge orthodox — or structuralist — conventions of fixed racial and cultural differences, with their attendant notions of 'purity', by presenting an ethnomusic-ological perspective of inter-community contacts and cross-currents.

Equally, however, the postmodern constructions of plural identities seen here dehistoricize and de-politicize ethnicity, turning it into the surface experience of cosmopolitan cross-currents. This depoliticization translates into a devaluation of community identity, which then must rely upon fixed and reiterated social practices as a way of presenting the appearance of cohesion. Disengaged from involvement with people outside of their communal milieu, Lucía's family appears blindly attached to their ethnic and patriarchal values and codes. The superficiality of this projection of community is highlighted by Bourdieu's concept of habitus, which at communal level allows for cohesiveness in the course of navigating through different fields and adapting to contingencies. Habitus, however, is engaged with field and this is sorely lacking in the film. Despite their 'centrality' to the script, Lucía's family is frozen in their material affluence and cultural rigidity.

The presentation of this ethnic community in *Alma gitana* further places the spotlight on contemporary Spain in its role as a competitor in the global cultural marketplace. Indeed, the 'Spanishness' that tourists come to savour in Spain (a perspective which views Spanish identity itself as 'other') is depicted here in the guise of flamenco, itself seen to be largely mobilised by *gitano*s. Lucía's brother, who we later learn is a severe patriarchal figure of *gitano* authority in her life, sings at the flamenco tablao Corral de la Morería whilst Antonio dances there. In so doing, the two men are engaged in the joint venture of presenting presumed *gitano* musical identity to tourists for their easy consumption. Ethnicity is thereby packaged for transitory diversion and flamenco is drawn into the global marketplace as another commodity for sale. Tourists are unable to distinguish Antonio's ethnic identity from that of the singers and other performers, so that *gitano* identity becomes indistinguishable in their minds from an overall 'Spanish' experience. Spanish culture, when viewed as 'other' by tourists and foreigners, becomes reliant upon *gitano* musical traditions. This move on the director's part is, however, not without its measure of ambivalence. On the one hand, it becomes necessary to emphasize the borders by which *gitano* ethnicity can be identified; thus Gutiérrez carefully highlights stereotypical aspects of *gitano* community identity by establishing a series of supposed norms in terms of social behaviour among *gitano*s. She therefore reproduces to a large extent the clichés of essential identity that are typical features of the (much derided) profile of the gypsy in the Western imaginary.[11] On the other hand, key *gitano* characters, such as Lucía, the heroine, Darío, the *gitano* pastor, and the music produced by the fusion group Ketama, are presented as open to cultural difference and mobility within the context of a shifting postmodern cultural scene.

Key scenes in *Alma gitana* emphasize fixed notions of *gitano* identity, while others seek to dismantle them. The black and red colours that mark the opening shot of the film evoke stereotypical visions of Spain — and gypsy — as culturally different 'other'. The camera dwells on this scene to the drawn-out cry of cante jondo in a metaphoric 'freezing' of this view. As Antonio's mother, whose ethnic identity remains unknown in the course of the film, is seen winding a black and red shawl around her in the midst of a dance, stark clichés of gypsy passion are called upon. The use of the two strong primary colours appears to indicate essential attributes of *gitano* identity. They are also the colours most associated with Spain in a global context, in particular with the images of Spain disseminated through advertisements for sherry, tourism, and 'passionate' popular culture. In this sense, Antonio's mother is both gitana and paya at once, an international symbol of Spanishness. Yet, the ambivalence surrounding her ethnicity also points to the constructed nature of cultural identity. Her son's ethnic classification as a *payo*, therefore, is less a matter of inherited identity than of conformity to dominant social codes. If he is a *payo*, it is not because we — or he, one assumes — are sure of this, but because it is more likely that he belongs to the group that forms a majority. Furthermore, the animosity between his father and his mother's *gitano* lover Darío point to his father's *payo* ethnicity in a presumed play of opposites. In addition, following the death of his parents, Antonio was raised by his *payo* uncle and aunt. However, the fact that Darío has been more of a father-figure to Antonio than his supposed 'real' father, together with the fact that he and Antonio's mother were lovers, places ambiguity not merely on the question of paternity but also on Antonio's 'real' ethnic identity. Gutiérrez's portrayal of ethnicity as construction is shot through with tension as her representation of *gitano* ethnicity calls upon a measure of fixity and innateness that is absent from the *payo*s. While Antonio as supposed *payo* does not need to exercise obvious traits of ethnicity in order to be endowed with such identity, the *gitano*s as a minority group must reiterate their ethnic practices in order to exist as a separate group. Indeed, any assumptions of *payo* ethnic identity that emerge from the film must be drawn from a contrast with the clearly laid out *gitano* ethnicity. In particular, *gitano* identity is marked by a strict adherence to patriarchal traditions and by emphasis upon the virginity of unmarried women, a perspective that is in line with Gay y Blasco's study on *gitano* identity.

At the same time, flamenco is portrayed as a form of *gitano* music that is open to change and adaptation. Its versatility surely suggests similar ethnic flexibility in the *gitano*s. The presentation of flamenco as hybrid song emphasises the improvisatory aspects of music, and by implication ethnicity, in shifting postmodern contexts. Rather than adhere to any fixed conventions or 'rules' in terms of musical expression, fusion flamenco emerges from encounters with cultural difference. The film juxtaposes Ketama, African musicians, and a Japanese singer, each with their own musical styles which blend to form hybrid songs, in the course of shared musical celebrations of ethnic diversity. This is foregrounded by the friendship of the protagonist Antonio with the members of the international group 'Congo Bongo'. At night in the Sala Caracol, Africans, Americans, Japanese, Spaniards, and *gitanos* come together in the performance of fusion music where flamenco lends itself to other 'ethnic' musical forms to become part of a youthful, musical celebration. Cultural identity, in this global context, is presented as contextually defined, processual, and contingent upon encounters with difference. Far from being perceived as a barrier, otherness appears here as an invitation to travel. However, as Smith states, 'while the diversity, rapidity and rhythm of "world music" is offered as a primary (and indeed solitary) practice of cultural creation and social action, elsewhere in *Alma gitana* heterogeneity is repeatedly associated with culpable confusion, even chaos' (2000: 172). The unmistakable associations established between world music, the consumption of drugs, such as cocaine, and sexual promiscuity are suggestive of a certain illicitness that cannot but tinge both the romance between Antonio and Lucía and the projection of flamenco as cultural encounter.

For Antonio and Lucía, who first meet in the Sala Caracol, musical performance coincides with the propensity to cross ethnic borderlines in the name of love. Here the performance of music and dance becomes equated with movement or passage — an association that is further emphasized by the repeated shots of Antonio and Lucía travelling through Madrid on the latter's motorcycle. The camerawork in the scenes which take place in the Caracol emphasizes the mobility of ethnic identity through its focus on groups of young people moving to the music. Rather than focus on individuals, the camera frames groups of ethnically diverse people sharing a musical platform. Most importantly, Antonio first sees Lucía dancing flamenco in the ladies' room at the Caracol, in a spontaneous flamenco outburst in the company of other young women. In contrast to the rigid cultural parameters of her home environment and despite the controlling presence of her elder brother, in the Caracol she can express herself in a new and more open environment. However, the implicit suggestion here is that only a gitana could dance so.

Further emphasis on the film's superficial treatment of ethnic contacts and negotiations, as opposed to divisions, is highlighted by the film's inevitable reliance upon binary oppositions with an uneven spread of power. The above-mentioned scene, where the lovers first meet, is a case in point: its dramatic impact is derived from two different sets of binary oppositions which inevitably reinforce the very unevenness of power that the film overtly seeks to negate. Firstly, the gender division arising from Antonio as the male standing at the entrance to the ladies' room, he alone in a typically machista vision of the man as unique and powerful, she surrounded by her girlfriends in an exoticised vision of the beloved supported by her (less attractive) female escorts. This is reinforced by the camera's emphasis upon his 'sighting' of her, thereby aligning us as viewers to this perspective of ethnic and gender 'otherness'. Secondly, there is a binary opposition in terms of ethnicity established through the viewers' 'knowledge' that Antonio is *payo* and Lucía is gitana, as are her female friends. Not just is the woman here surrounded and supported by her female friends, but they are also all gitanas. The result is that the overlaps of ethnicity at play on stage in the Caracol do not result in the ironing out of difference, but in a musical pastiche that has no great social or cultural repercussions. The African singers dress in traditional clothes, Antonio's ex-American girlfriend has a lingering accent which marks her 'origins' and Lucía must return at the end of the evening to the cloistered life of an unmarried gitana. Roots or 'essential' identity inevitably win over improvised cultural practice.

Diverse and colourful presentations of ethnic difference, as through the Japanese singer or the African women, avoid the possibilities of dealing with the question of social or ethnic inequality. Equally, the idyllic sense of community generated by fusion music does not extend into the 'real' world, where ethnic difference inevitably points to subaltern social status. While the film presents the viewer with examples of cultural hybridity, no effort is made either through the narrative or the cinematic technique to probe beyond hybridity into the question of power. Indeed, cinematic technique, with its 'otherizing' of the *gitano*s, often serves to dislodge the film's claim of addressing ethnic inequalities. In this context, Jacques Attali's statement that '[w]ith music is born power and its opposite: subversion' (1985: 6) is not borne out in the film, as the nocturnal activities at the Caracol fail to extend into the light of day. Antonio's *payo* relatives look down upon his involvement with flamenco as a sort of ethnic 'downgrading' that threatens to reduce his place in society. Similarly, Pocho, the illegal African immigrant, is detained by the authorities, in a move which presumably precedes deportation. Gutiérrez therefore establishes a further binary opposition in the film through the contrasts between the 'unreal' musical world of ethnic fluidity and the 'real' world of ethnic prejudice and barriers. What is more, her insistence on flamenco as primarily the musical expression of *gitano*s points to the ethnic 'origins' of this music, thereby charging it with an essential ethnicity that coincides with general stereotyping.

Gutiérrez is therefore unable to sustain a projection of ethnic identity as contextually determined social strategy and falls back time and again onto a reliance on stereotypes of fixed identity. The ethnographers Teresa San Román and Paloma Gay y Blasco likewise construct ethnic fences around the *gitano* communities of their focus in order to isolate and analyse the cultural identity of the latter. Gutiérrez as a filmmaker can be said to coincide in general with their view of *gitano*s as a subaltern minority within the overwhelmingly *payo* nation-space of contemporary Spain.

The concern amongst *gitano*s to preserve the 'purity' of their identity, stressed by Gay y Blasco, forms the basis for the transgression/cultural travel posed by a morally reprehensible love in *Alma gitana*. In keeping with Gay y Blasco's findings, a vision of the *gitano* community as firmly based upon binary oppositions forms an overall frame for the film's narrative of inter-ethnic relations. However, the film also attempts, despite its flaws, to explore the elasticity of ethnic boundaries contained in San Román's (and Bourdieu's) more flexible and historicized view of ethnicity as 'strategy'. Despite her close family ties, Lucía's participation in a larger community of fellow-students of her own age group places her on the overlapping zones of *gitano* and *payo* communities. In particular, she exemplifies the morally worthy gitana who nevertheless feels no overwhelming need to stay within the confines of her immediate social and family circle. Unlike her mother who always remains within the domestic environment, Lucía is able to articulate alternative and competing views with regard to how *gitano*s should live. On the one hand, she insists upon the maintenance of her own virginity, as also on the fact that gitanas only ever love one man in the course of an entire lifetime. On the other hand, she objects to the fact that her elder sister is being physically abused by her husband and states very strongly that she ought to leave him. In so doing, Lucía displays an ambivalence as regards 'correct' gitana behaviour, no doubt the result of her own cultural implication in the wider postmodern context of contemporary Spanish cultural fluxes.

Lucía's cultural location on the borderline of *gitano* ethnic practices is further evidenced by the fact that she is studying art conservation at university, thereby contradicting any stereotypes which associate gitanas with illiteracy and *gitano*s in general with low culture (music and dance). Gay y Blasco refers to a lack amongst gypsies of any durable cultural traces, such as painting or sculpture. Music, the cultural expression most commonly assigned to *gitano*s, is generally considered to be orally transmitted and hence pliable in the face of contextual demands. This view of *gitano*s as a 'transient' or migrant people, temporally associated with the present, coincides with stereotypes which associate *gitano*s not just with illiteracy but also with a lack of known or narrated linear and traceable 'history' which easily locates them as 'romantic other' to Europeans. By engaging, albeit as a student, in the heritage industry, Lucía assumes a place among those who fashion, lay out and construct a larger national and European cultural memory. As an art restorer, her rescuing of cultural traces contravenes the notion that *gitano*s are outsiders to the construction and maintenance of 'high culture'. This is all the more so in the context of her father's antique business. While his shop hints of many a *gitano*'s livelihood as 'chatarrero', his prosperous business nevertheless upgrades him to middle-class and even high-bourgeois status, making him indistinguishable from non-*gitano*s of the same class. It further emphasises the family's active role in the circulation of prized cultural objects, allowing them therefore a place in the construction of an archive at national, and not communal, level.

The delineation of marginality assigned to *gitano* communities by San Román and Gay y Blasco derives without doubt from the tight socio-economic conditions in which the *gitano*s of their studies live. There is therefore little ambivalence in their work around questions of power and hegemony. It is clear that *gitano*s squeeze in at the bottom end of social structures and have therefore little space from which to negotiate or manoeuvre their status. San Román's use of the term 'strategy', however, locates identity as contingent to contextual factors and denotes a degree of negotiation as ethnic practices alter according to environments and historical periods. Gay y Blasco's work tends to freeze the *gitano*s' own use of these culturally shared concepts into sets of binarily opposed and static paradigms. This automatically negates the possibility of any negoti- ation of power on their part. In this context, *Alma gitana* too fails to take into account any questions of hegemony despite brushing the issue, although not for the same reasons. The play between the different ethnic groups does not probe inequalities in its presentation of fusion as a smooth process, although these are evident in the subaltern status of the illegal immigrant Pocho, whose identity when questioned by the police must remain clandestine. Differences between the status of First World and Third World immigrants also emerge in this scene in the Rastro when the police ask Pocho for his documentation. Donna, Antonio's American ex-girlfriend, has to reply on Pocho's behalf, since presumably his accent would give away his origins. Apparently, Donna is not in danger of being unwelcome in Spain, whilst Pocho definitely is. What is more, the policeman leaves when she states that Pocho is her boyfriend from America. It therefore appears that a black immigrant from the United States is more welcome to the authorities than a black immigrant from Africa, implicitly throwing up the binary of First World against Third.

The reversal of stereotypes presumably intended by Gutiérrez to redress the balance of cultural preconceptions (but which results instead in an avoidance of confrontation with the question of social inequality and of the failures of multiculturalism) is most obvious in the economic affluence attributed to the *gitano* family and in Lucía's consequent material well-being in comparison to Antonio, as well as in the portrayal of *gitano*s as subjects of racism. In this context, Werbner and Modood write in their introduction to *Debating Cultural Identity* that

... anti-racists subvert their own anti-essentialist project by defining Whites as essentially oppressive, homogenous, immutable and essentially racist. . ...Rather than strategic essentialism . . . what is needed is strategic *deconstruction*: a continuous process of self-monitoring reflexiveness that explores the personal experiences of people of all 'races', while exposing the constructedness of all political categories . . . (1997: 11)

This statement perhaps most aptly points to a major failing that runs through this film: the mere juxtaposition of contradictory constructions of identity, whether ethnic or otherwise, fails to take into account identity's processual nature. Equally, the strategy of essentialism evident in the film lacks reflexivity, so that community as shared ethnicity appears brittle and inflexible. What we have instead is the mere juxtaposition of opposites, best exemplified by the two protagonists. Antonio's multiple part-time occupations as dancer, waiter, and dance student, together with the fact that he lives in a room in a shared flat, lead to the impression that his income is not much above the bread line. In contrast to Lucía's focused pursuit of her studies, Antonio is unable to fulfil any role satisfactorily. Furthermore, his loose and somewhat strained ties with his uncle and aunt, as well as his sense of abandonment caused by the traumatic death of his parents, mean that he, and not the *gitano*s, are floating in a perpetual and blurry present devoid of clear goals. In this sense, he is an indistinct protagonist, associated with the open road and his motorbike through repeated scenes which suggest movement and deracination. An early scene in the film, where Antonio as a child raises his hand to shield himself from the sight of his parents' car plunging to their death, blends across shots into a similar move as he dances on stage. The inference is that, with their death, the future closed in on him and his desperate pursual of flamenco translates into a search for meaning in the face of psychological and emotional fragmentation. The blending of the two scenes further suggests that the orphaned child is still present in the man, so that temporal depth in terms of evolution or linear growth from the past is ironed out, as are projections into the future. In this sense, Gutiérrez's presentation of Antonio as a typical postmodern subject, caught up in a series of synchronic and unrelated 'presents', serves to reinforce the fixed and essential traits of *gitano* identity which appear all the more rooted and unbroken in contrast. Lucía's unwavering pursuit of her studies then appears as one more expression of fixedness, despite its unconventionality in terms of general expectations of gitanas.

Nevertheless, Antonio's involvement in *gitano* culture reveals the potential permeability of the latter. Yet the idea of such permeability is also undermined by the possibility, however vaguely implied, that Antonio may in fact be of *gitano* blood, thereby substantiating an essentialist view of cultural as innate. He chooses to defy conventional expectations on his uncle's part that he should have a career in Law and attempts instead to enter the world of professional flamenco. Early on in the film, Antonio indicates the power of performance to dissolve or transcend constructed ethnic barriers when he tells a client in his uncle's bar 'cuando bailas, te vuelves un poquito *gitano*'. In the next breath, he tells the same client that 'el flamenco es universal'. Clearly, he has a vested interest in stating this view, since his future success as a *payo* professional depends upon the universal accessibility of particular ethnic art forms. When viewed in this light, however, flamenco, so firmly an attribute of the *gitano* in the conventional imaginary, shows itself to be stereotypically contradictory: on the one hand, it is apparently 'innate' for gypsies, on the other, it can be acquired by all. This ambivalence is reinforced by the many scenes in the film which focus on rehearsals and classes in dance studios: in contrast to the spontaneous dancing seen amongst *gitano*s at the wedding, flamenco, when practised by non-*gitano*s, is constructed into choreographies, studied and rehearsed. Its place, among *payo*s, is the studio or the theatre, i.e., strictly as 'performance', while, for *gitano*s, it offers expression for communal celebration, as in the wedding scene. The inference is that flamenco as cultural identity may be inherent for those born into a community but can only be gained access to by 'outsiders' through following a series of structured steps.

Gutiérrez's presentation of Darío, the Evangelical pastor and former lover of Antonio's mother, also presents multiple and contradictory readings. On the one hand, his position in the Church places him as a presumed leader of *gitano* integrity, colouring the latter with the notions of essentiality that arise from religious beliefs. On the other hand, Darío is seen to support the love affair, despite the threat that it poses to the supposed moral character of the *gitano*s. In her doctoral thesis, Gay y Blasco devotes one chapter of her thesis to the role of the Evangelical Church in providing a forum for the construction of *gitano* identity. In an interview with her,[12] she informed me that since the 1960s, when it was first introduced to Spain by a French gypsy pastor, more than half the *gitano* population of Spain has converted to Evangelism. She states that Evangelism has taken root so strongly largely because it provides a basis for the construction of *gitano* identity within the framework of a Biblical past and thereby a social or historical 'memory' in terms of the wandering peoples. This clearly implies that the Evangelical Church serves as a forum for the construction of community identity through shared belief in the imagined narratives of *gitano* history. Furthermore, the Evangelical Church offers a model for *gitano* values and thereafter monitors social practices. According to Gay y Blasco, the Church sanctions the patriarchal structure of family and society and accommodates the ensuing inevitability of male violence on women, whilst at the same time curtailing excesses. Pastors, always themselves *gitano*s, resolve disputes at personal and communal levels. Evangelical pastors, as exemplified in the film by Darío, have gained the highest status in *gitano* society that can be achieved, namely that of 'Tío', or Church elder and conflict mediator. In the course of their activities, they ensure that *gitano* morality is upheld, in the first instance by laying great stress on the protection of the virginity of unmarried women, regarded as the guardians of the community's overall virtue, according to Gay y Blasco. Gutiérrez's portrayal fits partly with Gay y Blasco's findings in that Darío is able to reconcile Lucía with her family and to negotiate with them and with Antonio on her behalf. Gay y Blasco's findings are stretched somewhat, however, when Darío is seen to shelter Lucía when she is in direct conflict with the rest of her family and the moral conventions of her community. In this way, Darío complicates the 'set' role of the pastor within the structures of the Church and at the helm of *gitano* morality. He is able to both maintain his social and spiritual role within the community whilst aiding a love that reminds him only too poignantly of his own past adulterous love affair with Antonio's mother. Indeed, he is instrumental in bringing the lovers together at the end. The love of God that he transposes to the human realm apparently makes no distinctions of ethnicity.

However, Darío's special relationship with Antonio, whereby he becomes a sort of 'bridge' between the opposed lovers as Antonio's 'father' and as Lucía's 'Tío', also poses particular problems with regard to the intended reading of the film as a projection of distinct ethnic groups: the possibility that he may be Antonio's biological father would 'explain' and 'justify' both the latter's love for Lucía and for flamenco in accordance with essentialist precepts which would understand this relationship in terms of shared blood. The indeterminacy that lingers on at the end of the film with regard to Antonio's own ethnic origins doubly undermines both the film's projections of ethnic difference as well as of the compatibility of cultural plurality. At the same time, this indeterminacy allows for the possibility that identity should be viewed as 'performance', and that it is hence possible to reformulate or reconstruct identity. Again, Darío is an obvious example of this and his association with music (it should be noted here that Peret is now best known for his evangelical flamenco CDs, in praise of Christ) suggests that identity, like music, is best explored through performance. This point is underlined by the scene of Gospel flamenco in the film, where *gitanos* jointly celebrate their Evangelical identity. Like the Evangelical Church itself, Gospel flamenco invents a 'place' for the *gitanos* and provides them with a route for the reformulation of identities. Darío, as pastor, expresses this when he tells his congregation that he had been a dead man until he found his faith. What is interesting here is the underlying contradiction in Gutiérrez's portrayal: on the one hand, Darío's 'new' born-again identity as an Evangelical Christian is proof of the constructed nature of all identities. On the other hand, the performance of flamenco as Evangelical music, albeit reinvented as fusion, points to the essentialist stereotype that flamenco is *gitano* music coloured with the essentialist or dogmatic 'belief' in the *gitano* alliance with God. This is a tension that Gutiérrez never manages to ease throughout the film. Nor is it an easy one to resolve: as in Atxaga's work, *Alma gitana* wrestles with the complexities of essentialism in such a way as to offer both positive and negative readings.

A key symbol in the film is the 'mantón', gifted to Antonio's mother by her lover Darío, worn by her when she danced. It was then left to Antonio upon her death and he later gifted it to Lucía. The 'mantón' then is returned to Antonio via Darío, and later given back to Lucía in a presumed reconciliation between the now estranged lovers as a token of undying love. This view of love as enduring and 'essential' is reinforced by the rapid shift from colour to black and white, whereby the scene is 'frozen' and hence eternalized. The use of black and white also presents contradictory readings. On the one hand, it projects love as an abstraction, romanticizing it by removing it from the more colourful matters of everyday. At the same time, it firmly places Darío's love affair in the past, opening the way for new experiences. When Lucía wears the shawl, she both confirms her implication in Antonio's story, uniting his present with his past, and asserts her own unique and different personality that is different from its previous owner's, despite continuing to wear it as a mantle of forbidden love, as her predecessor had done. Beyond its symbolic significance as a token of love across social and temporal boundaries, the use of the mantón also problematizes symbols of essential Spanish identity. Despite its modern associations with Spanish culture, the mantón de manila, as its name suggests, was introduced to Spain from the Philippines. At both communal and personal levels, therefore, the mantón underlines the point that notions of 'authenticity' and 'ownership' are contextual and subject to alteration. Equally, however, the mantón, like the dance, is fetishized in the course of the film's narrative by its symbolic value in terms of Antonio's obsessive need to reconcile himself with the trauma surrounding his parents, their abrupt death and the love triangle that he/we never manage to disentangle. Once again, Gutiérrez's is seen to depend upon stagnation and essentialism. Worth recalling at this point is Homi Bhabha's analysis of fetishistic disavowal:

Within discourse, the fetish represents the simultaneous play between metaphor as substitution (masking absence and difference) and metonymy (which contiguously registers the perceived lack). The fetish or stereotype gives access to an 'identity' which is predicated as much on mastery and pleasure as it is on anxiety and defence, for it is a form of multiple and contradictory belief in its recognition of difference and disavowal of it. (1994: 74–75)

Viewed in this light, the mantón appears both as the representation of originality or essentialism and as a statement of difference and anxiety. The passage of the shawl from Antonio's mother to Lucía thereby marks both continuity and the anxiety that comes with change and absence. In this context, the mantón acts as a metaphor for the many borders present in the film, fetishized in an attempt to disavow difference.

In *Alma gitana*, nevertheless, Gutiérrez clearly attempts not merely to express her dissatisfaction with irreconcilable cultural borders, but also to articulate ways of moving beyond such restrictions. However, the film is strewn with examples of contradictions, which show an inevitable reliance, despite her best efforts, upon the social conventions which result in such divisions. The setting of the film in the Madrid locality of Lavapiés underlines the multi-racial element of the film; Antonio moves from an American girl-friend to spending the night with a Japanese woman. Yet, the next morning, he tells his flat-mate 'hay una china en mi cama', thereby perpetuating the racially ignorant view that all Oriental people are 'chinos'. Lucía steps out of *gitano* tradition by meeting

Antonio in secret, but refuses to relinquish her virginity, thus reaffirming her ethnic difference from *payos*. Amara Carmona states in press interviews that she hesitated before agreeing to the final long kiss with Pedro Alonso set in the bus station, since it would not be seen as decent behaviour for *gitanas*. Her brother, Pepe Luis, has said in *El País de las Tentaciones* (Barrios 1995), that he allowed her to go ahead with the scene because it was, after all, only a film; in real life, he is sure that 'Si en la vida real les veo dándose un beso, les parto la boca. Aunque ella tuviera un novio, nunca se besarían o harían manitas delante de mí'. *Alma gitana*, in its narrative as well as in its making, therefore exemplifies the gap pointed out by Bourdieu between what people think is right (virgins must never kiss) and what they actually end up doing (it is alright if they kiss in a film, but not in real life). Clearly, in this case, Gay y Blasco's findings that *gitano* morality and bodily performance are one and the same is, in Bourdieu's words, a 'rule', which cannot encapsulate the 'strategies' or practices that *gitanos* have to resort to in the course of an acting career.

In a similar way, the issues that Gutiérrez proposes in *Alma gitana* can be used to 'think against' her. A primary critique that can be made of the film is the evident emphasis that has been placed on Antonio as protagonist. This is made clear through the uneven weighting, particularly at the start of the film, given to scenes which focus on Antonio, as opposed to on Lucía. Through familiarisation with his personal history, spectators are led to identify with Antonio. His desire to get to know Lucía thus becomes shared by the spectator; her elusiveness suffered by him in the early part of their relationship is suffered by us viewers as well. The frequent alignment of the camera with Antonio's line of vision further draws viewers into 'sharing' his experiences and emotions, thereby creating empathy with him. Such a strategy may have some ideological relevance, since Antonio, more than Lucía, is 'open' to other cultures and wishes clearly to explore what is different and unknown, thereby expressing Gutiérrez's own point of view; nevertheless, this alignment of vision between spectators and the male protagonist makes him the central protagonist of the film. Furthermore, this invites spectators to view Lucía from his angle, a perspective which is emphasized by repeated close-ups of her face at several key points in the film, thereby rendering her somewhat into an object of fetish, once again tinged with ambivalence. In particular, scenes such as the one in the Arab restaurant where they drink mint tea objectify her face through close-ups which view her from Antonio's position. While several shots place Antonio squarely in the middle of the screen, indicative of his central position, Lucía is often towards one end of the screen, at an angle from the camera. The extensive number of shots revealing Lucía's home life (with the camera aligned here not to her perspective, but observing her, i.e., so that we as spectators 'view' her at home) allow viewers to 'get to know' her, thus further emphasizing her status as being 'other' or outside of our, or Antonio's, midst. In this way, the *payo* world is presented as primary and *gitano*s, as well as other non-Spanish ethnicities, appear secondary. Such an impression is heightened by Gutiérrez's treatment of Antonio's friends from the group 'Congo Bongo'. Their presence on screen recedes to the point of disappearance as Lucía's involvement in Antonio's life increases. Pocho's fate at the hands of the authorities remains unknown at the end, but the likelihood of deportation looms large. When Lucía visits him in the police station, her own enclosure within family and tradition is mirrored by his confinement in the cell; nevertheless, as Gutiérrez stated in response to questions on Pocho following the screening of *Alma gitana* at the London Film Festival (17 November 1996), he remains in prison, unlike Lucía who can hope to break out of her confinement.

Gutiérrez's portrayal of a multi-ethnic Madrid is thus somewhat undermined by the limited exploration of the personalities of the non-*payo* characters. Indeed, their major contribution to the narrative is the visibility of cultural plurality provided by their racial difference. Gutiérrez allows them little more than their outward features to speak for who they are and to provide them with any sort of identity; viewers must therefore rely on their own assumptions — or stereotypes — of those nationalities, races, and communities in order to furnish them with any subjectivity. Furthermore, it is through their relation with Antonio that these African, Oriental, and American characters gain any presence at all, thereby serving to mark his own ideological tendencies towards openness. Antonio's first encounter with Lucía raises her to a situation of pre-eminence over the other non-*payo*s who occupy his life and who appear on screen. As her part in his life, and thereby in the film, is confirmed by the reciprocity of their desire, so the other ethnic characters get lost from Antonio's and our view. Thus a hierarchy based on nationality ('Spanish' over 'non-Spanish' or First World over Third) is established by Gutiérrez, who in her ordering of events reveals her own cultural empathy even as she attempts to expose racism. What is more, Gutiérrez endows the character of Antonio with psychological complexity and depth through the trauma of having lost his mother when still a young child, a trauma which marks his quest for flamenco and involves the viewer with him on an emotional level. Whilst flamenco is shown to be an unconscious or innate aspect of *gitano* identity, Antonio's conscious attempts to 'regain' his mother through flamenco is thus charged with an emotional weight. Furthermore, the traumatic loss of his parents provides a logic around his free-floating subject-position, liberating him from personal history and the weight of tradition. However, Lucía as the other leading character must rely on a stereotypical vision of *gitano* patriarchy for her origins and appears to be distinct from other gitanas solely in her pursuit of her studies and the propensity to love despite social prohibition. As a gitana, Lucía can get up at a wedding and dance spontaneously (although we know that Amara Carmona is a trained dancer (Barrios 1995: 6), proof that *gitano*s also have to learn to dance), while Antonio, as a *payo*, must struggle to dance with 'arte'.

Gutiérrez thereby perpetuates another stereotype surrounding *gitano*s regarding their 'natural' musicality. In the publicity surrounding the release of the film, Gutiérrez stresses her extensive contact with *gitano*s through the making of the film and her deliberate decision to avoid professional actors in an attempt to portray *gitano*s as they really are. She states that she was very impressed by their way of expressing their feelings through song and dance. This vision of the *gitano* as one whose 'natural' language is the musical coincides with an established stereotype that has been at the source of the gypsy myth not just in Spain, but perhaps especially there. In practice, it is a myth that has served as a source of livelihood for gypsies and as a validation for their existence. Indeed, the supposed musicality of the *gitano*s also serves a purpose in providing a 'screen' behind which they can protect themselves from the scrutiny of hostile gazes. Gutiérrez states that whenever she was with a group of *gitano*s during the filming of *Alma gitana*, they would inevitably break into song; one wonders whether they did so because she was there. Although she has stated that 'el futuro de la humanidad está en la mezcla de las culturas' and this is clearly the spirit which underlies the film (*Alma gitana* may equal 'universal spirit' if we are to take into account Antonio's implied view that 'lo *gitano*' can be universal), it seems that Gutiérrez herself has yet to overcome some of the biases that she speaks out against.

Alma gitana ends with the lovers travelling down the same road, but apart, with Lucía inside a coach and Antonio on his motorcycle. The ambivalent ending of the film, which projects the possibility of a 'happy ending' into the future for the lovers, perhaps expresses the self-contradictions and ambiguities involved in the formulation of what is clearly an emerging and developing view of cultural plurality for its director as well as for the majority of Spanish audiences. Perhaps this is best exemplified by the glass wall that repeatedly is seen to separate Antonio from Lucía, a transparent barrier that brings into view new perspectives that are out of reach. In three scenes in the course of the film, they see each other on different sides of the glass separation, twice through her father's shop window and once through the coach window. Each time the glass invites and complicates crossing; it acts at once as barrier and transparency. Moreover, each of these scenes is a brief moment of epiphany. On the first occasion, Antonio unexpectedly glimpses Lucía inside her father's shop, near the Rastro. He enters and there ensues an emotionally charged scene as he moves about and touches objects despite her request that nothing should be touched, thereby implicitly challenging her confinement within set codes. On the second occasion, Antonio appears outside the shop again and Lucía swiftly leaves the shop on a false pretext in order to meet with him. This time it is she who breaks out of the family enclosure in order to be with him. The third meeting through glass occurs in the final scene of the film, as they both set out for Sevilla. Again, the glass 'wall' between them blocks any real meeting but arouses the desire for this. Away from social reprobation, possibility is implied in the long stretch of road as they are coursing along. What matters in this account of forbidden love is precisely that there should be no 'happy ever after' as an ending; the absence of a positive final note in the lovers' favour places a question mark around of the fluidity of identity. Indeed, the final shot of Antonio pursuing Lucía in the coach down a main road posits identity in terms of a 'road movie', the travellers' journeys clearly incomplete.

Identity as process is necessarily hybrid, at play both with the idea of pure 'origins' and the possibility of new, reformulated mixtures. Whilst Gutiérrez on the one hand posits hybridity as a response to the exclusionary practices of essentialist beliefs in ethnicity, she also relies upon the latter as a base for the construction of fusion. This ambivalence, itself a feature of hybridity, results in inaction as regards social and political inequality. Equally, as we have seen, the emphasis on hybridity as an unmotivated end to itself cannot sufficiently explore issues of hegemony and counter-hegemony. The bourgeois *gitano*s of *Alma gitana* are representative of the commercially successful Habichuela family rather than of *gitano*s in general. Their middle-class status renders them as economic 'other' to the average *gitano*. Lucía's tight family strictures are useful, not in their reflection of *gitano* communities, but in constructing a series of opposites that gives shape to the film. The film's weaknesses in this regard arise from an inability to move beyond swings between identity as essential or as fluid. No reflexive analysis of the encounter with difference is sought, resulting either in inflexibility or in shapeless fluidity. Gutiérrez thereby encloses *gitano* identity in marginality, rendering community identity void of political force by projecting the *gitano*s as an inwardly-focused group. In his *Rethinking Ethnicity*, Richard Jenkins states that

The important thing to emphasize is that ethnic groups, indeed all groups, are institutions: patterns of social practice identifying persons that have become established over time as the 'way things are done' in a particular local context, and of which people in that context are conscious. Institutions are aspects of local social reality in terms of which and with reference to which decisions are made and behaviour oriented. (1997: 61)

In a postmodern context of plural social realities, then, ethnicity as an institution must both provide a ground of stability and mould itself to changes in interaction. This view ties in with Bourdieu's stress on habitus and field, whose interplay accommodates the taking of targeted positions or the movements of groups and individuals within those groups in the play of power. In the absence of such play, *Alma gitana*'s focus remains largely on what is an exoticised and superficial, if pleasant, love story between members of presumedly oppositional communities.

If *Alma gitana* can be read as a multiculturalist attempt at establishing tolerance for difference, then its 'embedded' construction of the *gitano* community can be seen to reify community as essence, exemplary thereby of the failings of multiculturalism. Of particular relevance here is the view, made explicit by the film, that ethnic identities and cultural differences are somehow 'set' and not processual or fluctuating. In this sense, the film undermines its own aims. Not just does the focus of the narrative around Antonio both open up the question of historical amnesia and its decentering consequences upon identity, but the projection of solid communal walls among *gitano*s gains meaning only in contrast to the former. Thus a basic binary frame for the film's narrative is constructed, resulting in a checkmate that blocks a view of identity as processual. No attempt is made at any point in the film to deconstruct this binary vision of identity. Community in the context of ethnicity is depoliticized in *Alma gitana*, serving merely to add exoticism to the colour of a postmodern and plural Madrid. By focusing on Lucía and her family as an enclosed group framed by timeless values and codes, the concept of community loses its temporal depth. The spatial restrictions placed upon it by such a portrayal further freeze it. Gutiérrez's imposition of hybridity through music onto such a scenario necessarily fails to engage with the mobility that accompanies processes of identity in late modernity. Hybridity then serves as pastiche, resulting in the postmodern failure to encompass historical dimensions.

1. The analysis presented in this chapter has been developed from my article 'Between Being and Becoming: An Ethnographic Examination of Border Crossings in *Alma Gitana* (Chus Gutiérrez, 1995)', *Tesserae, Journal of Iberian and Latin American Studies*, 5 (1999), 173–78.
2. This term, now accepted amongst ethnographers of gypsy identity, denotes a non-Gypsy Spaniard and will be used henceforth as such.
3. Existing analyses of this film have been referred to in the course of this chapter. Paul Julian Smith's examination of the 'proper' (2000) paves the way for a problematization of borders of identity. I shall do so in the specific context of ethnic identity, as shared ethnicity is generally considered to be a key aspect of shared community identities.
4. This concept of ethnography as travel is explored in detail by James Clifford in his *Routes* (1997).
5. In his essay, 'Culture's In-Between', Homi Bhabha (Hall and Du Gay 1996: 53–60) underlines the essentialism that lurks beneath multiculturalist positions, whereby culture is reduced to stasis.
6. Paul Julian Smith (2000: 174) states that such purists are also known as *flamencólicos*.
7. See Smith 2000: 170–74 for more details of the contradictory stances on ethnicity that are presented in this film.
8. See Gay y Blasco, 1999. I am also grateful to Paloma Gay y Blasco for allowing me to read her doctoral dissertation, upon which this book is based.
9. A visit to gypsy organizations in Spain, such as the Asociación de Mujeres Gitanas Romí Serseni in Madrid, provides ample evidence of the many socio-economic problems that affect *gitano* neighbourhoods in urban areas.
10. Gutiérrez stated at the London Film Festival that *gitano*s had been vociferous in their support of the film.

11. See Ian Hancock's compilation of gypsy history (*Roads of the Roma*, 1999) for details of persecution in Europe.
12. Gay y Blasco met me in Cambridge, October 1997

CHAPTER 5

THE CÓRDOBA PRISON PROJECT: TRAVEL, CONTINGENCY, AND COMMUNITY THROUGH FLAMENCO

This chapter problematizes the practice of flamenco as rehabilitation amongst *gitano* convicts in Córdoba prison.[1] The idea for this project, which seeks out a disciplinary overlap between cultural studies and ethnography, arose from an article in the *Independent on Sunday* (6 October 1996) which reported that flamenco was being practised in the penitentiary of Córdoba as a form of rehabilitation for long-term prisoners; the fieldwork during which much of the material for this chapter was collected took place in June 1998. In its course, this project is an attempt to question concepts of ethnicity and community identity within the enclosed space of prison and beyond it, in terms of the larger socio-cultural context of Andalusia. More precisely, my aim here is to examine the divergences between the discourses of community identities and their practices, which surround and emerge from the effort to prepare the *gitano*s for social reinsertion through flamenco. I shall argue here that 'essentialist' perceptions of divisions and hierarchies of community identities contrast in their stasis with the migrancy of liminal identity, the discourse of prison serving, in fact, to construct bounded fields which nevertheless are crossed by the subaltern in their experience of identity as survival through mobility.

An examination of the modern institution of prison and the practice of flamenco within it, therefore, sheds new light on the concept of community. Viewed in terms of ethnicity and social liminality, there appears more than a mere contradiction between the discourses and practices of community identities. A complex interweaving emerges from this contradiction, the discourse of prison seeking to confine identity on the one hand, the practices of prison precisely challenging such borders on the other, with each process dependant upon the other though straining away from it. Community as essentialized or as myth, as explored in the introduction to this thesis, is then balanced by community as fluid, mobile, and contextually contingent. Like the larger context of modernity itself, the notion of community is coloured with ambivalence, its imagined essentialisms a necessary antidote to its practised mobilities and reinventions.

The theoretical framework for my analysis is drawn from an alignment of James Clifford's re-definition of the ethnographic field, not as enclosed space, but as routes of travel with Homi Bhabha's postcolonial focus on the subaltern articulation of cultural differences. My claim is that in the case of the prison workshop, flamenco becomes a hegemonic tool of negotiation whereby the cultural ideal of rehabilitation is superseded by a social reality of complex negotiations and engagements. Despite essentialist discourses of fixed ethnic and other identities, community identity reveals itself through social practice to be mobile in the quest for empowerment. Its contingent adaptability and permeability to a range of contexts underline the open-endedness of the concept. Flamenco then becomes the vehicle whereby aesthetic endeavour refigures social relations. In this way, prisoners and prison authorities alike are seen as interstitial spaces that generate cultural change and movement. In the course of this process, 'essential' perceptions of community identities provide fields within which the identity can in fact be negotiated and thus become adapted to cultural contingencies.

Clifford writes against the grain of established traditions of anthropological practice, whereby Western ethnographers remove themselves from 'home' and 'visit' for an extended period of time the foreign 'other', whose ways they observe and record for posterior analysis once back 'home'. Clifford contests the validity in postmodern, postcolonial times of the spatial and hierarchical distinctions implicit in conceptions of ethnography as a practice of displacement from one fixed location to another and as attention by the intellectual to what is distinct and different from the self. He bases his arguments on Michel de Certeau's definition of 'space' as 'discursively mapped and corporeally practised' (Clifford 1997: 53–54), constituted by people's movements in, around and through it. Thus he states that the 'field' should be viewed as a 'cluster of embodied dispositions and practices' (1997: 71) rather than as a location, so that ethnography takes place as engagement en route. The borders that demarcate the field thereby reveal themselves as unstable and renegotiable, so that distinctions of inside and outside, home and abroad, center and periphery display their ambivalence. Thus today's world of blurred cultural and political borderlands forces ethnography to question its own practices in order to 'reinvent its traditions in new circumstances' (1997: 61). Ethnography's long-standing reliance upon travel must therefore be seen not as a 'getting to' but as a 'going through', as ethnographic subjects are constituted in processes of complex relations.

Clifford's questioning of the 'field' of ethnography and its related academic practices extends to a description of its overlap with cultural studies. He cites various examples where distinctions between ethnographic work and cultural studies become blurred, thus proving the invalidity of research practised on the premise of spatialized difference, both real and metaphorical. This vision of ethnography as mobile and flexible facilitates an overlap with Homi Bhabha on the temporal and spatial boundaries around complex, cultural conjunctures. Bhabha's postcolonial perspective revises modern conceptions of cultural difference and authority in order to reveal the ambivalence within such rationalized views of otherness. He states that cultural meaning is historically contingent and 'multi-accentual' (1994: 177), so that cultural differences are without common measure. The emphasis falls instead on the discursive articulation and rearticulation of culture 'as an uneven, incomplete production of meaning and value . . . produced in the act of social survival' (1994: 172). This view of culture as a strategy of survival forces a rethinking of conceptions of social identity and affiliation, as it sheds light upon the historical contingency and displacement of the subaltern who move through the overlapping fringes of the terrains of difference. Bhabha's postcolonial angle homes in on the edges of the ethnocentricities of modernity so as to tease out 'a range of other dissonant, even dissident, histories and voices. . .' (1994: 5). With their temporal attention focused on the present as a moment of displacement or crossing, the social reality of the subaltern is transitional.

Clifford's problematization of the ethnographic field extends to a questioning of the epistemic authority of ethnographic texts, stating that the textual nature of the discipline renders lived experience into translation as cross-cultural, hegemonic encounters are circumscribed into authoritative texts. This point is of obvious relevance to the writing of this chapter. Much of it is based on two interviews in Córdoba, one with the four *gitanos* to be mentioned here in the prison in the presence of the educationalist and the President of the Confederación Andaluza de Peñas Flamencas, and the other with the latter two on their own. The meeting with the prisoners took place, interestingly, in the prison chapel.[2] Earlier on, I had been requested not to ask awkward questions and to approach the *gitanos* as 'artistas', not convicts. During our meeting, the prisoners stressed more than once that 'el flamenco nos ha salvado, gracias a estos dos hombres',[3] referring to the educationalist and the President of the Peñas. This could of course be true, but it may also have seemed like a beneficial thing to say. Clearly, the encounter, which was after all an 'arrangement' through official routes, was somewhat forced and the only discourse readily available was institutionally sanctioned. Despite the hour spent together, the gulf was apparent between myself as an 'outsider', the officials who had taken me there and the prisoners who lived there. The gulf was not just one of cultural identity, but closely linked to it through obvious discrepancies in terms of the power to speak and act. The officials clearly showed me those prisoners whom they wished me to see and allowed me to be there only for as long as I was willing not to be awkward or too explicit in my questions. Like the prisoners, I too felt compelled to obey. It became all too clear to me that prison is a space that is politically charged in terms of power relations.

Furthermore, this political tension ensues from the attempt to present or articulate power 'relations' as power 'structures', or as given 'essentials', as a way of deflecting any challenge to authority. In the case of the flamenco workshop, ethnic identity was being enacted or repressed according to political determinations. The meeting was a performance on many sides. Nevertheless, the officials' cooperation in allowing me access to the prisoners, despite their having only a sketchy understanding of my project, spoke clearly of their desire to 'open' the prison space up through exposing the flamenco workshop. In so doing, they were obviously aware that they, as well as the prisoners, were subject to public scrutiny. By making this exception, and literally opening the gates of the prison, they unwittingly underlined the contextual contingencies that determine the enforcement of prison regulations. Nevertheless, it was also an opportunity to show such regulations at work. Given the predominant orality of their backgrounds, it is hard to imagine the inroads and fluxes through which the prisoners navigate their way through institutional life and after it. Much of this chapter is therefore reconstructed, tenuous. Behind the reiterated socio-cultural 'ideals' of the workshop organizers, only the song is discernible. The efforts to make music must therefore be considered for their performative potential. This, however, requires disentanglement from the structurally divisive discourses that surround both the concept of rehabilitation and the closely related concept of community.

Central to the project of the workshop as a site of rehabilitation is the concept of community as an organic entity. In this sense, community is reflected in the discourse of rehabilitation as bound by a common morality and as offering individuals membership of a unified group. Community also stands, in a tacit way, for what is 'right', as opposed to 'wrong'. The discourse and practices of punishment exile miscreants from community, whilst also placing re-entry into the latter as the desired target of the period of imprisonment. The notion of exile from community can in itself be compared, of course, to the religious notion of expulsion from paradise (I found it curious in this context that my meeting with the convicts should have taken place in the prison chapel — the religious discourse of expulsion/salvation thereby implicitly tied to discussions of the practices of the workshop). In this sense, no distinction is made in the discourse of rehabilitation between community and society, as the isolation of prison is seen to charge 'free' social contexts beyond the prison walls with the emotive force contained in the accepted concept of community. Furthermore, the physical isolation of prison excises prisoners from not just a larger social context, but also from daily proximity to their immediate family and friends. The belief in, or the 'imagined' memory of, community as a stable entity, i.e., community as 'home', therefore, sustains the years and activities of imprisonment. Further-more, in recognizable echoes of religious (i.e., Catholic) discourse, re-entry into community is only possible following a suitable period of repentance. Indeed, the very process of rehabilitation is possible only after repentance has set in. This focus on repentance falls in line with organic perceptions of community and is a central aspect of the imagined exaltation of community as essential and stable. In *Civic Repentance*, the communitarian Amitai Etzioni argues for the concept of repentance which would allow those who have violated the law to regain membership of their communities. He directly links the concept of civic repentance with that of religious repentance. Equating society with community, Etzioni states that

While the goal of reintegrative justice is to restore the offender to membership in community, this can occur only if the offender repents for his crime and makes reparations to his victims. In this way, an offender must earn his return to society by admitting and apologizing for his act and repairing the harm he has caused both his victims and the community. (1999: ix)

The concept of community thereby becomes central to the processes of repentance and rehabilitation, which cannot function without this anchoring notion. According to Etzioni,

Repentance is not merely or even largely a personal endeavour; it involves the other members of the community, including the victims of the offense, as well as the core values of the community. (1999: x)

Reintegration into community following the period of punishment thereby implies commitment to the core values by which community defines itself. Binarily opposed notions of 'good' versus 'bad', 'right' versus 'wrong', etc., are at work here, blocking any view of community identity as processual, contradictory, or fluctuating.

Indeed, prison discourse projects the practice of music not as aesthetic performance but as an exercise in preparation for re-entry into community that is closely harnessed to paying for their 'sins': the educationalist stated to me that 'aquí, ellos saben que el cante es a la vez placer y pena, cantando se sale de aquí'.[4] The discourse of rehabilitation constructs hierarchical divisions within prison, which are structured around traditionally essentialist and unified concepts of community identity. These fall into four overlapping categories within the prison which relate to ethnicity and degrees of empowerment: those of *payo*, *gitano*, official and convict.[5] Equally, as mentioned above, the process of rehabilitation assumes a stable and fixed socio-cultural — and in the case of the *gitano*s, ethnic — context outside the prison which then becomes the target for reinsertion. Indeed, the normalizing efforts of rehabilitation depend largely on fixed perceptions of identity and clear demarcations of distinct social and ethnic categories. It should be borne in mind here that, despite the many cultural and political changes that have occurred since the transition to democracy and despite Spain's membership of the European Union, Spain still has some of the longest prison sentences in Europe.[6] Drug-related crime (a major social problem[7] among the economically disadvantaged *gitano*s of urban areas) often received sentences of twenty years or more in the 1980s. The stay in prison thereby is of considerable duration for most convicts and prison provides the major communal forum within which identity evolves over two or more decades for many of the men concerned.[8] Nevertheless these perceptions of group identities are themselves plural and complex in their constructions: on the one hand, the *gitano* convicts are identified as sharing both *gitano* ethnicity and the liminal status of convicts; similarly, the prison officials share both their hegemonic *payo* ethnicity and the social authority gained from their policing role in the prison space. On the other hand, the enclosed walls of the prison turn all those inside it, convicts and officials alike, into a social grid where identity is constantly being negotiated even in the attempt to impose and contain the latter through processes of normalization.

The term rehabilitation implies clear boundaries between the 'self' as civic society and the 'other' as the deviant or criminal. In this context, the *gitano*s in prison are doubly 'otherized': not just are they convicts, but they are also members of an economically disadvantaged ethnic underclass. This reinforced exclusion from hegemonic fields ironically strengthens essentialist readings of their musical propensities, thereby enhancing their own abilities to use the music as a vehicle that traverses fields of established discourse. This is particularly so, since the borderline between self and other works at a range of different levels, from the attitude of the prison authorities towards the *gitano*s to the very perceptions of flamenco in a larger national or international forum. Flamenco has long provided the Western imaginary with a location for passion, a location which both contrasts with and serves to underline the supposed rationality of the West through exoticized or fetishized constructions of gypsy song as 'other'. Popular definitions of the word 'flamenco' blur the music with the dance style and the Andalusian with the gypsy, yet imply that these are separate and interdependant components of a single regional and cultural expression.[9] It would appear that the *gitano*, with his supposed darkness of skin, eyes, and temperament exemplifies in extreme the southern Spaniard when viewed as exotic or passionate Other. Consider the following description by William Washabaugh of the singer El Agujetas, father of one of the principal protagonists of my project:

He was dressed all in black. His billows of curly black hair framed a scarred face that Clint Eastwood would covet. . .And then Agujetas began to sing, though at the time I would have said that his voice was not singing, so much as ripping and tearing at his soul. Standing about two feet from my face singing fire . . ., Agujetas had *me* transfixed and my *wife* stunned. (1996: x–xi).

The singer mesmerizes his audience, stuns them, with this unbridled onslaught of embodied emotive otherness. Yet it is this very otherness that offers him fame and the material means by which to control his singing career, as seen in Abel's documentary cited below. It could therefore be said that the binary opposition thrown up by the position of marginality assigned to the *gitanos* between the convicts, on the one hand, and the prison officials and the peña authorities, on the other, reflects the social reality existing in wider cultural circles.

Washabaugh's initiation to flamenco is by no means unique. Nor is Agujetas's ability to conjure up heart-wrenching emotion.[10] Throughout its history, flamenco has propelled itself on guarantees of emotive heights (or, to use Mitchell's term, 'catharsis') which have allowed its practitioners the means to a living. If today it offers visions of impassioned alterity[11] to non-Spanish audiences, its evolution since the seventeenth century has depended upon doing much the same for those wealthy enough to afford such frenzied visions within Andalucía. Its early development as the musical expression of an urban underclass sustained by the sponsorship of wealthy patrons, or señoritos, has left it a legacy of association with the socially marginal.[12] Nowhere does flamenco seem so 'authentic' as when articulated by those whose nameless and insignificant lives form the very dregs of society, namely those members of an underclass further marginalized by incarceration. Thus, of the *cante jondo*, or deep song, repertoire, the *saeta carcelera*, sung originally by convicts behind bars, has traditionally been considered the most 'authentic', and hence moving, of songs of repentance sung during the Holy Week period.[13] That prison populations in Andalucía have long been largely comprised of a motley underclass who together fall under the ethnic label of *gitano*[14] leads to a triangle of cultural associations between the multiple connotations surrounding the words '*gitano*', 'prison', and 'flamenco'.

Córdoba prison's flamenco workshop was set up over ten years ago in order to draw *gitano* prisoners, the majority of whom are there on drugs-related charges, into participating in educational activities. Such workshops aim largely to divert prisoners from established drug dependencies and to prepare them for re-insertion into society. The *gitanos*, who are largely illiterate or partially literate, have, according to the prison authorities, consistently been resistant to other forms of rehabilitation and yet willingly opt for this project. Clearly, this willingness has been understood by flamenco and prison officials as a sign of their innate propensity for this art form, a propensity which derives directly from their ethnicity and which therefore binds them to their communities. A professional guitarist, Rafael Trenas, trains them in lyrics and techniques under the close supervision of the 'educador' or educationalist in charge of the prisoners, Antonio Estévez, himself qualified in criminology[15] at the Sorbonne University, Paris. The choice of music ranges from the long-standing prison flamenco tradition to other conventional forms of cante, such as bulerías, tarantos, and siguiriyas. Estévez's close personal friendship with Don José Arrebolas, President of the Confederación Andaluza de Peñas Flamencas, has led to the National Penitentiary Flamenco Song Contest in which convicts from all over Spain are invited to take part. It should be said here that while in Córdoba, the prisoners have the choice of attending the workshop for practice, other prisons in the rest of Spain do not offer flamenco as rehabilitation. Held biennially in the Córdoba prison, the Song Contest is sponsored by the Confederación, itself dependant upon funding from the Consejería de Cultura de la Junta de Andalucía. Prisoners who choose to participate from other prisons in Spain are transported to Córdoba for the occasion, often spending weeks inside the windowless vans, or 'jaulas' as the convicts called them, which carry people and goods between prisons in different cities. Winners of this contest earn remissions on their sentences and prize-winners from prisons elsewhere in the country can apply for transfer to Córdoba in order to continue their flamenco training. Of the three penitentiary song contests held so far, Antonio de los Santos El Agujetas, son of the Agujetas mentioned above, was the winner on one occasion and another *gitano*, José Serrano Campos, won twice. In recent years, these singers have been allowed to perform at public peña gatherings of flamenco aficionados, accompanied by the educationalist. In 1997, Agujetas and Serrano were taken to studios in Granada under the auspices of the Confederación de Peñas in order to record the compact disc, *2 gritos de libertad* (released in Granada, March 1997). It is hoped by prison authorities and peña organizers alike that the release of this disc will lead to increased professional recognition for the two singers with possibilities for future work, as well as create awareness in the larger public of the artistic talent that lies 'buried' in prison. In late 1997, both Agujetas and Serrano were released from prison, the former for having completed his foreshortened term and the latter on 'libertad condicional', whereby he has to report back from time to time.

The project undertaken by the workshop presents contradictory readings: on the one hand, flamenco in conventional discourse is considered to be the musical lament of the socially underprivileged, its practice by convicts particularly appropriate since incarceration epitomizes the social constraints and liminality of the practitioners. On the other hand, communal reinsertion is sought through such music, turning it therefore into a bridge for communal participation. Roles appear to have switched and what emerged as the expression of trauma among social outcasts has become the means of re-inserting them, or perhaps inserting them, into their 'native' communities. As gateway to a wider forum, the prisoners and the educationalist alike avail of flamenco for access to wider communal circles at large. The educationalist clearly plays a crucial role in determining the form rehabilitation takes. In general, rehabilitation is considered a central aspect of the imprisonment process, whereby the denial of personal freedom should serve to reshape or reform the individual. Its professed goal is the successful (re)insertion of the individual into society, providing him where possible with the means to make a living without resorting to crime. Prison therefore aims to provide a bridge between deviant marginal communities and the social mainstream.[16] As a rule, therefore, rehabilitation aims for a definitive break with identity as experienced prior to entry into prison. As such, the prison stay and the rehabilitation process mark the deliberate loss of a former identity and the establishment of a new, 'better', one. Re-emergence into society after the prison stay is projected as a new 'lease' of life, based upon a refashioned subjectivity. Therefore, a premise of rehabilitation is surely the notion that identity is non-essential and constructed according to will and circumstance. This contradicts the discourse by which flamenco as rehabilitation is promoted, whereby the *gitanos* are urged to express their 'natural' cultural selves and flamenco is understood to be the musical expression of a marginal and unruly ethnic group. The benefits from going along with such rhetoric are clear. Estévez described *gitanos* as generally a marginal people, given to apathy, disorganized and living only for the present. The flamenco workshop and contest, he said, offered a few of them the chance of some social status. For the *gitanos* with musical talents, flamenco as rehabilitation implies a possible shift in social status from convict or criminal to 'artista'. The recording and release of the compact disc has obviously made this almost tangible: Serrano said to me with reference to the CD 'para nosotros es una cosa muy grande'; Agujetas implied his hopes for the future through an unfinished sentence 'una vez que salga el disquito. . .'.[17] Involvement in flamenco at least means the occasional sortie to peñas and the social visibility and participation so long denied to them. From the invisibility of prison, they shift to the spotlight on stage. The workshop also means in some small way that within prison, they can echo the cultural happenings seen on television and thereby partake in a larger cultural life.

The location of the prison on the peripheries of Córdoba acts as a spatial metaphor for the workshop's marginal engagement with any larger flamenco environment. The existence of the workshop itself hangs currently in the balance after the departure of the former prison director who was himself a flamenco 'aficionado'. Its day to day running, and the attention it has received in flamenco circles, derives from the close friendship between the educationalist and the head of the Andalusian peñas. In such a context, prison officers and convicts are both not just on the fringes of the mainstream, but also in close contact within the tight space of prison and largely mutually dependant upon one another for their flamenco identity. Despite the very clear rules of hierarchy that determine individual and group positions within this space, convicts nevertheless seek daily to negotiate their liberties through gaps or unexpected openings in the power structure. For example, the two singers who have sung at regional peñas usually request permission to spend the whole night out of prison, reporting back only later the next day, thus snatching time to visit family and friends and engage in 'normal' social activities, such as having drinks in bars. Similarly the organizers of the workshop seek access to the outside world whenever possible through journalists, such as those who covered them for the *Independent*, performance at regional peñas or even through my own interest in their project. Indeed, it is possible to state that the slippage and movements of status and identity occur not just through the interstitial spaces between these normalizing structures, but also because of the temporal instability of these very structures. Thus the use of flamenco as a tool of rehabilitation can also be the vehicle by which cultural identity travels and crosses ethnic and other thresholds, for both prisoners and officials.

Indeed, the choice of flamenco as a form of rehabilitation raises questions with regard to the premises from which the latter proceeds. The use of creative arts as rehabilitation in prisons is widespread in Spain and elsewhere, a case in point being the flourishing theatre group run by Elena Cánovas Vacas in Yeserías prison, Madrid.[18] A report titled 'Music in Criminal Justice Settings' (1996), published by the Unit for the Arts and Offenders in Devon makes clear that the arts offer prisoners a way to refashion perceptions of themselves and hence to revise their social attitudes. It offers them an interest that could continue when released and that could even provide them with a livelihood, as with some of the actresses from Yeserías who have gone on to act for television.

What is different about the Córdoba project is that the flamenco workshop calls upon the perceived ethnic identity of the prisoners, thus requiring them to draw forth aspects of their socio-cultural experiences and identifications with community from prior to entering prison. It further depends upon perceptions of 'essential' identity, innate talents or propensities guaranteed by ethnicity, since all the prisoners taking part are *gitano*s. In general, the practice of the arts in prison aims to provide a new, as yet unencountered, dimension to prisoners' lives, allowing them a fresh route through which to explore possibilities for constructing positive social identities. In the Córdoba project, however, the workshop calls upon old associations, ruptured and left behind by the trauma of the criminal event(s) and subsequent legal processing. Thus the practice of rehabilitation involves the metaphorical return, in one way or another and despite the enclosed prison space, to the very communal environment that presumably led to their involvement in crime. Flamenco as cultural memory is closely associated with the social and communal landscapes which surrounded the convicts prior to prison. At the same time, the enthusiasm with which *gitano* prisoners subscribe to this form of 'rehabilitation', which they find easier or more worthwhile than other forms, derives from the belief, shared with the officials, that flamenco is part and parcel of *gitano* cultural expression. Organic notions of community are thereby called upon in order to warrant musical interests in the present. The assumption, of course, is that the return to community by definition implies a return to a shared code of ethics. Equally, these very 'organic' or essentialist concepts of identity tend, in hegemonic discourse, to attach marginality and criminality to *gitano* communities, whereby re-insertion could imply a return to criminality. In the course of my interview with the prisoners, Agujetas said '(el flamenco) yo ya lo traía dentro. . .', whilst all of them also agreed that 'el flamenco nos ayuda a salir de aquí'. A paradox arises, therefore, in terms of rehabilitation: on the one hand, its aim is to lead the convicts out of crime and into mainstream society; on the other, it avails of essentials linked to their pasts which do not allow for the possibility of new constructions and projections of identity.

This conundrum can perhaps be understood, however, in the light of the compact disc, as well as Mitchell's comments (1994) on the marketability of flamenco as cathartic song. The mediatory element between contradictory projections of flamenco is perhaps the notion that flamenco acts as a form of repentance, whilst also having evolved as a means to a livelihood for the urban poor. Parallels between religious discourse and prison discourse became too obvious to ignore in the course of this project. So also the notion in the wider culture that cante jondo is a song of lament. Furthermore, and as Mitchell has pointed out (1994), it is a lament sung to a paying audience. If, as is stated by all those involved, the release of the disc is a culminating point in the rehabilitation process, then the use of flamenco can be justified, not as a return to origins, but for the audible remorse that charges the song, as well as the marketability of the cultural product and the social status provided by musical recognition. 'Innate' ethnic expression, marketed as the song of a gypsy prison community, has a commercial appeal which, therefore, can provide a way out from the underprivileged socio-economic conditions which led it to originate in the first place. The heightened cathartic appeal of such flamenco for a lay audience is even more 'authentically' moving than other forms of cante jondo.

Nevertheless, it is still impossible to disentangle notions of 'original' *gitano* identity from the social ideals set by prison authorities, whereby the professed aim is to divest convicts of their participation in a criminal underclass, and the means by which they attempt to achieve these. Rehabilitation through flamenco remains a blurred issue devoid of clear tenets despite, or perhaps because of, the apparently 'essential' demarcations that appear to define its contours. The entire scenario is set up according to a series of preconceived essential contrasts based on difference and hierarchy. Firstly, the workshop places *gitano*s under the tutelage of *payo*s, in terms of both the guitarist and the educationalist, subordinating the one ethnicity to the other in keeping with social norms. Secondly, the personal and communal criminal histories of the *gitano*s, their liminal status as convicts, segregates them from those who permit them the practice of the *cante*. The policed space of prison means that educationalist and guitarist represent authority to the extent that the *gitano*s must acquiesce to the requirements placed upon them in order to earn further favours. The impotence of the *gitano*s contrasts with the rights exercised by the authorities to 'visit' flamenco upon them or not. The contrast is reinforced by the evident desire of the *gitano*s to practice flamenco, making it an ideal tool for the construction of institutional obedience. Such disciplinary boundaries apparently turn the workshop into a fenced zone of bipolar confrontation with difference, where the 'unruly other' (i.e., the *gitano* convicts) is relentlessly plied in the fashion of the 'disciplined self' (i.e. the *payo* authorities).

Clifford's plotting of the ethnographic course has been compared to the image of an airport where multiple encounters take place within contexts of travel and translation. Nothing could be further away from the enclosed and ordered space of prison. Yet, like the ethnographic 'field', the flamenco workshop presents rehabilitation as a contestable site, epitomizing the contradictions of the ethno-musical negotiations outside of its walls. For Clifford, his questioning of the ethnographic 'field' acts as a metaphor for the discipline itself, which he views as an 'invention' that begs constant redefinition. Thus he states:

There are no natural or intrinsic disciplines. All knowledge is interdisciplinary. Thus, disciplines define and redefine themselves interactively and competitively ... by appropriating, translating, silencing and holding at bay adjacent perspectives. (1997: 59)

The professed certainties of ethnic difference and community identities along which prison practice operates can, in the light of this statement by Clifford, be seen as a way of managing power fluxes which occur there. Thus the myth of the *gitano* as 'flamenco auténtico' differentiates *gitano*s from the other convicts in the prison, who are, by default, *payo*s, but only to create a majority for the former since eighty per cent of the inmates are *gitano*s. Furthermore, this supposedly innate propensity allows them to take part in this rehabilitation activity whilst 'believing' that they are only expressing what is 'natural' to them. What then appears to the authorities as obedience can also be interpreted as acts of self-assertion that are potentially threatening, since if the *gitano* is seen as authentically flamenco, he is also seen as authentically truant. If a propensity to flamenco and to criminality is seen as intrinsic to *gitano* identity, and yet rehabilitation (whose goal is surely the distancing from such deviant expression of ethnicity) is attempted through the former, then a bizarre paradox emerges from the overlap of the concepts of rehabilitation, truancy and music. At the same time, for the authorities, the flamenco workshop allows them to draw boundaries around the prisoners through techniques of reward and punishment. These extend from increasing or decreasing the number of cigarettes allowed per day for singing well, to allowing, or not, week-ends spent at home, from denying the man the privilege of taking part in the workshop if he does not 'deserve' it, to re-instating him once he has earned this privilege through good behaviour in other areas of prison life. Thus the authorities know that they can touch the perceived core of *gitano* identity whilst offering the workshop as a kind of seduction for the furthering of it. In this way, the authorities also affirm their rights and highlight their own boundaries.

Equally, the undeniable temporal burden of imprisonment is thereby shifted around. As manager of the rehabilitation process, the educationalist's role is obviously pivotal. Interestingly, the educationalist also acts as the manager for the two singers who feature in the CD, arranging their visits to the recording studio and liaising in the drawing up of their contracts. Opportunities for the *gitano*s to practise flamenco, to perform outside or even to be allowed into the workshop depend on his recommendation and approval. In the course of their 'doing time', he, together with the prison director, decides how the prisoners' time is spent. Estévez said that his job was also to 'do things' with the prisoners, to be an 'animador', to provide them with occupational therapy that would allow the time to pass. He viewed his role in their lives as a combination of mentor, teacher, and psychotherapist. Given their low literacy levels, he stated that they took 'naturally' to music. Clearly, the predominant orality of *gitano* societies allowed a privileging of the propensity for music and rhythm. The music also took their minds away for a while from a drug habit that only a few ever really overcome. Thus Estévez said 'cuando ellos están cantando, se desconectan (de la droga)'. Equally, Manuel, one of the other prisoners I met, said of prison life that when they are out exercising in the patio or practising in the workshop, 'tocamos las palmas, estamos cantando y nos quitamos la tarde'. The implication in these two statements is that the music allows the *gitano*s to both remove themselves from the drug dependency, albeit temporarily, that marked their entry into prison and also to do away with the weight of time that hangs on them there. Timothy Mitchell's perception of flamenco as psycho-drama or catharsis opens up the further possibility of exploring the workshop's potential for providing a release from both the trauma of the criminal event and the temporal and spatial rupture implied in the prison stay. Improvising the lyrics of a taranto that he sang when I met him, Agujetas chose the words '. . . y en esta cárcel, yo me muero. . . '. He was thus able to say through the song what he could not have freely said in the presence of the officials. The performance of the song also allowed him the use of facial and hand gestures that heightened the sense of entrapment and despair implicit in the lyrics.

In this context, Martin Stokes writes 'Music then does not simply provide a marker in a prestructured social space, but the means by which this space can be transformed' (1994: 4). In the light of Manuel's comment quoted above, it could equally be stated that music allows time to be transformed. Not only is the enclosure of prison or the dead-end of addiction overcome for a while by flamenco, but also the extension of time in prison, which is contrasted by the reduction of space, is thus foreshortened. It could be then said that music allows a different discourse by which experience, and thus identity, can be formulated and thereby 'invented'. Traditional organization of prison society can thus be re-organized or even subverted as new constructions of temporal and spatial experiences allow where possible for diverse cultural constructions.

Indeed, the marked distinctions between the authorities and the prisoners are perhaps not as stark as would appear from the way in which they are apparently laid out. The educationalist, Antonio Estévez, the former director of the prison, Francisco Velasco and the guitarist Rafael Trenas are all three *payo*s who grew up in *gitano* neighbourhoods. Their personal associations with flamenco go back a long way and they perceive flamenco to be a core part of their lives and formative to their own sense of identity. Estévez and Velasco are close friends of José Arrebola, President of the Confederación Andaluza de Peñas Flamencas. Run on funds from the Junta de Andalucía which are filtered to them through the Confederación, one or more peña exists in most Andalusian cities. Their purpose is decidedly 'purist': to keep alive the traditions of flamenco and to maintain it as an 'art' and not a commercialized product. Peñas regularly stage shows by young performers, commented upon and informally guided profession-ally by the more established artists, many of whom are *gitano*s (though some only for professional purposes),[19] who are viewed as the bedrock of tradition. An unspoken 'ethnic' and gender distinction exists nevertheless when it comes to running the peñas and holding the purse strings. Whilst performers tend to be from both communities and sexes, the Presidents and managing committees of the bigger peñas are *payo*s as are most of the panel in adjudicating boards at the many competitions organized on a regular basis. The most obvious binding factor among those who run these clubs is their common vision of flamenco as a 'treasure'. Peña organisers come from a variety of walks of life, generally middle-class: Antonio Núñez, President of the peñas of Cádiz, works for Radio Cádiz and Pepe Arrebola, the overall head of the Confederación, is a regional sales manager for Sureña beer. For these men, flamenco is an 'afición' and hence almost a 'family' matter. At the same time, they consider themselves the custodians of the art, although, in order to believe that they are holding on to it, they must engage in continuous negotiations, taking the art with them as they follow the cross-currents of such arrangements. Funds from the Junta de Andalucía have not risen in over eight years and so must be sought from members' pockets or through their links with companies who can be persuaded to sponsor events. Arrebola repeatedly emphasized the lack of funds needed to run the workshop in prison. He said that neither the Ministry of Culture nor the Ministry of Interior provided financing. He was able to apportion some of the money made available to the Confereración de Peñas by the Junta de Andalucía, but this did not amount to enough to pay for the professional guitarrist's fees. Arrebola stated to me that 'todo lo que estamos haciendo es tercermundista' with reference to keeping the workshop and competitions alive. The sociability of the Andalusian lifestyle opens the way for complex networks of personal and professional relations which often result in the indefinite deferral of the scheduled. What is more, the professional becomes visibly embroiled with the socio-cultural. Thus Arrebola is able to justify taking time off from his demanding job to attend to peña matters, by promoting his brand of beer at these gatherings. Therefore it does not seem too far-fetched to propose that, for Velasco and Estévez, the professed aim of rehabilitation perhaps serves as somewhat of an excuse for drawing flamenco into their professional lives, allowing them to integrate aspects of their own socio-cultural and communal experiences.

In this sense, the prison authorities reveal themselves as more committedly 'flamenco' than many of the prisoners who are supposedly genetically so. Their determination to carry on with the 'prison peña' despite a lack of proper funding, since neither the Ministry of Justice, the Ministry of Interior or the Dirección General de Instituciones Penitenciarias make any extra provision for it in their requirements regarding rehabilitation, is evident in the fact that they have on occasion had to dip into their own pockets to keep the workshop running. The prison workshop's greatest impact is not within the penitentiary institutions but rather within peña circles: 'Están en la calle o están en la cárcel, pero *son* flamencos', said Estévez of the *gitano*s. The roots of this flamenco essentiality are perceived as embedded in their *gitano* ethnicity, since they consider flamenco to be the "natural" expression of the *gitano*. At the same time, however, both Arrebola and Estévez state that 'el flamenco es una forma de ser' and also that 'allí aglutina todo, *payo* y flamenco', thus implying hybridity in the evolution of the music. Essential conceptions of flamenco thus coincide with an awareness of its flexibility and transferability; perhaps this paradox can be understood through Arrebola's comment that his task was to ensure the new generations would 'mover el repertorio'. In his introductory comments to the compact disc, *2 gritos de libertad*, Arrebola describes the workshop as a

peña de altas paredes, muros de granito, puertas grandes de hierro que impiden la libertad de lo humano y cerrojos de sonidos negros escalofriantes, que en ningún momento podrán impedir la libertad del conocimiento, de la expresión, de los sentimientos y del grito sagrado del cante.

Flamenco is seen here as a 'divine' vocation, a birthright which cannot be contained by restrictions to personal freedom; indeed it is implied that perhaps it is heightened by such constraints, as if prison were some dark night of the soul. Thus Arrebola describes the winners of the Penitentiary Contests as 'dos magníficos cantaores dignos de figurar en los carteles más importantes de *nuestro* flamenco'. The image is quasi-religious;[20] the disc itself, proof that flamenco officialdom can nurture the art. The prison matter of *gitano* rehabilitation clearly overlaps with the attempted preservation of musical traditions in an overall cultural context of slippage, experimentation, and change. Woven into this preoccupation, nevertheless, are the constrictions and pressures of the moment with their many social implications. Thus the fourth Penitentiary Song Contest, planned for October 1997, had still not taken place when I did my fieldwork due to financial constraints and the educationalist's prolonged ill health. A change in prison director, this time, as already stated, someone without personal involvement in flamenco, casts further doubt on the plausibility of the contest. The workshop has been suspended on occasion when the organizers have had to attend to other professional responsibilities or when funds have been lacking. Tradition also bows to the choice of cante for practice, moderated to suit the musical experience and preferences of the prisoners. The range practised is mostly in the style of Camarón de la Isla, whose music is well known to them, rather than the older and more 'traditional' cante from the 1920s of Manuel Torre, for example. Arrebola's phrase 'mover el repertorio' can thus be interpreted as both keeping traditions alive and shifting, or adding to, the repertoire, as a way of ensuring its survival. The ambivalence of the phrase points to larger indeterminacies in terms of official practices.

The *gitanos* that I met in prison presented a variety of attitudes to flamenco. Some had no awareness of the music prior to coming to prison. Others had varying repertoires learnt from their socio-cultural milieux. One claimed that he was a distant cousin of the world-renowned flamenco dancer Joaquín Cortés. Of the two winners, José Serrano had sometimes sung in *salas de fiestas*. Married, with five children, three of whom were conceived while he was in prison, and a grandchild in Sevilla, Serrano was sentenced to a twenty-year term for assisting in homicide. Serrano said that he was thirty-eight years old, but Estévez stated that he neither has a birth certificate nor did he have a *documento nacional de identidad*[21] when he entered prison. His repertoire of songs is limited and when asked what he would do when released, he said 'cantar si me sale algo y volver a lo mío, que es vender lotería'. Illiterate still and uncertain of his age, Serrano's focus has consistently been on reuniting with his wife and family. Indeed, his prison term was extended longer than necessary, despite the remissions earned from winning the Contest twice, for having 'forgotten' to return after weekends spent at home. In spite of such 'bad behaviour' which would normally warrant being grounded, Serrano was permitted to appear from time to time at public peña events. The other prizewinner, Antonio Agujetas, carries with him the legacies of his name.[22] Son of El Agujetas and grandson of Agujetas Viejo, he comes from one of the best known 'familias cantaoras' of Jérez de la Frontera. His father El Agujetas rose to international success, but abandoned his deaf-mute wife and eleven children, four of whom are also deaf-mute.[23] The aura surrounding the Agujetas name is one of predestined tragedy, a 'natural' disposition to cante grande or the deepest of deep song. For the flamenco purists, the father's alienation from his community meant that the spotlight shifted to his son Antonio Agujetas. Nevertheless, in 1981, Agujetas was sentenced to twenty-two years in prison for repeated drug-related assaults. His attendance at the workshop was part of the usual prison life of head counts, shared cells, and time-tabled duties. He has a considerable repertoire of cante and a recognizable

likeness to the singing style of his father. The stark contrast exists between, on
the one hand, the absence of family support for Agujetas with an almost total
absence of visits or contact from 'home', according to the educationalist, and,
on the other, the audible oral transmission of singing styles between himself and
his father despite their estrangement. Interestingly, despite his closeness to the
older forms of cante grande and despite their keenness on tradition, the panel at
the Penitentiary Song Contest awarded the first prize twice to Serrano, whose
style is more akin to those of contemporary singers such as Camarón (much
derided in the 1980s by flamenco purists for 'polluting' the song through hybrid
ventures) or Pansequito. Professed cultural ideals of preserving traditions are
thus dislodged by the surrounding social reality of shifting undercurrents in
musical tastes.

As for the matter of flamenco as rehabilitation, it remains painfully
questionable in terms of achieving the professed goals, whether these be
communal reinsertion or material empowerment. Since his release, Agujetas has
performed at peñas and has found occasional employment at tablaos, where he
has inevitably had to comply with contemporary musical tastes which require
cante to harmonize with the guitar and to give precedence to the dance.[24] Thus
the unharnessed cante grande of his paternal line has to reinvent itself as it
accommodates shifts in the surrounding socio-cultural contexts. According to
the President of the Peñas of Cádiz, Sr. Antonio Núñez, with whom he is in
touch, much of the rest of his time is spent in bars. In terms of reintegrating into
community, Sr Núñez stated that none of his relatives had been willing to offer
Agujetas a permanent home. He had therefore been moving between relatives
and friends and had yet to find a permanent base. Sr Núñez also voiced fears
that he would give in again to old drug habits. The compact disc recorded by
him and Serrano in March 1997 took time to be launched, but is now widely
available throughout Spain. Its release on a wider commercial scale had to await
its official media launch by the Confederación de Peñas for well over a year after
its release. This supposedly tangible evidence of rehabilitation, convincing in its
social visibility, was delayed for so long due to financial pressures and
uncertainties in the Confederación. By June 1999, a year after my fieldwork, the
flamenco workshop had been temporarily suspended owing to the educationalist's ill health. However, there were plans to resuscitate it as soon as he
returned to work.

The complexities surrounding the music emerging from the prison underline
the migrancy of cultural identities. Such a move away from culture conceived in
binary terms reveals the prison workshop as a site for a politics of everyday life.
Despite its social invisibility, it appears not on the peripheries of society, but as
an interstitial space where tradition is reinscribed through the contingencies and
complexities of subaltern lives. As such, it is necessarily performative. Clifford's
plotting of the field as embodied route opens the way for Bhabha's focus on the

on-going negotiations that take place at interstitial zones. If the *gitanos* are obviously subaltern when viewed through the prism of institutional categories, then the peña organizers are also subaltern in their manoeuvrings to gain recognition and funds, knowing that their movements only rustle the edges of larger sanctioning bodies. The workshop thus becomes as much a site for the reformulation or reconstruction of their identities as for rehabilitation of the prisoners. In either case, rehabilitation ceases to denote a kind of preparation for the future, a suspension of the present in anticipation of something better. Nor can it be justified as a means of anointing the tablet of tradition, for this too can only be recreated in the present. The time of flamenco as rehabilitation is clearly in the here and now, an engagement with the fluxes of the present as a way of getting on. Agujetas's trajectory through prison and beyond it most clearly depicts the rehabilitation intended in the workshop not as an enclosed site but as on-going process. The inherited identity of his musical traditions, his liminal status as a newly-released convict and social expectations of acclaim reveal his cante as split in its efforts to engage with the present as a means of overcoming it. From this perspective, the projections of alterity commonly assigned to flamenco are no more than a veneer for expressing the invention and re-invention of the cultural self. Flamenco thus becomes doubly performative, a transitional text that shows cultural identity, like ethnicity, as experiential process. Despite its intentions of social rehabilitation, the prison workshop must therefore be remembered as an intermediary space of cultural renewal, politically and socially charged by the passage of the cante.

What is more, the reiterated premises of fixed or essential community identity and ethnic difference upon which the workshop and much of prison routines are based only serve to open up routes through which identities, those of prisoners and officials alike, can travel across space and time. The ambivalence as to whether flamenco is innate to the *gitanos* or a social construction remains an issue of debate that could perhaps be resolved if viewed through the repeated musical practice of rehearsal and performance. In the course of my meeting with the prisoners, Serrano stated that 'ya hasta el morir con el flamenco, lo llevamos dentro', his use of the first person plural indicating his membership of a community bound by a common musicality. Furthermore, this musicality appears innate and essential in the light of this statement, rendering community organic. Agujetas had said much the same earlier in the interview (as quoted above), but at this point he intervened, stressing 'Pero hay que practicarlo, hay que practicarlo'. Viewed through the metaphor of the workshop, community identity, whether *gitano* or other, is best reiterated through practice; this involves openness to other discourses and to temporal and spatial ruptures. At the same time, community as fixed, organic entity remains an important feature of the imaginary, despite the many practical challenges to such a notion. Social practice as survival through mobility traverses the fixed discourses of prison and other institutions, adapting to contingencies and embracing hybridity in the course of its travels. The survival of the workshop depends largely on the determination and perseverance of those involved in it, themselves caught up in other competing projects and activities. Arrebola repeatedly stated that dedicated flamencos were a minority group, implying here the cooperative efforts of everyone in the workshop, but he said that their effort was to 'seguir matando el gusanillo'. The theoretical overlap provided by Clifford's perspective of ethnography as route and Bhabha's view of culture as survival forces a rethinking of community identity in terms of ambivalence and transition. No longer stable or fixed, community identity appears contingent and indeterminate, open-ended and, like the cante, constantly on the move, propelled by time and through space. Attempts to maintain it dislodge as much as they 'preserve', as seen in the workshop's jagged, uphill efforts to navigate the song through uncertain temporal and spatial terrains.

1. This chapter is an extended version of the chapter titled 'Elusive Song: Flamenco as Field and Negotiation Among *Gitano* Convicts in Córdoba Prison' (Nair 2002).
2. Entry into prison provided me with a practical experience of the presence of concentric boundaries, as a series of doors had to be opened and shut in order to gain access into the chapel, which is located in an interior space.
3. During the meeting Agujetas demanded an extra cigarette from the educationalist for having sung for me and was given it. He then asked me for some reward for the meeting. I was, however, unable to give him anything, since the officials had stipulated that I should neither give nor receive anything from the prisoners.
4. In conversation following my interview with him, Córdoba, June 1999.
5. The question of gender is pertinent here. Córdoba's prison has a women's wing, where several of the convicts are *gitanas* — indeed, according to the cited article in the *Independent on Sunday*, some of these women are the wives of the male convicts. At the time this article was written, the women also participated in the flamenco workshop; however, by the time I did my fieldwork, the female participation had stopped due to insufficient funds. A clear gender hierarchy thereby emerges, privileging the male over the female and rendering the female gitana convict the most marginalized in the system of prison classification. This extreme liminality of *gitana* convicts is corroborated by the report titled *Mujeres gitanas y sistema penal* carried out by the Proyecto Barañi (date unkown), which states that 'una de las características de las mujeres gitanas es su invisibilidad en nuestra sociedad, similar a la que sufre el colectivo general de las personas presas. Ello hace que el colectivo de reclusas gitanas sufra esta característica, por partido doble' (p. 10).
6. This was confirmed to me by the prison rehabilitation officer, Antonio Estévez.
7. The Asociación Secretariado General Gitano in Madrid has details of various programmes which attempt to both stem drug-related issues and counsel families of those held for drug dealing. Increasingly, the social workers and mediators are *gitanos* themselves.
8. Of the four men I interviewed, one of them, Justo, said he was nineteen years old. In prison for seventeen years, Antonio Agujetas began his sentence at a similar age.
9. Bernard Leblon states that following the Spanish Constitution of 1978, Andalusia expressed its cultural difference from the rest of Spain through the symbol of flamenco (1995: 95)
10. Dominique Abel's recent video-documentary of this singer, *Agujetas Cantaor* (Ideal Audience, 1999), shows him to be self-exiled from community, living instead in a house away from his hometown of Jeréz de la Frontera in the company of his Japanese wife and refusing to be in touch with family members. Interestingly, Agujetas's rejection of

community in the organic sense causes him to be described by the film-maker as 'personalidad muy libre y original, mitificado', thereby equating alienation from community with mythification.

11. See Grenier and Guibalt (1990) for a more general discussion on the 'other' on anthropological perspectives of music.

12. Steingress relates the flamenco 'afición' to the transmission of extremes of emotion to the audience through the song. He connects this to the social 'alienation' experienced by a growing modernity. (1991: 16–32)

13. See Mitchell (1994) for details of the practice of saetas during Holy Week.

14. Mitchell (1994) explores the ethnic and social mixtures present in the antecedence of contemporary gitanos: gypsies, moriscos, Jews, ex-convicts, sailors, etc. Far from being ethnically unified, gitanos, he states, are the product of a hybrid culture, best recognized by their membership of a socio-economic underclass.

15. Tierney describes this discipline as 'the study of crime, of attempts to control it, and attitudes to it' (1996: 11). This is also implicit in Conklin's (1995) study of the subject. The current crises in criminology have occurred because post-structuralist perspectives in related disciplines force acknowledgement of the discipline's arrival at crossroads, whereby criminology must review its own tenets.

16. Writing about the history of flamenco, Gerhard Steingress states that 'el cante "nació" como antítesis frente a una cultura de masas nivelada y represiva. El "grito" del cantaor y el contenido de la copla que interpretó de manera individual supuso una protesta contra toda una sociedad saturada e hipócrita. El personaje del "gitano" sirvió de símbolo de esta resistencia cultural, como personificación de la libertad frente a la nivelación, de la marginalidad frente a la integración social forzada' (1991: 114). Steingress thereby stresses the opposition between flamenco as an aesthetic form and mainstream society's normalizing drive. Rehabilitation through flamenco then becomes a contradiction in terms.

17. I was able to tape the prison interview, although the quality of the recording was poor given the acoustics of the chapel.

18. See Creative Time, a collection of papers from The 2nd European Conference on Theatre and Prison (10–13 April 1996), University of Manchester.

19. In this context, it is worth noting Gerhard Steingress's statement that 'De este modo, "gitano" no designó ni lo étnico ni lo racial sino ciertas características psicológicas y sociológicas que la sociedad burguesa atribuyó a los gitanos. La noción "flamenco" se aliaría a esta imagen gitanesca de los gitanos y sirvió para caracterizar hábitos artísticos muy peculiares y enraizados en un ambiente subcultural determinado. Por su parte, los artistas que ejecutaron este papel se consideraron "flamencos" en el sentido de "gitanos artísticos" o "artistas agitanados"' (1991: 181). Racial connotations of gitano identity overlap in this sense with artistic affiliations, rendering the former into performance or construction.

20. Both Steingress (1991) and Mitchell (1994) explore the popular religiosity that accompanies attitudes to flamenco, Steingress calling it 'una sustitución artístico-secular' (1991: 85). In my conversation with the prisoners, it was evident that the 'discourse' of religion (in terms of sin, punishment, pardon, salvation, etc.) easily ran alongside the parallel discourse of rehabilitation from crime.

21. The lack of the D.N.I., in this and any other gitano convicts, may serve to reinforce the notion that the gitano community is in some way pre-modern by not possessing the classificatory documents attached to modernity. In this way, gitanos can further be fetishised in the modern imaginary as 'wild' or 'untamed' and, hence, resistant to the methods of rehabilitation used on other, non-ethnic, prisoners.

22. See Don Pohren 1988: 351–52.

23. Caterina Pasqualino states the following about El Agujetas: ' Sur Agujetas courent des rumeurs si extravagantes qu'elles confinent au mythe. Peut-etre est-ce que l'absence du personnage sur la scene locale favorise la légende…En partie vérité et en partie affabulation, ceel-ci mérite d'etre rapporté, non seulement parce qu'elle est considérée comme l'eexplication de la force de son chant, mais aussi parce qu'elle est un modele qui sert de refence a la communauté de San Miguel' (1995: 95). See pages 94–98 of her thesis for details of the rupture between the singer and his family.

24. See P. Manuel (1989) for a discussion of social shifts in flamenco styles.

CHAPTER 6

MOVING PICTURES: COMMUNITY, PLURALITY, AND
RELOCATION IN PHOTOGRAPHS OF NORTH-AFRICAN
IMMIGRANTS IN BARCELONA

This chapter focuses upon photographic representations of the Moroccan
immigrant community living in the Barcelona locality of Ciutat Vella.[1] The
photographs aim both to record current social and ethnic practices among the
Moroccans and to construct a sense of community through shared ethnicity.
Given the racial and ethnic diversity of Ciutat Vella — home not just to
Moroccans, but also to Pakistanis, Turks, Chinese, Philippinos, Catalans, and
several other 'nationals', as the many arrows on a street corner off Plaça San
Agustí which point diversely to cities such as Karachi, Shanghai, Manila,
Marrakesh, etc. will attest — the construction of such community must be seen
as multi-sited and inevitably subservient to the global economic shifts that have
given rise precisely to this diverse immigrant presence. It is impossible to ignore
the political economics surrounding migration as a feature of globalized
capitalism. For migrants, the political and social contexts within which ethnicity
is firstly transported and then enacted is coloured by the effects on the host
nation of economic and cultural globalization. Questions of ethnicity thus
become appropriated by various political discourses, so that the cultural issues
surrounding the subaltern lives of migrants provides fuel for a series of political
or ideological 'positions'. The relatively recent phenomenon of migration into
and through Spain means that no in-depth analysis has yet been made of these
issues in the Spanish context. Nevertheless, my intention in this chapter is to
examine the narratives and practices of ethnicity and community identity within
the context of migrant experiences. Complex overlappings of community
affiliations co-exist in the locality of Ciutat Vella and no reading of the
photographs is ever complete. Equally, the concept of community or any other
attempt to frame identity in group contexts must be considered here as open-
ended and necessarily deferring onto otherness. The particular focus will be on
the means by which migrants seek recognition of themselves in the course of
displacement and are thus able to construct a communal 'self' that is distinct
from and recognizable to the new socio-cultural context in which they live.

Indeed, the question of the self's relation to the other, so central to concepts
of identity, is rendered visible through the ethnically diverse populations of the

contemporary Western metropolis. In the shifting urban landscapes which ensue from such multiplicity, not only is the 'national' seen as plural, but the imagined edges of the nation are revealed as scattered and fragile. Following in the wake of Spain's transition to democracy and entry into the European community have come the northward strivings of economic migrants from the African continent, both Maghrebian and sub-Saharan. Spurred on by received images of Western prosperity, the 'ilegales', as they are familiarly called, have been arriving in growing spurts since approximately 1985 and making their uncertain way through rural and urban zones. While many of the sub-Saharan migrants are refugees, the majority of the Maghrebians, mostly Moroccans, come for economic reasons. The increasingly visible presence of these migrant communities in the main Spanish cities turns the latter into a multiplicity of spaces and tempos, where there are no linear narratives which can sufficiently articulate the experiences of diaspora.

In what is a strange echo of Spain's own sudden leap into postmodernity, with its attendant focus on capitalist modernization and plural identity, the immigrants depart abruptly from the still predominantly oral contexts of their native and largely rural communities in order to stake a claim in the material prosperity of the West. In so doing, they must also complicate the predominantly handed-down cultural memory that locates and organizes such oral communities living in rural and often remote regions.[2] What follows instead are experiences of temporal and spatial dislocations, whereby the tenets of localized communities no longer hold. Indeed, it is important to bear in mind that these tenets were disturbed prior to their leaving: the dream of the West arises for the Moroccans in some considerable measure from stories of 'success abroad' and from the idealized images relayed by satellite television which throw light upon the economic backwardness and lack of infrastructure in their own country. Most of Spain's Maghrebian communities come not from the larger towns or cities of Morocco, but from the Rif region and from the south of Morocco. Within a framework of globalized late capitalism, the displacement of traditional, more 'organic', values of community identity takes place not merely through displacement from a fixed location, but also by the arrival of change via technological media to local environments. The articulation of cultural identity therefore comes up against an impasse, as temporal ruptures occur between present and future. As the ground for the shared experience of the present fractures, there are no linear discourses which connect the constructions of a cultural past reiterated through orally transmitted, memory-based narratives to a future shot through with the capitalist dreams of postmodernity. Furthermore, cultural memory, the basis upon which community identity reconstructs itself, attempts enactment in strange and indeterminate places. With the spatial dislocation involved in the act of migration, cultural memories become scattered, even as the immigrants strive in their new contexts for the means with which to recognize themselves and thereby ask for recognition.

The photographs of Moroccan immigrants living in Barcelona taken by a Catalan photographer, Núria Andreu Castellvi will be considered in this context. My aim is to assess the repercussions of migration and relocation on community identity by examining issues related to cultural memory and ethnic identity as social practices. I also wish to consider the role of photography in the construction and dissemination of community identity. The examples of Moroccan cultural life in Spain captured by Andreu raise questions with regard to remembered ethnic identity in the face of displacement. Equally, the ambivalence of these photographs invites multiple readings for, whilst they are framed by a Catalan viewer on the 'outside' of Moroccan immigrant experience, nevertheless the different ways in which different spectators in a postmodern, cosmopolitan Barcelona are likely to process these images must also be considered. The spatial and temporal disjunctures surrounding the performance of such identity and the dissemination of its image in postmodern contexts must, therefore, surely force a refiguring of the very concepts of ethnic identity and community.

The theoretical framework for my analysis relies upon the juxtaposition of contemporary reassessment of the ethnographic task and approach in the late twentieth century with Eduardo Cadava's exploration of Walter Benjamin's imagination of history through the language of photography. The ethnographers I draw upon are George Marcus, who calls for 'a multi-sited research imaginary in the midst of general transition' (1998: 9) and Elizabeth Edwards, who assesses the place of still photography in anthropology. Cadava probes Benjamin's writings in order to uncover the convergences between photography as flashes of the past and historical understandings. Ethnographic theory which attempts to question its own premises proves very useful in understanding Andreu's focus on representing the ethnic identity of an immigrant community. The question of recognition (both that of the immigrants by the 'host' community and that of the immigrants by them — 'selves', given the fragmented and multiple narratives of identity characteristic of spatial and temporal displacement), however, is usefully explored through Cadava's views of Benjamin on history. Therefore, my analysis of the photographs will draw upon Marcus and Edwards, while my conclusion will rely upon Cadava.

Andreu's work focuses on the Moroccan inhabitants of Ciutat Vella, near the Ramblas in Barcelona, in order to portray aspects of their social and communal lives in the Catalan capital. In particular, she attempts to put forward visible expressions of ethnic identity which serve to differentiate the immigrant community from the surrounding cultural and social contexts. Their overall aim is to inform the local Catalan community about the nature of the Moroccan ethnicity that is now in their midst and thereby secure a stronger neighbourhood understanding. Therefore nearly all of her photographs on this subject seek out those cultural signs, events and actions which connect the community with their native contexts. This marks out the migrants' otherness to Spanish viewers, thus implying the latter's otherness to them, whilst also affirming the presence of the 'other' in the midst of the 'self'. This emphasis upon cultural difference aims to establish an acceptance of plurality within the neighbourhood whereby the 'other' can enter into a dialectic with the 'self' and thereby prevent the possibility of oppositional or racist attitudes and approaches.

Andreu's earlier training as a photographer led to the start of her career in 1992, when she collaborated with the organization S.O.S. Racism in the former East Germany.[3] This collaboration was triggered by a wave of racist attacks on refugee camps, which sheltered Kurds. It led to a series of photographs of immigrant refugee camps and of anti-racist events in various German cities. The following year, she moved to Madrid and through S.O.S. Racism's office there, was introduced to ATIME, Asociación de Trabajadores Inmigrantes Marroquíes en España, whose organized protests against the Ley de Extranjería she photographed. Since 1996, Andreu has been carrying out photographic coverage of the Moroccan population in Ciutat Vella as part of her collaboration in an on-going long-term social project titled Xenofília. This project is set up by five non-governmental organizations based in Barcelona (Associació per l'Estudi i la Promoció del Desenvolupament Comunitari, Cooperacció, Entrepobles, Mon 3 Universitaris per al Tercer Mon and Sodepau), themselves funded in part by the Spanish government in accordance with European community directives on the integration of immigrants and in part by the Generalitat de Catalunya and local town-halls. The Xenofília project falls in line with Barcelona's overall drive towards making local communities responsible for the well-being of their localities through positive neighbourhood practices. Its aim is 'la solidaritat e integració de persones immigrades i autoctones al barri de Ciutat Vella' (Andreu 1998). It is clear that the participating non-governmental organizations view Xenofília as a way to fulfil an important social task through promoting cultural awareness among the 'indigenous' community which can lead to strong neighbourhood ties.

The premise from which this project departs can best be understood by its name as described in the 1996 *Memoria* on it written by the editor Dris Buisef (himself attached to Cooperacció) and financed by the Dirección General de Migraciones (based in Madrid):

Xenofilia, como nombre, es una palabra formada por la raíz griega *xenón* — extranjero — y *phyleo* — simpatía, aceptación, amor — , que se opone a la palabra xenofobia, formada por *xenón* y *fobia* — antipatía, rechazo, aversión. Ha sido, para los promotores del proyecto, una manera al mismo tiempo directa, expresiva y ágil de darle la vuelta simbólicamente al auge del sentimiento de racismo, exclusión y marginación hacia los extranjeros que, veniendo de diversos países del Sur, se instalan para trabajar y vivir en nuestra sociedad (1996: 7).

The deliberate play of binarily opposed associations between the word *xenofilia* and the implicit *xenofobia* relies in each case upon a set of fixed concepts of *ego* and *xenón,* or self and other. Furthermore, the foreigner is seen as someone from 'outside' who comes to settle in 'nuestra sociedad'.[4] The insufficiencies of such perceptions in a context of postmodernity are evident; so also the difficulty with achieving sentiments of 'xenofilia' when the subaltern or liminal are not necessarily located as marginal, but are themselves constituent of a motley social fabric.

This focus on the border crossings which initiate immigrant experience both complicates the perceived integrity of the national space and serves to reinforce the sense of unbreachable peripheral boundaries by locating the 'other' as a perpetual 'guest'. In this way, the *Memoria* confirms that national frontiers are maintained by the drawing of invisible borderlines between 'self' and 'other', whilst also pointing to a long history of imperial and colonial contact and relation between the two. The remembrance of colonial contacts can, once again, be double-edged: on the one hand, the immigrant thus appears less 'foreign' or at least as a foreigner in 'our' mould and therefore more acceptable; on the other, it perpetuates the subalternity attached to postcolonial subjects, thus reinforcing the sense of Western hegemony of which the 'self', as nation, is a part. In this context, during my meeting with him in January 1999, Dris Buisef clearly outlined to me three areas of focus in the Xenofilia attempt to create awareness, and hence acceptance, of Moroccan immigrants in Barcelona: firstly, the geographical location of Morocco as Spain's southern neighbour; secondly, the many centuries of Islamic rule in Spain, whereby 'Moroccan' cultural memory merges with that of Spain; thirdly, and more recently, Spain's colonization of northern Morocco with the resulting spill-over of Spain onto the Moroccan mainland, the last vestiges of which are the small, but significant, colonies of Ceuta and Melilla. Moreover, he emphasized that it was important to portray Morocco not as an unified space of culture and religions, but rather as a mosaic of Judaism, Islam, and Christianity with attendant linguistic and cultural diversity.[5] For the purposes of Xenofilia's cultural awareness programme, it must be assumed that this vision of the 'other' as diverse makes possible an acceptance of diversity in the 'self'. In addition, Buisef's report provides details of the contemporary 'market' for immigrant labour by outlining the flow of migration to and from several Western countries, including Spain, since the beginning of the second half of this century and by pointing to reasons why such labour is currently needed in Spain (such as for reasons of low birth rate, etc.). A stress on the large number of Spanish emigrants living around Europe and America further makes migration more acceptable and in some ways less 'foreign':

... aún hoy día, un 4% de la población española sigue emigrada (una cifra que muchos medios de comunicación y analistas del fenómeno migratorio se guardan de difundir) (1996: 22).

Therefore the report provides ways in which the 'self' (in this case, the nation) can be enhanced through solidarity with the 'other' (the foreigner).

Thus, in his conclusion to the *Memoria*, Buisef writes that

No se trata de que un puñado de gente más o menos altruista, más o menos voluntaria, más o menos activista vaya sembrando maneras de ver, de vivir y de hacer. Se trata, antes que nada, de un reto: el de nuestro futuro, el de nuestra convivencia, el de nuestra democracia (1996: 53).

Once again, the word 'nuestra' brings to mind the question of who 'we' are and how we know ourselves. Tolerance of difference is important, it would appear, not for the mere sake of dialectic or openness, but in order to safeguard the future, in economic, political, and cultural terms, of a 'self' which acknowledges its own diversity.

As these words imply, the project proceeds along the clear assumption of a borderline between immigrant and local communities.[6] This is further evidenced in the title of the photographic exhibition organized as part of Xenofília, where Andreu's photographs were displayed between 25 April 1998 and 30 May 1998 at the Sala Arpi (owned by the photographic equipment company ARPI, who sponsor her work by supplying her with materials) in Barcelona: 'Trencant Fronteres' (Breaking Frontiers). In her introduction to the exhibition, Andreu describes the subject of her work, the locality of Ciutat Vella, in the following words:

Un espai que compartit al centre de la ciutat, el barri de Ciutat Vella a Barcelona esta sotmes constantment als canvis urbanístics i socials. Com un cor que batega, al ritme del temps i de l'espai que li toca viure, s'expandeix en una atmosfera densa, a vegades difícil de comprendre. (1998)

The boundaries that she is referring to are therefore not merely those of ethnic difference, but also those of the enclosed space of Ciutat Vella, which has now become the space of cross-overs of cultures and ethnicities. Thus Ciutat Vella becomes metaphoric of the 'national' space, now transformed and expanded by the foreign presence. In his review of her exhibition, Josep Catalá Domenech writes of her photographs that:

En ellas aparece objetivado el espacio humano que surge del incesante cruce de fronteras en que se ha convertido nuestro mundo. Y si las fronteras ya no pueden equipararse al territorio, es que su característica principal no es separar, alejar o distanciar, sino unir. Las imágenes de esta antología muestra el instante extraordinario en que esta unión se produce, dejan constancia del momento en que la múltiple confluencia de fronteras acaba por anularlas todas (1998).

Thus the immigrant presence in Ciutat Vella displaces all existence there into borderline positions. Ethnicity, therefore, must itself be lived on a shifting edge.

Andreu goes on to evoke this dialogue with alterity that underlines her photographs, as also the shared temporal and cultural experience of diversity:

El gest d'un moment que reivindica la seva presencia solidaria en nuestro entorn, el de tots. El contacte dels rostres amb l'aire que omple la placa i els carrers, iguals o diferents a d'altres. Els nens continuen jugant, els joves parlant, les dones passen i desapareixen. Les imatges es refereixen ja a un passat, evocant l'existencia d'aquest temps, que es el nostre. (1998).

Clearly, Andreu is attempting to address the confusion that she perceives as resulting from the presence of ethnic difference in the heart of Barcelona. This confusion, 'difícil de comprendre' in her own words, also arises from the above-mentioned cross-over of different temporal and historical experiences lived by those in Ciutat Vella. As she states, the images which refer to a 'foreign' past (such as those which commemorate the cultural and religious practices of the immigrants' original communities) are also those of the here and now. Thus expressions of cultural memory as seen in the photographs bring into the centre of Barcelona a temporality which derives from another space, that of rural Morocco. The photographs then become symbolic of both temporal and spatial cross-overs — and hence, as she states, cultural confusion or entanglements.

Perhaps this apparent confusion referred to by Andreu can be understood to arise from the blurring of a stress upon accepting cultural difference with the stress on 'integration' as a positive or socially beneficial act. This is an emphasis that is made equally by Andreu as by Buisef in the *Memoria* on Xenofilia:

Fugint dels topics i de les formes utilitzades pels mitjans de comunicació per expressar les diferents situacions vinculades amb la població immigrada que viu a la ciutat, aquest reportatge s'elabora des de un punt de vista mes subjectiu, implicant-se amb la problematica actual per a sensibilitzar a l'espectador, tractant la vida i loes costums dels immigrants a la nostra ciutat, mostrant també les diverses actuacions del Projecte Xenofilia i d'altres col.lectius que treballen per la solidaritat e integració de persones immigrades i autoctones al barri de Ciutat Vella (1998).

This projection of integration is based upon the assumption of the fixed polarities of indigenous and migrant communities. On the one hand, the visible markers of ethnic identity serve to delineate the contours of cultural differences cohabiting a shared space. On the other hand, the concept of cultural integration implies a projection of unity that must therefore be somehow drawn from sources other than ethnicity or cultural memory. The question arises as to how to construct unity out of difference, even without taking into account the instability of such differences.

Integration becomes even more problematic within a postmodern context of flux, whereby the identities of both 'inmigrante' and 'autóctono' are multiple and shifting. In this context, Cesarani and Fulbrook write in the conclusion to their edited volume (1996) that:

... whatever the differences of culture, dialect, religion or economy, if immigrants are accepted by host communities as having a legitimate claim to belonging, their integration is less problematic than if the differences are construed as insurmountable barriers to a sense of common humanity (1996: 216).

Thus a necessary condition for integration is the willingness to share space with difference as well as to focus on what is common over a period of time and within a space, rather than on what is different. The photographic exhibition can be read therefore at the most basic level as visual documents which testify to the cohabitation of different ethnic groups in Ciutat Vella, a textual confirmation deemed necessary as a step towards integration. Indeed, the photographs thus signify much more than the immigrant life they portray: implicit in their viewing is what remains unseen but tremendously pertinent to the issue of integration — the social, economic, political, ethnic, and cultural repercussions of the immigrant presence to the supposedly 'indigenous' or non-immigrant (hence 'settled') population. More to the point, the immigrant presence speaks of displacement and travel, with its inevitable repercussions on all these aspects of those who are seen as, or who view themselves as, 'settled'. Therefore, the question still remains as to the feasibility of integration within an overall socio-cultural and political context of competing pluralisms and social flux. The visibility of cultural (and religious) differences, in other words the public performance of community or ethnic identity, becomes charged with political content and functions as a signifier which is aimed at mobilizing responses. In this context, it is worth recalling Richard Jenkins' statements (1997) that ethnicity is transactional and therefore power is central to inter-ethnic and intra-ethnic relations. Dissemination through the media or in a public forum such as the Sala Arpi of such cultural messages makes them all the more powerful and far-reaching. Simultaneously, however, they must compete with other agents of different cultural and political allegiances who hold other agendas, thus giving rise to rivalries and cross-currents which bear witness to the collapse of traditional concepts and processes of integration. Writing about the French experience of immigration, Sami Naïr states that, whilst the major preoccupation of the republican concept (of citizenship)

was the concern with universalism, the proposed model of an abstract ideal as the goal of all ordinary citizens, equality as the *sine qua non* of communal life, the construction of a neutral public space — the new concept is centred on the individual subject, rejects the abstract project, prioritizes liberty over equality and opens up the public space to the clash of cultural particularisms. (1992: 44–45)

The question can therefore be asked whether Andreu's photographs are just one more display of ethnic 'particularism' in the cultural marketplace and, if so, is their goal of integration at all viable in an overall context of fluidity and flux. Regardless of the extent to which integration is possible within a postmodern context, such 'particularisms' should be understood as the result of migrant and scattered cultural memories which become charged with political, ideological and, most importantly, economic resonances through dislocation and travel. For precisely these reasons, however, and despite their efforts to the contrary, the migrants' enactment of cultural memory through rupture and displacement will differ from the orally transmitted performance of culture among those whose temporal and spatial experience has yet to be disturbed and for whom collective integration is a given.

Andreu's work evidently proceeds from an ideological position which aligns her with organizations which seek to orient and accommodate immigrants from the Third world in the West. She is avowedly 'anti-racist'[7] and wishes to work for a more tolerant attitude towards difference and for greater opportunities for such minority groups. Her work aims to open up traditional attitudes in Catalunya and the rest of Spain which view the nation as enclosed. A premise of her work, therefore, is the notion that the nation, prior to the 'foreign' presence, is generally understood to be unified and integrated. Beyond any artistic efforts in her photography is the ethnographic[8] intention of her work.[9] Her pictures aim primarily to construct a narrative of identity in terms of 'realist' photography; furthermore, and perhaps even superceding the realist intention of her work, this narrative is one that is ideologically fired since its aim is social change or 'reform'. Xenofília uses her photographs in several of their publicity leaflets and, interestingly, has availed of one of her pictures of Kurdish refugees in Germany for a leaflet informing Moroccan immigrants of help they can get in Ciutat Vella in order to find accomodation. The leaflet, which is trilingual (Arabic, Catalan, and Spanish), does not state that the photograph is of Kurds nor does it acknowledge Andreu as the photographer. Andreu, however, showed me the leaflet as an example of the uses to which her work has been put. The assumption, of course, is that the photograph reveals no visible ethnic or racial difference between the Kurds who are represented and the Moroccans that are targeted. While the former are political refugees in Germany and the latter economic migrants in Spain, any distinctions in their positions are thereby blurred. What binds them then must depend on the surface racial similarity visible in the photograph and the obvious restricted economic and social conditions that they share in the host countries. Like the majority of Moroccans, the Kurds have dark hair and light skin. The photograph, which shows several young men (again an evocation of the predominantly male influx of immigrants, which raises demands for more freedom for 'reagrupamiento familiar', an on-going matter of political and legislative debate) and a woman in one, rather small, living room, evokes the cramped domestic circumstances of immigrant life. The hands of two other men can be glimpsed on either side of the photograph. The message is that there are too many people and too little space in the room for the camera to be able to capture them all. Of those who are visible, one man holds a television remote control in his hands, while two others play with a gameboy. Once again, the sense of 'passing time' or endless waiting recalls the extended queues and anonymity that accompany immigrant experience. Clearly the photograph is emblematic of the Moroccans as well as of the Kurds and can therefore broadcast a common message for the two groups. In the face of ethnic hostility, it appears that organizations such as Xenofilia seek to raise a counter-discourse of their own that will serve to signify their political positions and claims for tolerance (this brings to mind the clear example of such counter-discourse provided by the name 'Xenofilia').

The constructed nature of their rhetoric, which mirrors the structural features of dominant discourses, becomes transparent once the surface use of the photograph is known. The photograph obviously permits a fluid cross-over of projections of identity based on a degree of shared, if spatially fractured, experience. What binds the two sets of immigrants then must depend on the surface racial similarity visible in the photograph and the obvious restricted economic and social conditions that they share in the host countries. Clearly, the use of a photograph of Kurds in Germany in an information leaflet intended for immigrants in Spain can be problematic (no doubt this being the reason why no mention of authorship is attached to the photograph). The implication is that immigrant identity, regardless of location, can be expressed in the same terms, thus levelling subalternity by disregarding the particulars of place and time. This levelling of different immigrant groups erases the historical particularities of each community. Yet Andreu — and presumably the organizers of Xenofilia who avail of this photograph — do not appear aware of this apparent disregard for important cultural differences between immigrant groups and locales of emigration. The focus is instead on the present, where the photograph comes in as useful. It must then be surmised that Andreu's is a postmodern lens whose contrasts and juxtapositions can be viewed as both levelling difference and providing a public platform, however improvised, for the latter.

Furthermore, Andreu's representations of subaltern ethnic groups should also be considered in the light of her career's progression. Clearly, her photographs mark out a professional terrain and area of expertise, one where very few other Spanish photographers have as yet ventured. She is highly regarded by ATIME[10] and other non-governmental organizations, who consider her work as extensions into the public realm of Moroccan immigrant identity. The exhibition of her work, which is subsidized in part by ARPI, provides as much publicity for the latter as for the subject matter, thereby helping to promote their products by appealing to new clientele. It is therefore impossible to isolate Andreu's ideological stance from the wider social and economic contexts which influence it and in which it is obviously implicated, with the attendant stress on social visibility and marketability. It is also important to bear in mind Andreu's relations with the subjects of her photographs. She states that while many of the photographs were taken with the knowledge and consent of the subjects, nevertheless some were taken without their awareness. Her photographs concentrate largely on the public life of the Moroccans, an arena that is predominantly male-dominated, given the strict adherence to Islam in the community and the predominance of men over women in terms of immigrant population.[11] Her own position vis-a-vis them as a woman, as a non-Muslim, and as a Spaniard has, she states, placed constraints upon her freedom to photograph. Andreu's photographic work, therefore, provides a convergence of cultural text, social constraints and ethnographic intent. What emerges from here are several questions pertinent to on-going debates in contemporary ethnography.

George Marcus's 'Requirements for Ethnographies of Late-Twentieth Century Modernity' is triggered by an article in the *Radical History Review* which problematizes 'the question of who or what controls and defines the identity of individuals, social groups, nations and cultures' (1998: 58). As his title suggests, Marcus attempts to reassess practices in realist ethnography which continue to rely upon such framing concepts as 'community, subculture, traditions and practices' (1998: 61). He does so by laying out a set of practices which are based on a reassessment of the culture of late modernity and subsequently require a break with some of the founding tropes of ethnography. Marcus probes the concept of the spatial in ethnography and asks for a break with traditional understandings of community. He states that 'culture has been mapped literally onto locality to define one basic frame of reference orienting ethnography' (1998: 62). Cultural identity, he insists, is simultaneously produced in different places for different purposes and should be viewed as a 'process of dispersed identity' (1998: 63). The latter, therefore, should always be viewed as multiple and multi-sited. Marcus also probes the question of history and temporality and asks for a break with the practice of historical determination in explaining the ethnographic present. He states that realist ethnography relies upon Western historical metanarratives; instead he foregrounds the traces and expressions of scattered memories as clues to the present. Furthermore, Marcus moves away from a structuralist approach to cultural analysis towards a privileging of the senses, whereby ethnography becomes more visible and sayable through overlapping sets of associations and experiences. These requirements evidently depend upon a 'remade' observer in terms of the ethnographer's own sense of purpose.

In the same way as Marcus urges ethnographers to look beyond the traditional boundaries of the discipline, so does Elizabeth Edwards reassess the role of still photography in visual anthropology by looking beyond the disciplinary edges to wider photographic discourse. According to Edwards, visual anthropology in general privileges film as the main visual medium with 'political, structural or expressive possibilities' (1998: 53). The photograph, states Edwards, has usually been relegated to archives of documents, since the assumption is that it freezes

COMMUNITY, PLURALITY, AND RELOCATION   155

and frames time, experience, and history. In particular, Edwards writes against this traditional use of still photography as a realist medium. In place of an oppositional conception of visual production, where the realist is seen as polarized from the expressive and anthropological document is seen as polarized from art, Edwards writes for a dialectic which seeks the 'interaction of anthropology and still photography on and beyond the discipline boundary' (1998: 53). Thus the still photograph, for Edwards, frames the confluence of anthropology with other forms of articulation and expression, such as the contemporary visual arts. Positioned on the borderline of ethnography and creative visual expression, the still photograph can act as an ideal medium for reversing or altering what Edwards refers to as 'the traditional anthropological categorization of peoples and experience' (70). It is thus a multi-dimensional and ambivalent site of fluidity which invites questions and offers perspectives rather than make closed statements. Photographs therefore are filled with possibilities and thus signify the opening up of the anthropological boundary. Contrary to traditional perceptions of the photograph as 'closed' and 'still', it marks a moment of cultural experience poised in mid-flight. In this sense, photographs directly challenge anthropology's traditional encapsulation of the 'other' through the 'framing' of culture within fields demarcated by the anthropologist, thus decentering and repositioning traditional concepts of history, experience, and identity. The multiple dimensions of historical experi-ence, central to cultural identity, are brought together in the spatial and temporal intersections of photography, so that the photograph is at once revealing and ambiguous.

Marcus and Edwards coincide in their efforts to travel beyond the confines of traditional anthropological discourse in their search for new forms of interpreta-tion and new understandings. While Marcus examines conventional practices and assumptions or tropes, Edwards explores the possibilities of constructing new meanings from photographs. Both are concerned with the production of texts of ethnographic knowledge and the means by which such texts are interpreted. If ethnography's role is to analyse culture, then it must also take into account its own processual implication in the latter. As Marcus states (1986: 168), 'the ethnographic position of authority' on culture must give way to an awareness of incompleteness and ambivalence. The same is true of Edward's view of photography. This point is of relevance to Andreu's photographs. If her aim has been to realistically portray her subjects in order to produce an ethnographic text on immigrant cultural identity, then the resulting incompleteness of her efforts should open up further possibilities. Her photo-graphs should therefore be considered for the questions they pose, rather than for any certainties they appear to offer. This is all the more so when considering her photographic training and material indebtedness to ARPI, who no doubt housed her exhibition as significant of photographic potential in its many dimensions. Similarly, ensuing from anthropology's implications in larger cultural contexts is the reminder that cultural studies too operates within multiple sites and tempos.[12] The interdisciplinary dimensions of cultural studies render any analysis incomplete and open to further questions. Thus any attempts, such as this, to critically analyse Andreu's ethnographic attempts should be viewed in the interrogative rather than in the affirmative.

The photographs which follow were presented to me by Andreu as sets of sequences, each set being constructed out of shared location and time for the subjects involved. Nevertheless, when I went to see Andreu, they were not arranged in any order but were shown to me out of a pile of other examples of her work, all relating to Moroccans in Barcelona. Any reading of the photographs therefore will depend, firstly, upon Andreu's sequencing of them in terms of the narratives they are intended to contain, which in turn leads to my own arrangement of them. The photographs here were all part of the Trencant Fronteres exhibition. They depend to a great extent on general preconceptions and understandings of Islam among the viewers, since the predominant visible markers of ethnicity are drawn from religious affiliation rather than race or national identity.

Furthermore, it would appear that Moroccans themselves closely link the practice of Islam with what they perceive as 'their' cultural and ethnic identity. Thus mosques, such as the one in Carrer Hospital, are important cultural centres which work in close alliance with non-governmental organizations, such as those involved in the Xenofilia project. According to Colectivo Ioé (1995), the observance of Islamic rituals becomes somewhat watered down in practice through the experience of migration and relocation. Moroccans, especially those (mainly young men) who come without their families, often find themselves slipping from the practice of prayer five times a day or beginning to join Catalan friends or colleagues for a drink. Parents may tolerate children eating pork at school dinners but not in the home. Women may drop the headscarf in order to increase their chances of finding work by looking more socially acceptable. Such ambivalence in the practices of daily life can, however, make the observance of special religious events all the more important. By highlighting specific cultural points in the calendar, immigrant communities are able to maintain a grip on what they perceive as their ethnic identity not merely as individuals or on a personal basis, but as a community. The rituals of religion become signifiers which relay onto spaces and times deemed as 'original', thus providing a sense of linear continuity, albeit in passing and imaginary, in the face of displacement. Equally such signifiers carry political messages for recognition and for more 'space' in the host environment. The act of constructing and acknowledging a 'self' therefore coincides with visibility to and acknowledgement from the 'other'.

The five photographs which make up the 'Plegaria comunitaria' perform just such a function for the Moroccan community.[13] Through the practices which mark this communal prayer ceremony, the Plaça de l'Escorxador becomes transformed into an Islamic forum. In the first picture, Andreu has framed four rows of men kneeling over in Islamic tradition, their foreheads to the ground (Picture 1). Their shoes have been removed and placed before them. Several of the men have covered their heads with the white cap that is usual in such ceremonies. Andreu stated (personal interview, January 1999) that although she had received permission from the Imam who conducted the ceremony to be there on the day, she was unable to photograph the men freely. She said that when she went to the front of the congregation in order to photograph the men, the Imam asked her, as a woman, to step back to where the women were seated. The picture was therefore hastily snapped against his wishes. The objection was in accordance with Islamic custom whereby women are not supposed to stand or sit before men when the latter are in prayer. Nevertheless, the flexibility of traditional Islamic practice can be glimpsed not just in the ease with which a public square has been turned into a prayer space, but also in the mere fact of Andreu's presence as a woman and as a non-Muslim at such a ceremony. It must be surmised, therefore, that the Moroccans collaborated with her because they were perhaps aware of the political potential of having such photographs taken, whereby Islam is witnessed as occupying an undeniable space in the heart of a European city.

The next photograph shows some rows of women, presumably located behind the men, sitting on a Moroccan rug which has been laid out on the square (Picture 2). The women are all dressed in traditional clothes, their hair covered in scarves. Behind them is a sculpture by Joan Miró and, further still, are high-rise apartment blocks. The square, now staging the colours, sounds, and rites of Moroccan ethnicity, lies nevertheless in the heart of postmodern Barcelona. The Moroccan rug thrown on the public space both proclaims the presence of 'another' ethnicity and suggests the ease with which it can be rolled up and put away. The relocation of Islam speaks also of deracination.

In the next picture, Moroccan women embrace each other in traditional style following the prayer (Picture 3). One of them holds a baby in her arms. Despite the women's traditional clothes, the child's warm jacket speaks of a temperate climate that is at odds with the practice of this ceremony as it might be at 'home'. The architecture in the background adds to this sense of make-shift ethnic practice. In the fourth picture, the Imam hands out dates to the congregation (Picture 4). With strong religious and cultural connotations attached to it of happiness and prosperity, the date, together with mint, is symbolic of Moroccan ethnicity. Indeed the fifth picture shows two women standing in front of Miró's sculpture, mint leaves in their hands (Picture 5). Both pictures highlight the hybridity which accompanies the performance of remembered ethnicity. The rigorous rules of Islam have been adapted to fit with changed social and cultural circumstances. Similarly, and despite the evidence that ethnicity is an imagined construction, its very versatility underlines its potential to provide communal solidarity and offer new avenues to empowerment. Hence the political weight that is inevitably attached to such ceremonies and the importance attached to visibility in public. Furthermore, it is not just the immigrants' practice of ethnicity that is hybrid: the new spaces that are thus occupied and transformed are also hybridized by the different narratives of identity that are played out on them. For viewers of the photographs who are familiar with the Plaça de l'Escorxador, Miró's sculpture appears in a new light when flanked by the rites of Islam. The narratives thrown up by such mixes are hybrid, multi-dimensional, and transitory. Everyone knows that once the rugs have been rolled up and the dates eaten, the space of the square will offer itself up to other, very different, performances of identity.

The Eid el Kebir sequence marks the observation of this major Islamic holy day in Barcelona. The sacrificial ritual begins with the feeding of the sheep by the children of the family. Here, in the first photograph, they are seen in a large field on the outskirts of Barcelona, Prat de Llobregat. Implicit is the distance between this field and where they actually live, Ciutat Vella (Picture 6). The viewer would no doubt understand that they have had to come here in order to fulfill this religious obligation, since there are no provisions for carrying it out near their homes. Also implicit is the revulsion that the neighbours would feel should this act of animal slaughter have taken place in their midst.[14] The isolated location of Prat de Llobregat away from the center of Barcelona acts as a metaphor for the immigrants' position in society and the alienness of their cultural inheritance. In the background other groups of Moroccans can be seen as they unpack from vans and set up the equipment for the ritual slaughter. The picture suggests a 'camp', which can be dismantled after use, suggestive of deracination. The wind which catches the little child's hair further speaks of impermanence, although the children are seen to comply with tradition. The second photograph shows men trying to catch a sheep (Picture 7). Their obvious shared amusement and enjoyment implies the joyfulness for them at the impending slaughter, thrown into relief by assumptions of horror on the part of a non-Islamic public. It is clear in the picture that Western, and still largely non-Spanish,[15] concepts of cruelty to animals fails to hold significance for those concerned. Behind them is the farmhouse from which the sheep were purchased. The third photograph of this sequence shows a whole family engaged in cleaning the carcass (Picture 8). Interestingly, Andreu has no photographs of the slaughter itself, which follows the sacrificial prayer led by an imam. This is firstly because Islam forbids pictures or images in the context of prayer and, secondly, because only men take part in this religious act. Thus only the 'social' aspects of the holy day could be framed by Andreu. The fourth photograph in this series underlines the larger social and political contexts within which this Islamic act must occur: as the men clean the carcasses, the Spanish police watch from a discreet distance and a plane suggests the proximity of the airport (Picture 9). Implied in the police presence is the asking of permission to use the field for these purposes, itself symbolic of the immigrants' disadvantaged social position. Also in evidence is the monitoring of communal activities and the hint of threat as members of the establishment survey the outsiders within their territories. It could well be possible that the police intention is one of protection: i.e., to ensure that the immigrants are not disturbed by any locals who may object to the celebrations or who may question their use of the fields. Nevertheless, the police presence also speaks of expectations of unruliness or disorderly behaviour from the immigrants, thus confirming common stereotypes attached to foreigners and any economic underclass. Furthermore, the practice of Islam is thus rendered somewhat subversive, as if in defiance of established norms.[16] The fifth photograph shows the carcasses being strung up on racks to bleed and then be gutted by the butcher (Picture 10). The bearded man stands by with a carrier bag which bears the name of a local (and inexpensive) supermarket in Ciutat Vella. The simultaneous cleansing of several sheep implies the presence of several families who must all share one space and thus blur their distinctions and view themselves instead as one community.

The sixth photograph shows a Moroccan woman video recording the events of the day, while another police van watches in the distance (Picture 11). In this sense, the police surveillance acts as an echo to the woman's own surveillance of the events, albeit with different intentions in mind. This is complicated by Andreu's own surveillance of the police as well as the woman, with her own very different set of intentions. The role of the video camera in identity constructions has been explored from various angles.[17] In the context of the Moroccans, who are economic migrants, the recorder speaks very evidently of the acquisition of material objects associated with the West. The video of the holy day confirms at once the adherence to Moroccan traditions and the shift to a European standard of living, which includes such appliances as a television and a video player. It echoes Andreu's photographic act in that it suggests the transportability of the Eid el Kebir event from the margins of Barcelona to countless other locations, which could perhaps even be those left behind in Morocco. The final photograph in this series marks the end of a successful day, as the kebabs made from the sheep are shown off to the camera (Picture 12). The age and appearance of the people in the photograph are a reminder of the relative youth of the immigrants in Spain, most of whom are still below the age of forty.

By focusing on the issue of animal slaughter, the Eid el Kebir photographs shown to a Catalan public must provide stark images of ethnic alterity in terms of social and cultural values and norms. They suggest a culture gap between host and guest community that is almost always at the core of debates on tolerance of diversity. Such a gap carries with it the suggestion of irreconcilable difference and borders of opposition. From a European perspective, understandings of ethnic identity of Muslim immigrant communities often devolves into the practices of Islam, irrespective of whether the people concerned are Moroccans, Algerians, Kurds, etc.[18] Implicit in such a view is the rigidity of such practices, since they are prescribed in detail in the Koran. However, the Eid el Kebir photographs would suggest otherwise to those familiar with the observance of this day in a solely Islamic context. Indeed, the Moroccans themselves might read in the photographs the signs and symbols of displacement, as culture is performed as improvisation in strange settings. Immigrants to Barcelona from rural areas of Spain might note surface similarities with local practices of *matanza*, while Muslims, be they Moroccans or other nationals, may note the importance of the absence of pork as a marker of distinct ethnic and community identity. Striking to the eye is the absence of traditional Islamic clothes in the photographs. Nowhere is there evidence of the veils that Islam prescribes for women in public or the djellabas that men usually wear for traditional occasions. All the men and children photographed are in casual Western clothes, while the women appear to make a concession to 'tradition' by wearing headscarfs. If those unfamiliar with contemporary Morocco may regard the lack of 'otherness' in the dress worn for this ritual occasion as a departure from Moroccan practice 'at home' and thus as a sign of adaptation to life in Europe, Moroccan spectators may well find such clothing 'normal'.[19] Those unfamiliar with Islam might perceive the rigidity and persistence of cultural norms in the pictures; nevertheless, those who have lived in Islamic cultures would be struck by the flexibility and provisionality of the rites. The Koran stipulates that a sheep should be bought and fed in the family home for a month prior to the sacrifice, a norm that is followed in general. In Barcelona, the sheep were bought from a farmer who housed them until the day of the slaughter. While the latter generally takes place in the family home, the open, unprotected stretches of Prat de Llobregat poignantly pose a question mark around the issue of home. This is reiterated in the last picture, where the meat is shown to have been grilled on skewers, suggesting an open fire. While in Morocco, the sheep would be cooked in a domestic kitchen, the skewered meat is further suggestive of the contextual flexibility of remembered ethnicity. In this context, Mr Derdabi of ATIME spoke of the pride of the Moroccan people at having their religious festival photographed and exhibited to the public in Barcelona. Multiple spatial and temporal connections emerge from this exhibition. Not just is a 'marginal' immigrant event centralized by its location in a gallery, but Islam is brought into the here and now. If the initial perception expected of those Spaniards and Catalans who view the photographs is one of alterity, then this equally throws into question the certainties of the non-immigrant self. As visual documents of cultural memory re-enacted, the photographs bring into the midst of Barcelona the rituals of 'other' ethnicities through the act of spatial migration. Thus, the very viewing of these photographs implicates the self with other, in the same way as cross-currents of spatial movements are established. Such migration in turn causes multiple temporal experiences to be experienced simultaneously. While the photographed events arise from the cultural memory of the immigrants, as they attempt to reconstruct remembered identity, their efforts at commemoration also establish the temporal rupture of displacement.

Andreu's presence at the Eid el Kebir celebrations was welcomed by those taking part and she states that she was asked to join them in the meal. The publicity provided by her camera obviously allowed the immigrants to view her as a means of social travel through the 'transmission' of the photographs. It would appear that, like the actions of the day themselves, the photographs act as tangible artefacts or documents of cultural memory. At the same time, these very texts serve the ARPI gallery as a way of promoting themselves as 'different' from other competitors in the market, just as they provide Andreu with a hallmark to her professional reputation. Thus the question of ethnicity and cultural memory becomes embroiled with capitalist expansion as it emerges in the midst of spatial and temporal multiplicities.

Questions about the multiple dimensions of space and time are again raised in a set of three photographs taken inside the home of a Moroccan woman in Ciutat Vella during the fasting month of Ramadan. The first picture shows a corner table with various objects, such as a vase, some glasses and a framed photograph (Picture 13). On the lower shelf are further objects and a telephone. Hanging on the wall next to this table is the calendar for Ramadan, stating the times at which the fast should be started and broken each day. Ethnic identity is suggested by more than the calendar: the glasses on the top shelf bring to mind the sweet black tea so familiar to Moroccan daily life. Paul Rabinow states that tea was introduced to Morocco only in the eighteenth century by the English and did not become popular until the mid-nineteenth. Yet, as he adds, 'tea and sugar have a tyrannical and obsessive centrality in Morocco' (1977: 35), he states. The next photograph focuses on another wall of her living-room, this time a wall cabinet with more objects and a television screen showing a family seated in yet another living room around a meal laid out in front of them (Picture 14). The photograph made little sense to me beyond the image of an image until Andreu explained the context to me: the television screen was relaying images of the Ramadan fast being broken on Moroccan television. Above the screen is a photograph of the owner of the flat when she was younger. The third photograph completes the set with the owner and her two daughters breaking their own fast at the same time as the people on Moroccan television (Picture 15). Behind them on the wall is a basketball net, suggesting the multiple uses of the limited space they inhabit: living room, dining room, and playroom all at once. A Catalan newspaper lies on the table next to the large plate from which all three eat, in the Moroccan way. Cultural and linguistic hybridity emerges from the two languages juxtaposed in the room as does temporal and spatial ambivalence. Similarly, the family's location in Spain overlaps with that of Morocco through the shared temporal experience which, nevertheless, also raises issues of displacement, as ethnic identity must rely upon technology for expression. The projection of ethnicity is a gesture of loss as much as of affirmation. The cramped, foldable table at which the woman and her children eat in the company of the 'imagined' ethnic community on television suggests a future dismantling. Like the Eid el Kebir scenes, once again community identity and cultural memory appear as constructs or performances which could be removed or replaced in the same way as the television could be switched off.

Disposability is once again present in a sequence of three photographs taken by Andreu without her subjects' knowledge. From across a square, Andreu has photographed the search and arrest by the Catalan police of a group of young Moroccan migrants. The first of these photographs, which she calls 'Pidiendo documentación', shows a group of three or four young men sitting on a bench in the square and being questioned by police (Picture 16). The act of interrogation is evident from the notes being taken by the police, who tower over the immigrants, although one of them is perched on the back of the bench with his legs on the seat (a posture which although perhaps unwitting is also suggestive of subversion). Curiously, the man in the foreground who is passing by appears more interested in looking at Andreu's camera than at the scene that is taking place on the other side of the square. Could it be that the recording of the event holds more interest than the event itself? Certainly his disinterest in the event itself can be read as a sign that such interrogations are not out of the ordinary and that the photographing of it is what is extraordinary. The police vigilance, seen in the Eid el Keir sequence, takes on more sinister notes here. Their standing posture adds an extra touch of authority over the seated, and hence physically lower, immigrants. As Andreu's title suggests, the police would be checking the legality of the Moroccans in Spain. More subtle, but nevertheless valid, aspects of immigrant experience are thrown up by the photograph: the migrants are young men, presumably recently arrived. Time appears to hang heavy on their hands, a phenomenon all too familiar to immigrants, particularly those who are recent arrivals and have yet to find employment:

Al llegar aquí me aburría y quería volver a mi país. Porque no había nada. . .veía a la gente diferente y, no sé, un cambio muy grande. No sabía ni una palabra de castellano. . .me sentía fatal. (Colectivo Ioé 1995: 212).

The clear sunlight and their obvious idleness in the square suggests that it is day-time and these men are presumably either without work or shift workers. Their gathering on the square also suggests that perhaps they have minimal domestic and economic circumstances, which force them to meet up in public places.

The next photograph in this sequence is called 'Contra la pared' (Picture 17). As the name suggests, two policemen and a policewoman are holding the three immigrants against the wall and are frisking them. The immigrants have their hands either up against the wall which they are obviously forced to face or behind their back. The policemen have their hands on the immigrants' bodies. The search takes place outside the doorway of a block of flats, next to a launderette which is shut. As they search the men, an elderly man enters the block of flats, apparently oblivious to what is taking place around him. His disregard speaks volumes: Xenofilia's project of neighbourhood solidarity now seems wishful given the attitude of local residents to the fate of the immigrants. The powerlessness of the immigrants with regard to the police is exacerbated by the lack of concern from ordinary citizens.

The last picture in this sequence is called 'Detención ilegal' (Picture 18). The camera frames the group of three police officers taking one of the immigrants away with them. He appears to be putting his jacket back on, as if he had been forced to remove it during the earlier search of his person. Isolated now from his peers and surrounded by police officers, the immigrant now appears truly enmeshed in the structures of authority, his fate in their hands. Reduced now to a mere number or a document in the possession of the structures of national vigilance, the young man in the picture will remain unnamed and unknown. Andreu's support for his situation becomes evident not just from her secret recording of the incident but also from her interesting title for this photograph: the arrest, and not the immigrant, is illegal. What she clearly perceives as abuse of the law on the part of the police amounts to the denial of personal and communal space to the immigrants, since their presence is not deemed valid on Spanish soil. Deprived of space, immigrants cannot enact their ethnic or cultural identity for lack of a forum. Consequently they can neither be recognized by others or even recognize themselves.

This set of photographs strikes a vibrant chord in the narrative of ethnic identity that runs through Andreu's work on Ciutat Vella. While most of her photographs document the positive, even celebratory, performances of ethnicity as an affirmation of immigrant relocation to the neighbourhood, these pictures show the other, darker, side of migrant situations. Cleaved, then, to the unmistakeable, if tentative, attempts to reconstruct remembered ethnicity is the facelessness that looms over and threatens migrant experience, the dissolution of identity into invisibility. The photographs rescue the migrants from oblivion, centering them in their obvious subalternity within the policed space of the locality. Equally, the photographic act and the dissemination of the image occur too late for those concerned, imposing upon them a double anonymity. The photographs challenge the Trencant Fronteres exhibition's attempts to reflect images of a harmonious community of cultural difference in Ciutat Vella, whilst also revealing the hidden tensions which underlie migration from the Third World into Europe.

The next sequence of photographs shows examples of daily life in Barcelona for the different members of the immigrant community. In the first one, some men are being trained in construction work, an area that frequently employs immigrants as casual labour (Picture 19). The photograph at once signifies their participation in Catalan society and also their subaltern position within the latter, given the often temporary and unreliable nature of the work. The second picture shows a group of school children from the Ciutat Vella area. Racial diversity (a mix of Asian, African, Spanish, Philippino, etc.) is evident in their faces, yet they form a group that is clustered together (Picture 20). Ethnic differences do not seem to interfere in their integration. However, the inner city look of the building behind the playground speaks again of economic subalternity, which thereby becomes a defining factor of their socio-ethnic identity. In the third picture, a Muslim man, wearing the traditional cap, enters what appears to be a disused shop in a run down street (Picture 21). Over the entrance is a sign in Arabic that reads 'masjid' or mosque. Clearly, a shop interior has been converted for communal use as a mosque. The 'nerve of national identity' (Cesarani and Fulbrook 1996: 60) is put into question by the signs and symbols of Islamic ethnicity inscribed on the streets of Barcelona. Catalan identity must thus be viewed as transnational and multi-dimensional, connected to other cultures and ethnicities through global networks of migration. This point is reinforced by the next picture, as the day of Saint Joan is celebrated in the neighbourhood of Ciutat Vella (Picture 22). Catalan women try out the Moroccan tea and musical instruments set up by Moroccan neighbours in the street festivities to celebrate the day. When considering the overlap of Islamic rituals with expressions of Moroccan identity, the sight of the Catalan woman in shorts, sitting with her legs apart, is at variance with general Moroccan behaviour. Yet, such diversion from the norm is deemed acceptable because of the ambivalent circumstances in which the cultural memory of immigrant communities can find a platform. Overlapping the distinctly Catalan festival are the tastes and sounds of ethnic alterity as remembered cultural expression explores new hybrid ways of enunciation.

Different ethnographic narratives emerge from Andreu's photographs. While her aim is a realistic portrayal of immigrants, her use of black and white is a clear attempt at abstraction, which heightens the elusiveness of ethnicity. Black and white photographs also draw upon an established tradition of photojournalism. In that sense, this allows the photographs to give the impression of 'breaking news' and thus gain impact on the viewer. Nevertheless Andreu's photographs go beyond any merely documentary or 'realist' objectives. They also visualize the traces of scattered identity, in Marcus's terms, which highlight points in the complex and multi-dimensional migratory processes of ethnicity.

While the photographs rely upon a general understanding of Islam and Morocco, they nevertheless reinscribe the latter through the experiences of migration and relocation. Equally, the photographs shed light upon the cultural fluxes of Catalan identity, as Barcelona is revisited through migrant lives. They fragment as much as they unite the immigrant experiences, so that community identity appears as a patchwork that is contextually assembled, reinvented or dismantled. The mediation of space with time, or perhaps, spaces with times, destabilizes fixed notions of cultural memory and ethnic identity reliant upon a single space and a single, linear time.

In his *Words of Light, Theses on the Photography of History* (1997), Eduardo Cadava explores Walter Benjamin's conception of history through the language of photography. His point of departure is provided by the following quote from Benjamin:

The true picture of the past flits by. The past can be seized only as an image which flashes up at the instant when it can be recognised and is never seen again. . . (Cadava 1997: 3).

Cadava states that the flashes and images of history as perceived by Benjamin therefore provide a link with photography that is present throughout the latter's writings. The photograph is the space of multiple relations between, for example, the image, reproduction, loss, memory, forgetting, and mimesis. Cadava likens this uncertain space to Benjamin's conception of history not merely as the movement of thoughts, but also as their arrest. The photograph, like history, becomes a caesura, a temporal fragment that projects dialectical constellations of past and future, as 'time becomes and disappears' (1998: 61) in the present. In his *Illuminations* (1968), Benjamin states in this context:

To articulate the past historically does not mean to recognize it 'as it really was'. It means to seize a memory as it flashes up at a moment of danger (1968: 225).

History, like the photograph, is, therefore, that flash of the moment before memory is forgotten.[20] Photographs therefore are the rescued traces of memory of a history, which defies direct representation.

Benjamin's imagination of history through the specular offers a convergence of new technological media and historical understanding in the time of modernity. The global movements of postmodernity further complicate the problem of history. For migrants, be they the Moroccans in the photographs or the larger populations of the urban centres, abrupt spatial and temporal shifts occur in the whirlwinds of a media-oriented late capitalism. The immigrants' cultural memory becomes all the more fragmented when caught up in the competing and synchronic signs and discourses of Spanish regional and national identities. As Spain grapples with the problems and issues attendant to its own cultural and historical memory/amnesia, what becomes apparent is the emergence of competing and multiple histories in the face of cross-winds of splintered temporality. Diverse cultural texts, therefore, struggle to respond to the question of community identity in the face of disjuncture, be they through literature, the visual arts, music, etc. Nevertheless such texts should be considered within the contexts in which they appear. They are also contributions to wider and fluctuating contexts of cultural multiplicities, characteristic of postmodernity. What emerges are often new, hybrid dimensions of cultural identities[21] constructed out of specific spatial and temporal axes. Cultural recognition, itself reliant upon a shared cultural memory, can thus at best only be partial and temporally bound, perceived from diverse perspectives and scattered, in the same way as plural narratives attempt to construct history in many ways, places, and times. Cultural memory and ethnicity can at best be caught in traces and held fleetingly. Like the handful of snapshots here, they can be shuffled and displaced, projected or not according to context and circumstance. Multi-cultural incentives such as the Trencant Fronteres exhibition, therefore, are challenged in their anti-racist intentions by the slippage of the very discourses upon which their understandings of alterity rely.[22] In this context, the exhibition's attempt to acknowledge the ethnic 'other' must also be read in the light of continual and multi-directional challenges to the arrest of identity. The act of cultural translation implicit in the exhibition equally attempts to construct borders in the face of this slippage or movement. Despite the exhibition's own photographic attempts to capture ethnicity, the snapshots of cultural memory are relocated and resignified in the present. Ethnic identity and shared cultural memory therefore emerge, not as unified, linear, or located, but as hybrid, incomplete, and migrant.

The concept of community identity must thus be re-imagined as no longer fixed to specific locations, such as Morocco or Spain or even as tied to axial routes, such as Morocco–Spain; instead it can best be understood as scattered nodal points in the cross-overs of diverse migratory flows traversing given spaces. Viewed in terms of mobility, currents and contradictory undercurrents, community identity defies its prior traditional or 'organic' and enclosed spatial premises by exposing the porosity of borders, whether regional or national. Marcus's attempt to re-position ethnography in the late twentieth century is an acknowledgement of late modernity's rupturing impact on cohesive, linear narratives of identity. Community identity becomes simultaneously de-localized and transnational. The photograph, as a temporally ambivalent medium, is, as Edwards states, a space of fluid encounters and fleeting projections of identity. Attempts to construct and articulate the immigrant community's identity should therefore be read as interrogations, tentative in their ambiguities. Equally, ambivalence surrounds possible readings or interpretations of the photograph — at once a space of oblivion and of refiguring — which, as Benjamin points out, puts forth a constellation of narratives from the image. Recognition in the face of dis/re-location, in the double sense of the process by which a community recognizes itself and the cultural platform through which it seeks recognition from others, is reliant upon the 'flashes of the moment' afforded by such material traces.

1. This chapter is an extended version of an earlier article published in the *Journal of Spanish Cultural* entitled 'Albums of No Return: Ethnicity, Displacement and Recognition in Photographs of North African Immigrants in Contemporary Spain' (Nair 2000).
2. The sources for information on the origins of the majority of Moroccans in Spain are interviews with Mohamed Derdabi, head of ATIME, Barcelona and with Juanjo of the NGO, CEAIM, Jeréz de la Frontera.
3. Information about Andreu's professional history and political beliefs was given to me by her in the course of our interview. Some of it is also written in the brochure introducing the Trencant Fronteres exhibition.
4. In this context, it is worth considering Richard Jenkins' definition of the relation with otherness, particularly in the context of ethnicity: 'Our "cultural stuff" will ... reflect our interaction with Other(s): how those Others categorize and behave towards us, how they label us. Nor is this all. Our categorizations of Others, and the routines that we evolve for dealing with them, are also intrinsic to our cultural repertoire. Social interaction at and across the boundary will necessarily involve categorizations: of "us" by "them", and of "them" by "us".' (1997: 168). Furthermore, Jenkins stresses in his conclusion the following call for rethinking ethnicity: 'That there are limits to the plasticity of ethnicity, as well as to its fixity and solidity, is the founding premise for the development of an understanding of ethnicity which permits us to appreciate that although it is imagined it is not imaginary' (1997: 169).
5. Indeed, it is possible to state that Morocco remains possibly the most culturally diverse among Islamic nations, with important Jewish communities dating back to the fifteenth century as well as numerous French communities from colonial times. While Arabic is the official language, Berber is spoken by many of those from the Rif region and French is commonly used in the cities. In parts of the north of the country, such as Larache, Tetuan, etc., Spanish is still in use.
6. See Homi Bhabha's critique of multi-culturalism in his essay 'Culture's In-between' (96: 53–60), where he explores the insufficiencies of such a social approach which depends on viewing cultural identity as fixed.
7. Interview with Andreu on 19 January 1999.
8. This is a curious, and very contemporary, reversal of the 'traditional' colonial assumptions of ethnography.
9. Interestingly, Andreu mentioned that she had tried to arouse interest in her photographs from the Anthropology department of the Universidad Autónoma in Barcelona, but they had not yet responded. She is happy for her work to be circulated in academic circles.
10. I contacted Mr Derdabi of ATIME to ask whether there were any Moroccan photographers in Barcelona or Madrid. He then put me in touch with Andreu.
11. ATIME estimate that seventy-five per cent of the Moroccan population in Spain is male.
12. Marcus mentions cultural studies as just on the other side of the anthropological boundary (1998: 4).
13. Copies of all the photographs referred to are to be found at the end of this chapter.
14. Despite the prevalence of Spanish rural rituals, such as the 'matanza', Andreu stressed that there was little understanding of the importance of the Eid el Kebir sacrifice among non-Muslims living in the Ciutat Vella area. Local mosques therefore offer a forum where the arrangements for observing this day can be organized with minimum disturbance to the neighbourhood.
15. Critiques in the public media around the ethical dimensions of bullfighting have pointed to the low awareness of this issue in Spain in general, with a subsequent continuation of negative behaviour patterns towards animals.
16. The questions which arise around the political repercussions ensuing from the practice of Islam in Europe form an important branch of migration studies. As Buisef states in his *Memoria* on Xenofilia, Spain's membership of the Schengen states affords it a strong

alliance through a sense of shared space. Other Schengen states, such as Germany and France, can provide Spain with clear examples of how to 'deal with' Islam in their midst, through much longer experience of immigration from Islamic countries, such as Turkey. The empowerment which results from this alliance of European nations tightens the control of 'others' who attempt to enter such space.

17. Sherman and Planell are just two examples, but both reiterate the importance of video in constructing and reflecting back upon projections of identity. A relevant exploration of video usage amongst migrants is in Olwig and Frostrup (1997: 86–100).

18. See Blommaert and Verschueren (1998: 94–98).

19. Dr Laïla Ibnlfassi, a former colleague from London Guildhall University, provided me with information on the uneven use of the veil in Morocco today. Previously worn by urban women as a dress of decency, the veil has now largely given way to the use of the headscarf. Conversely, rural women have increasingly adopted the use of the veil in a belated appropriation of urban fashion.

20. Caygill (1998) also presents Benjamin as a visual thinker and relates this to Kant's concept of experience.

21. See Chambers (1994: 9–48).

22. See Bennett (1998) for various perspectives on social tolerance and multiculturalism.

PICTURE 1.

PICTURE 2.

PICTURE 3.

PICTURE 4.

PICTURE 6.

PICTURE 7.

PICTURE 8.

Picture 9.

PICTURE 10.

PICTURE 11.

PICTURE 12.

PICTURE 13.

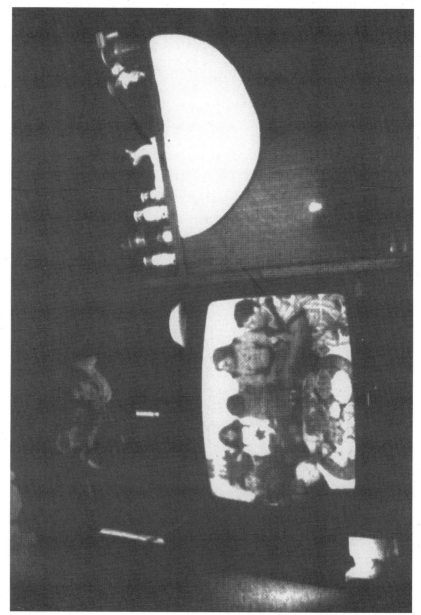

PICTURE 14.

PICTURE 15.

PICTURE 16.

PICTURE 17.

PICTURE 18.

PICTURE 19.

PICTURE 20.

PICTURE 21.

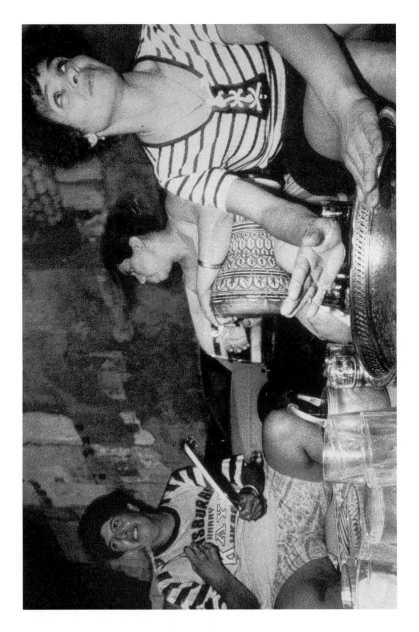

PICTURE 22.

AFTERWORD

COMMUNITY AND REFLEXIVITY

As the preceding chapters show, this study of community must remain in the interrogative. Attempts to draw clear-cut conclusions on community would result in a discursive stasis, whereby the larger context of modernity and postmodernity — as late modernity or an intensification of the tensions between discourse and practice that characterise modernity — would be lost. The notion of community in postmodern Spain can be seen to be foregrounded in political and cultural contexts over emphases on nation or state. Nevertheless, community is itself a problematic concept: necessarily fluid in order to survive in current contexts, yet loaded with the fixed structures attached to tradition, it is at once shifting, flexible, and evocative of security. It also alters notions of citizenship, no longer bound by the rigid categories of modern discourse, but following diverse socio-cultural courses. Ironically, it is community's very 'embodied', grass-roots connotations and smallness of scale in the imaginary which give it the mobility and flexibility to act as an efficient, if alterable, vehicle for communal identities in the midst of present-day ambivalence and displacements. Indeed, in terms of contemporary Spain, the complexities and unevenness of this larger cultural context are of paramount importance with regard to the concepts, narratives, and practices of community identities.

Whilst wishing to remain open-ended, this analysis will seek, nevertheless, to probe established ways of apprehending both the concept of community and the disciplinary parameters for the study of this concept. The question of boundaries, acting simultaneously as fixed markers of difference and as shifting points of contact, arises in both contexts, as does the question of how to 'know' without losing sight of the contingency of all knowledge. I shall, therefore, aim to end this book by extending my problematization of community as 'field' to a questioning of the construction of distinct disciplinary zones. In particular, as the interdisciplinary methodology and theoretical framework used for the analyses of community here show, I shall problematize boundaries and overlaps in the humanities, most especially between ethnography and cultural studies. By drawing a parallel between community identities and disciplinary arenas, I hope to raise questions which are as pertinent to widely held concepts of community in contemporary contexts as they are to the construction of academic discourses and areas of study on this most commonplace of terms.

This problematization of community can thus be viewed overall in terms of the shifting relation between Self and Other. The postmodern or late modern Self, aware of contextual instabilities, pluralities, and displacements, cannot distinguish itself so readily from an equally ambivalent Other. Indeed, the bourgeois notion of the modern individual as 'self-made' denoted a social project which sought to construct individuals via social discourses. This awareness of the pluralities of the Self as well as of the latter's shifting boundaries has lately become both intensified and complicated. As borders blur and choices proliferate in late modernity, difference is no longer relegated to relation with otherness but becomes a defining aspect of an increasingly plural and diverse Self, at both individual (as made evident in Atxaga's depiction of *El hombre solo*'s central character, Carlos) and communal levels.

REFLEXIVITY IN THE CONTEXT OF COMMUNITY

In abundance, on the move and dissociated from land and place, community identities are thus denoted, not so much by the embodiment usually connected with community, but by reflexivity and active or conscious choice. As Delanty states

Reflexivity has become more important today as a result of the multiple bonds of belonging, roles and identities. Communication is the means of dealing with situations which are multiple and discontinuous. [. . .] Learning to live with cultural uncertainty defines the reflexive situation of the self. This is more than a question of the cultural choices of the life-world but is also the central dimension in the encounter of Self and Other. (2000: 161)

Delanty goes on to emphasize the centrality of communication to this view of reflexivity, stating that 'contemporary societies are increasingly being integrated through communication, rather than by ideology, dominant value systems, elites or institutions' (2000: 161). Indeed, it could be argued that increased trans-cultural and transnational communication have successfully undermined the apparently essentialist discourses and narratives of modernist ideologies and institutions, such as the nation-state. So also, as Atxaga states in his introduction to *Obabakoak* (1989), such communication — intrinsically linked without doubt to rapid advances in the technology of communications, as witnessed by the connectivity made possible by the world wide web — alters the specificity of place, layering indeterminacy onto previously distinct communities. The persist-ence in Spain of tradition and an orality-based sociality well into the late twentieth century, coinciding with a period of deliberate engagement with late modernity, throws up a chequered cultural landscape of narrative fragments whereby community proliferates via deterritorialization. The curious juxtaposi-tion, to varying degrees, of tradition and late modernity paves the way for a technology-based communication that, nevertheless, bears certain traits to oral communication. In particular, new postmodernist forms of communication are contextual and immediate, not formally structured and bound within patterns of discourse. They differ, however, in that the very notion of accessibility that is synonymous with such communication provides an optionality and fluidity not found before.

Indeed, as early as 1982, Walter Ong had highlighted the shifts in orality within a larger context of advanced technology. In his seminal work *Orality and Literacy*, Ong distinguishes between what he terms as 'primary' and 'secondary' orality. Primary orality consists of the traits of cultures which have not yet experienced the predominance of literacy. Secondary orality, on the other hand, denotes the kind of orality experienced today in the electronic age and in the midst of literacy. While both forms of orality share several features, in particular the power of the spoken word to bind community through emotive audience response, they nevertheless also display major differences related to interdependency of the oral with the written and with mass dissemination through complex and advanced communications systems. In addition there is a marked difference with regard to the degree of self-consciousness or reflexivity experienced by literates. Ong analyses primary orality at length. The spoken word in such settings becomes an event or an act, so that thought, once enunciated, is directed outwards into the communal forum. Furthermore, for cultures which are primarily oral, the transience of the utterance allows for a flexibility and reinvention that is contingent upon contextual factors. Memory thus functions differently from literate societies, where great store is laid by fidelity to the inscribed text. Oral memory, according to Ong, functions more as a patchwork by connecting remembered formulae with the vocalist's on-going situation and audience. Thus, Ong states that:

The oral song (or other narrative) is the result of interaction between the singer, the present audience and the singer's memories of songs sung. In working with this interaction, the bard is original and creative on rather different grounds from those of the writer (1982: 146).

Oral memorization, therefore, conforms to social contingencies and circumstances. In this sense, primary orality offers itself up to the demands of the 'market' through improvised interaction. Unlike a written or recorded 'text', the oral performance cannot be revisited or revised. Indeed, it is this temporal adaptability of the oral utterance, whereby the word or song is suspended in the present, that gives it a sense of 'originality'/'essentiality' or, to use a word more favoured purists, 'authenticity'. This view of orality as a strategy of survival emphasizes the fluidity and cultural mobility of such cultures. Equally, rather than level orality with unified space as earlier anthropologists have done, oral transmission, viewed from this angle, appears on the move, reinvented and engaged with the present.

To be noted here is clearly the contrast that arises from Ong's study of oral cultures and conventional notions of tradition as the stable, unified cultural precursor to modernity. Indeed, Ong ascribes cultural fixity to literacy, assigning fluidity and improvisation to orality. These very features are foregrounded, according to Ong, in more recent contexts whereby literacy combines with easy access to technology. Unlike primary orality, secondary orality is lived in terms of self-consciousness, itself the result of engagement with literacy and communication. The communal identity fostered by secondary orality far exceeds the local, tangible audience and extends, through technological communication and, by implication, through international commerce, to distant and diverse points of the global village or, more to the point, global villages. This kind of orality, unlike its predecessor, leads to a reflexive construction of delocalized communities, a defiance of spatial enclosures and the fixedness of the printed word. As Ong says, 'secondary orality promotes spontaneity because through analytic reflection, we have decided that spontaneity is a good thing' (1982: 137). Central to secondary orality, therefore, is the determination to partake reflexively and through technological communication in the construction of community identities.

COMMUNITY, INSECURITY, AND RISK

In his recent work *Community: Seeking Safety in an Insecure World* (2001), Zygmunt Bauman underlines the enduring emotive appeal of community in current cultural contexts. In particular, he stresses the security imagined in terms of this notion, whereby the isolation and displacements of modernity can be mitigated. As Bauman points out, the myth of community that associates it with paradise lost tinges it with both nostalgia and hope. The modernist quest for community, in all its imagined integrity, is, however, without end:

We miss community because we miss security, a quality crucial to a happy life, but one which the world we inhabit is ever less able to offer and ever more reluctant to promise. But community remains stubbornly missing, eludes our grasp or keeps falling apart, because the way in which this world prompts us to go about fulfilling our dreams of a secure life does not bring us closer to their fulfilment; instead of being mitigated, our insecurity grows as we go, and so we go on dreaming, trying and failing. (2001: 144)

What Bauman indicates is that the concept of community is itself contingent upon the lived experience of insecurity — in other words, the myth of community hangs on its own precariousness.

In this sense, community needs to be read not merely in terms of its conventional connotations of security, as Bauman initially suggests, but also in terms of its alterity. Any approximation to the notion of community must thus take into account the unarticulated — and perhaps unimagined — absences, silences, and failures of community. Most importantly, community needs to be read in terms of risks or insecurities. Indeed, this point is forcefully brought out in the considerable body of work produced individually and separately by Giddens, Beck, and Lash in their development of the notion of risk in late modernity. By centralizing technology within a globalizing economy, Beck, for example, develops the twin concepts of risk and reflexivity, both aspects of what he calls a 'new modernity' (1992: 21). In his preface to *Risk Society: Towards a New Modernity*, Beck states that 'the gain in power from techno-economic "progress" is being increasingly overshadowed by the production of risks' (1992: 13). For Beck, these risks bring about a reflexivity in the experience of late modernity, whereby a new understanding is sought for the ruptures and risks of modernity. Nor should reflexivity be thought of as a means of avoiding risk. Harking back to Berman's description of modernity as 'maelstrom' (1983), risk becomes a defining feature of life in modernity, and the reflexivity which characterizes late modernity becomes the means of engaging with such risk. Such reflexivity opens up the possibility of grasping the concept of community against its conventional grain.

Community as 'double-framed' and contradictory, as the construct of reflexive discourses and capitalist-oriented agencies, is seen to be particularly resurgent in contemporary Spain.[1] Here its multi-dimensionality in terms of locality, wholeness, emotive closeness, open-endedness, and smallness all combine to foreground its appeal as a means of leaving behind the Francoist state apparatus which sought to unify nation and identity. However, given Spain's full participation in the heady cultural exchanges of globalized postmodernity, community also allows for distinct ways of participating in transnational and transcultural forums. Rather than providing security, community becomes an agent of risk and, as such, open to possibilities. The rushed economic alignment with Europe in the post-Francoist period, the hurtling race to be accepted as part of the First World and the dizzying experimentations with culture and identity of the 1980s and early 1990s witnessed a resurgence of community, not in terms of its traditional connotations, but as representative of a new cultural, economic, and political turn. The concept of reflexivity in terms of community, particularly relevant in this context of new Spanish political and cultural identities, opens up a third space for the latter, separate from its mythical essentialisms and its lived scatterings. By accelerating the processes of modernization, Spain's entry into late modernity marked the definitive rupture with certainties of place and time. Cutting across the unified abstractions of nation and society, the necessarily diasporic condition of modernity's migrants constructs community in the wake of displacement. No longer a *given*, no longer necessarily synonymous in memory or experience with security, no longer wedded to land, community is best perceived in terms of its shifting boundaries. There emerges then a new reflexivity, giving rise to community in the awareness of the collapse of myths of certainty. In this context, Lash describes reflexive communities in the following way:

These communities are reflexive in that: first, one is not born or 'thrown' but 'throws oneself' into them; second, they may be widely stretched over 'abstract' space, and also perhaps time; third, they consciously pose themselves the problem of their own creation, and constant reinvention far more than do traditional communities; fourth, their 'tools' and products tend to be not material ones but abstract and cultural. (Beck, Giddens and Lash 1994: 161).

This reflexiveness in community seeks out the encounter with risk as a means of survival and navigation through new, uncharted courses. Otherness, as Delanty has said, becomes a way for seeing the Self.

Equally pertinent in terms of reflexivity is an awareness of the question of empowerment and hegemony arising from the cultural patterns of such communities, tendencies which are nevertheless compatible with notions of contingency. Useful here is Bourdieu's development of the inter-related notions of habitus, field and practice (outlined in the fourth chapter). For Bourdieu, habitus denotes the on-going activities of mediated, flexible categories or schemata. It allows for a reflexivity which can uncover the unthought — and thereby, as yet unmediated — categories which accompany social and cultural practices. The heightened reflexivity of community therefore translates into a heightened contingency, whereby alterations to practice arise according to context. In his theoretical attempts to overcome subjective–objective dichotomies, the unthought categories of Bourdieu's mediated schemata are not contrary to conscious practice, but are there to be interpreted through reflexivity (Bourdieu, 1984). Fields, peopled not so much by agents, discourses, or ideologies, as by unthought bodily practices, open up contingent spaces in the struggle for hegemony. Far from undermining determined fields, then, reflexivity becomes a hegemonic tool in that it allows for an awareness of power and direction. The notion of reflexivity, clearly a key aspect of Bourdieu's academic contribution to the social sciences, thus translates in the context of community into a means of empowering the latter precisely through awareness of its own insecurities.

DIALOGIC COMMUNITY AND INTERDISCIPLINARITY

Much of Bourdieu's work has focused on the role and implications of the academic in the construction of particular disciplines. Indeed, this forms the basis for his theoretical focus on subjectivist–objectivist binaries and, consequently, for the formulation of his key contributions to the social sciences. As Jeremy Lane's recent book on Bourdieu (2000) demonstrates, the latter's work draws interesting connections between academia, the mass media, and the culture industries, all closely implicated in the production of diverse discourses of identity within the context of late modernity and advanced capitalism. Central to these connections is the notion of reflexivity, made clear in his numerous analyses of the role of the social scientist vis-à-vis the object of his or her analyses. As Bourdieu emphasizes in *An Invitation to Reflexive Sociology* (1992), he sees no opposition between the academic autonomy of the social scientist and the society or culture of study. Rather, academic discourses are themselves weighted with unthought, unconscious, and unmediated categories which beg scrutiny in their very construction. Writing on Bourdieu's idea of reflexivity, Wacquant states that:

First, its primary target is not the individual analyst but the *social and intellectual unconscious* embedded in analytic tools and operations; second, it must be a *collective enterprise* rather than the burden of the lone academic; and, third, it seeks not to assault but to *buttress the epistemological security of sociology*. (Bourdieu and Wacquant 1996: 36)

As Lane points out (2000: 10), Bourdieu writes within the French context, but his work is useful in interpreting other national and historical contexts. In particular, the notion of reflexivity, closely linked to the socio-cultural effects and experiences of late modernity, can shed light on the post-colonial and post-structuralist emergence of diverse disciplinary discourses.

As key features of late modernity, both risk and reflexivity mark the numerous intersections of discourses, narrative traces, and disciplinary routes. The ambivalence of community outlined here must surely lead to questioning the specificity of academic disciplines. The problematization of community as 'field' underlines the porosity of boundaries in contemporary cultural contexts and can be extended to a scrutiny of the humanities. From this ensues the risk of the undermining of autonomy, the loss of the distinction, and specific nature of particular fields, whether these be communities or, at a different level, academic disciplines. Indeed, an implicit questioning of any such specificity must arise from the interdisciplinary analytic approach that I have employed. Equally, however, this thesis is an effort to contribute to the burgeoning field of Spanish cultural studies. It is also an attempt to explore the overlap between post-colonial reworkings of ethnography and cultural studies. To what extent can a discipline, such as cultural studies, mark out its terrain precisely when it is traversed by numerous other disciplinary, economic, political, and cultural discourses? By what means can an 'academic discipline' be defined when it is so intricately implicated in the shifting world around it? As sustaining academic specificity becomes a risky venture, the notion of reflexivity is once again of relevance. Clearly, risk must work with reflexivity: it is precisely by taking the risk of being swept over by other discourses that specific discourses can then be reflexively constructed.

Giddens (a key analyst of late modernity cited in the introduction) argues that social theory is a key aspect of a fluid social world, whereby reflexivity, a defining property of late modernity, allows for a double bind between theory and practice, rendering the two mutually interdependent. Like Bourdieu, Giddens stresses the intersections of structure and action as the focal point for studying society, and, by extension, culture. As Tucker states in his book on Giddens,

Social theory heavily influences the very conceptual categories that people use to understand their lives, as many of social theory's concepts become part of a society's self-comprehension. (1998: 3)

This mutual reliance is explained by Giddens as follows:

social practices are constantly examined and reformed in the light of incoming information about those very practices, thus constitutively altering their character (1990: 38)

What emerges is an intersection between the everyday and the expert, which in fact allows for the emergence of reflexive discourses and practices. The current reworkings of ethnography that have informed much of this book are key examples of such disciplinary refigurings that have taken place in the light of poststructuralism. Rather than threaten academic autonomy with dissolution, it is this very reflexivity which also enables the production of specific disciplinary discourses, that remain nevertheless contingent and open to revision. Viewed in this light, both sociology and cultural studies are seen to be dialogic, their discourses poised on the contextual and open to reinvention. Gidden's theorization of the reflexive mutuality of academic discourse and cultural practice is particularly relevant in the case of contemporary Spain. Postmodernity in Spain is shot through with resonances of the popular, the silenced, and the local, joining voices with the global, the transcultural, and the transnational. To analyse Spanish culture is to engage across boundaries with a range of interdisciplinary issues. In this sense, the study of community in current Spanish contexts forces a dialogic encounter across disciplines and a reflexivity of such disciplinary mobility and inter-reliance to the same extent as it reveals community identities themselves to be both contingent and migrant.

1. Writing on 'The Postmodern Urban Condition', Michael Dear and Steven Flusty come up with an interesting new term: '*Commudities* are commodified communities created expressly to satisfy (and profit from) the habitat preferences of the well-recompensed cybergeoisie' (Featherstone and Lash 1999: 78).

BIBLIOGRAPHY

PRIMARY TEXTS

Andreu, N. 1998. Trencant Fronteres photographs.
Atxaga, B., 1989. *Obabakoak* (Barcelona: Ediciones Bolsillo)
——, 1995. *El hombre solo* (Barcelona: Ediciones Bolsillo)
2 Gritos de libertad, compact disc of flamenco sung by Agujetas, A. and Serrano, J., produced by J. Delgado (Granada: March 1997)
Gutiérrez, C. 1995. *Alma gitana,* video
Llamazares, J. 1985. *Luna de lobos* (Barcelona: Seix Barral)
——, 1985. *La lentitud de los bueyes/Memoria de la nieve* (Madrid: Ediciones Hiperión)
——, 1988. *La lluvia amarilla* (Barcelona: Seix Barral)
——, 1990. *El río del olvido* (Barcelona: Seix Barral)
——, 1994. *Escenas de cine mudo* (Barcelona: Seix Barral)

INTERVIEWS

Interview/conversation with Atxaga, B., London: 15 April 1999
Interview with Gay y Blasco, P., Cambridge, October 1997
Telephone interview with Gutiérrez, C., London–Madrid, January 1998
Interview/conversation with Llamazares, J., London, 25 October 1997
Interview in Córdoba prison with Agujetas, A., Serrano, J., Justo and Manuel together with Arrebola, J. and Estévez, A., 21 June 1998
Interview with Arrebola, J. and Estévez, A., Córdoba, 21 June 1998
Interview with Núñez, A., Jerez de la Frontera, 19 June 1998
Interview with Juanjo, CEAIM: Jerez de la Frontera, June 1998
Interview with Andreu, N., Barcelona, 19 January 1999
Interview with Buisef, D., Xenofilia, Barcelona, 20 January 1999
Interview with Derdabi, M., ATIME, Barcelona, 21 January 1999

SECONDARY TEXTS

Aart Scholte, J. 2000. *Globalization: A Critical Introduction* (London: Macmillan)
Abel, D. 1999. *Agujetas Cantaor,* video
Adorno, T. 1973. *Negative Dialectics,* trans. by E. B. Ashton (London: Routledge)
——, 1984. *Aesthetic Theory* (London: Routledge and Keegan Paul)
Appadurai, A. 1988. 'Putting Hierarchy in its Place', *Cultural Anthropology,* 3: 36–49
——, 1990. 'Disjuncture and Difference in the Global Cultural Economy', in M. Featherstone (ed.). 1990. *Global Culture: Nationalism, Globalization and Modernity* (London: Thousand Oaks; New Delhi: Sage)
Attali, Jacques. 1985. *Noise: The Political Economy of Music* (Minnesota: University of Minnesota Press)
Baah, R. N. 1996. 'When the Dead Reappear to Comfort the Living: Julio Llamazares and the Poetry of Silence, Loneliness and Death', *Selecta: Journal of the Pacific Northwest Council on Foreign Languages,* 17: 51–54
——, 1997. 'Julio Llamazares' Unstoppable Journey to the Past: A Comparative Study of *La lluvia amarilla* and *Escenas de cine mudo*', *Selecta: Journal of the Pacific Northwest Council on Foreign Languages* 18: 71–82
Bauman, Z. 2000. *Community: Seeking Safety in an Insecure World* (London: Polity Press)
Beck, U. 1992. *Risk Society: Towards a New Modernity* (London: Thousand Oaks; New Delhi: Sage)

——, 1994. A. Giddens and S. Lash, *Reflexive Modernization* (Cambridge: Polity Press)
Benjamin, W. 1968. *Illuminations*, ed. by H. Arendt (New York: Schoken Books)
——, 1985. *One Way Street and Other Writings* (London: Verso)
Bennet, D. 1998. *Multicultural States: Rethinking Difference and Identity* (London: Routledge)
Berman, M. 1982. *All That Is Solid Melts Into Air* (London: Verso)
Bertens, H. 1994. *The Idea of the Postmodern* (London: Routledge)
Best, S. and Kellner D. 1991. *Postmodern Theory* (London: Macmillan)
Bhabha, H. 1994. *The Location of Culture* (London: Routledge)
——, 1996. 'Culture's In-Between', in S. Hall and P. du Gay (eds), *Questions of Cultural Identity* (London: Sage), pp. 53–60
Blommaert, J. and Verschueren, J. 1998. *Debating Diversity* (London: Routledge)
Bollaín, I. 1999. *Flores de otro mundo*, video
Bourdieu, P. 1977. *Outline of a Theory of Practice* (Cambridge: Cambridge University Press)
——, 1984. *Distinction: a Social Critique of the Judgement of Taste* (Cambridge: Harvard University Press)
——, 1990. *The Logic of Practice* (Cambridge: Polity Press)
——, 1998. *Practical Reason* (Oxford: Polity Press)
——, and Wacquant, L. 1992. *An Invitation to Reflexive Sociology* (Cambridge: Polity Press)
Brinker-Gabler, G. 1997. 'Exile, Immigrant, Re/Unified', in G. Brinker-Gabler and S. Smith (eds), *Writing New Identities: Gender, Nation and Immigration in Contemporary Europe* (Minneapolis: University of Minnesota Press), pp. 264–92
Brooksbank Jones, A., 1997. *Women in Contemporary Spain* (Manchester: Manchester University Press)
Bottomore, T. (ed.). 1991. *A Dictionary of Marxist Thought* (Oxford: Blackwell)
Buisef, D. 1996. Memoria, Introduction to Xenofilia Project (loose type written sheet)
Bullón de Mendoza, A and Diego, A. 2000. *Historias orales de la Guerra Civil* (Barcelona: Ariel)
Cadava, E. 1997. *Words of Light: Theses on the Photography of History* (New Jersey: Princeton University Press)
Calvo Buezas, T. 1998. 'From Militant Racism to Egalitarian Solidarity: Conflicting Attitudes to Gypsies in Spain', *Journal of Mediterranean Studies*, 7: 13–27
Canclini, N. G. 1995. *Hybrid Cultures*, trans. C. Chiappari and S. L. López, (Minneapolis: University of Minnesota Press)
Carlón, J. (ed.). 1996. *Sobre la nieve, la poesía y la prosa de Julio Llamazares* (Madrid: Espasa Calpe)
Castles, S. and Davidson, A. 2000. *Citizenship and Migration: Globalization and the Politics of Belonging* (London: Macmillan)
Catalá Domenech, J. 1998. Exhibition Review of Trencant Fronteres (loose typewritten sheet)
Caygill, H. 1998. *Walter Benjamin: The Colour of Experience* (London: Routledge)
Cesarani, D. and Fulbrook M. (eds). 1996. *Citizenship, Nationality and Migration in Europe* (London: Routledge)
Chambers, I. 1994. *Migrancy, Culture, Identity* (London: Routledge)
Clifford, J. 1997. *Routes* (Cambridge: Harvard University Press)
Cohen, A. 1985. *The Symbolic Construction of Community* (London: Tavistock)
Colectivo IOÉ. 1995. *Presencia del sur: marroquíes en Cataluña* (Madrid: Editorial Fundamentos)
Conklin, J. E. 1995. *Criminology* (Boston: Allyn and Bacon)
Delanty, G. 2000. *Modernity and Postmodernity* (London: Thousand Oaks; New Delhi: Sage)
Edwards, E. 1997. 'Beyond the Boundary: a consideration of the expressive in photography and anthropology', in M. Banks and H. Morphy (eds), *Visual Anthropology* (New Haven: Yale University Press), pp. 53–80
Elorza, A. 1995. 'Some Perspectives on the Nation-State and Autonomies in Spain', in H. Graham and J. Labanyi (eds), *Spanish Cultural Studies: The Struggle for Modernity* (Oxford: Oxford University Press), pp. 332–35
Emerson, R. 1960. *From Empire to Nation: the Rise to Self-Assertion of Asian African Peoples* (Cambridge, MA: Harvard University Press)
Etzioni, A. 1995. *The Spirit of Community* (London: Fontana)
——, 1999. *Civic Repentance* (Maryland: Rowman and Littlefield, Inc.)
Farrell Krell, D. 1992. *Heidegger and Life-Philosophy* (Bloomington: Indiana University Press)
Featherstone, M. and Lash, S. (eds). 1999. *Spaces of Culture: City, Nation, World* (London: Thousand Oaks; New Delhi: Sage)
Fraser, R. 1979. *Blood of Spain* (London: Pimlico)

Gabilondo, J. 1998. 'Terrorism as Memory: The Historical Novel and Masculine Masochism in Contemporary Basque Literature', *Arizona Journal of Hispanic Cultural Studies*, 2: 113–46
Gay y Blasco, P. 1995. 'Sex, Gender and the *Gitanos* of Madrid' (unpublished doctoral thesis, University of Cambridge)
——, 1999. *Gitanos of Madrid* (Oxford: Berg)
Giddens, A. 1990. *The Consequences of Modernity* (Cambridge: Polity Press)
——, 1991. *Modernity and Self-Identity: Self and Society in the Late Modern Age* (Cambridge: Polity Press)
Graham, H. and Labanyi, J. (eds). 1995. *Spanish Cultural Studies: The Struggle for Modernity* (Oxford: Oxford University Press)
Graham, H. and Sanchez, A. 1995. 'The Politics of 1992', in H. Graham and J. Labanyi (eds), *Spanish Cultural Studies: The Struggle for Modernity* (Oxford: Oxford University Press), pp. 406–18
Grenier, L. and Guibalt, J. 1990. 'Authority Revisited: The "Other" in Anthropology and Popular Music Studies', *Ethnomusicology*, 34: 381–97
Hamilton, C. 2000. 'Re-membering the Basque nationalist family: daughters, fathers and the reproduction of the radical nationalist community', *Journal of Spanish Cultural Studies*, 1: 153–72
Hancock, I., S. Dowd, and R. Djuric, 1998. *The Roads of the Roma* (Hatfield: University of Hertfordshire Press)
Harvey, P. 1996. *Hybrids of Modernity* (London: Routledge)
Haywood, P. 1995. *Spain: Government and Politics* (London: Macmillan)
Herpel, S. 1997. 'Entre la memoria y la historia: la narrativa de Julio Llamazares', in P. Collard, I. Jongbloet, and M. E. Ocampo Vilas (eds), *La memoria histórica en las letras hispánicas contempráneas* (Geneva: Droz)
Herzberger, D. 1995. *Fiction and Historiography in Postwar Spain* (Durham and London: Duke University Press)
Homer, S. 1998. *Frederic Jameson: Marxism, Hermeneutics, Postmodernism* (Cambridge: Polity Press)
Izurieta, I. 1994. 'Orality and the Production of Basque Texts', *Torre de Papel*, 73–80
Jameson, F. 1981. *The Political Unconscious* (London: Methuen)
——, 1990. *Late Marxism* (London: Verso)
——, 1991. *Postmodernism, or, the Cultural Logic of Late Capitalism* (London: Verso)
Jarvis, S. 1998. *Adorno: A Critical Introduction* (Cambridge: Polity Press)
Jenkins, R. 1997. *Re-thinking Ethnicity* (London: Sage)
Jordan, B. and Morgan-Tamosunas, R. 2000. *Contemporary Spanish Cultural Studies* (London: Arnold)
Juaristi, J. 2000. *El bucle melancólico* (Madrid: Espasa Calpe)
Kaminski, B. 1991. *The Collapse of State Socialism* (Princeton: Princeton University Press)
Kearney, R. (ed.). 1996. *Paul Ricoeur The Hermeneutics of Action* (London: Sage)
Kenna, C. R. 1997. 'Memoria y tiempo en la narrativa de Julio Llamazares' (unpublished doctoral dissertation, University of Stanford)
Kinder, M. 1997. *Refiguring Spain: Cinema, Media, Representation* (London and Durham: Duke University Press)
Kropotkin, P. 1972. *The Conquest of Bread*, ed. by P. Avrich (New York: New York University Press)
Labanyi, J. 2000. *Postmodernism and the Problem of Cultural Identity* (Oxford: Oxford University Press)
Laclau, E. and Mouffe, C. 1985. *Hegemony and Socialist Strategy* (London: Verso)
Lane, J. F. 2000. *Pierre Bourdieu: A Critical Introduction* (London: Pluto Press)
Leblon, B. 1995. *Gypsies and Flamenco* (Hatfeld: University of Hertfordshire Press)
Lechner, F. and Boli, J. (eds). 2000. *The Globalization Reader* (Oxford: Blackwell)
Llamazares, J. 1995. *Nadie Escucha* (Madrid: Alfaguara)
——, 2000. 'Pueblos abandonados', *El País Semanal*, 30 April, 66–71
——, 1997. 'El Placer de Mentir', lecture given at Instituto Cervantes, London, 21 October
Luxemburg, R. 1972. *Selected Political Writings*, ed. by R. Looker, trans. by W. Graf (London: Cape)
Macklin, J. 1995. 'Memory and Oblivion: personal and rural identities in the narratives of Julio Llamazares', in R. Christie, J. Drinkwater, and J. Macklin, *The Scripted Self: Textual Identities in Contemporary Spanish Narrative* (Warminster: Aris and Phillips), 31–48
Manuel, P. 1989. 'Andalusian, Gypsy and Class Identity in the Contemporary Flamenco Complex', *Ethnomusicology*, 33: 47–65

Marco, J. M. 1988. 'Julio Llamazares sin trampas: entrevista realizada por José María Marco', *Quimera*, 80: 22–29

Marcus, G. E. 1998. *Ethnography Through Thick and Thin* (New Jersey: Princeton University Press)

Martin, A. 2000. 'Modulations of the Basque Voice: an interview with Bernardo Atxaga', *Journal of Spanish Cultural Studies*, 1: 193–204

Martín Corrales, E. 2002. *La imagen del magrebí en España: una perspectiva histórica siglos xvi–xx* (Barcelona: Edicions Bellaterra)

McDowell, L. 1996. 'Spatializing Feminism: Geographic Perspectives', in N. Duncan (ed.), *Bodyspace* (London: Routledge)

Mitchell, T. 1994. *Flamenco: Deep Song* (London: Yale University Press)

Monticone, R. 1986. *The Catholic Church in Communist Poland* (New York: Columbia University Press)

Nair, P. 1999. 'Between Being and Becoming: An Ethnographic Examination of Border Crossings, in *Alma gitana* (Chus Gutiérrez, 1995)', *Tesserae, Journal of Iberian and Latin American Studies*, 5: 173–88

——, 2000. 'Albums of no return: ethnicity, displacement and recognition in photographs of North African immigrants in contemporary Spain', *Journal of Spanish Cultural Studies*, 1: 59–73

——, 2002. 'Elusive Song: Flamenco as Field and Negotiation for the *Gitanos* in Córdoba Prison', in H. Graham and J. Labanyi (eds), *Constructing Identity in Twentieth Century Spain: Theoretical Debates and Cultural Practices* (Oxford: Oxford University Press), pp. 41–54

Naïr, S. 1992. *Le Regard des Vainqueurs: les enjeux français de l'immigration* (Paris: Grasset)

Olizaregi, M. J. 1998. 'Bernardo Atxaga: El escritor deseado', *Insula, Revista de Letras y Ciencias Humanas*, 623: 7–11

——, 1999. 'Bernardo Atxaga: Candidato al Andersen', *Cuadernos de Literatura Infantil y Juvenil*, 119: 30–36

——, 2000. 'La trayectoria literaria de Bernardo Atxaga', *Sancho El Sabio*, 13: 41–56

Olwig, K. F. and Frostrup, K. (eds). 1997. *Sting Culture: The Shifting Anthropological Object* (London: Routledge)

Ong, W. 1982. *Orality and Literacy: The Technologizing of the Word* (London: Methuen)

Ortiz, C. 1996. 'Obabakoak: El infinito virtual', *Cincinnati Romance Review*, 15: 106–12

Otero, A. 1996. 'A viaje por el río del olvido', *Revista Monográfica*, 12: 237–46

——, 1997. 'Luna de lobos de Julio Llamazares: la memoria popular en un espacio mítico', *Romance Languages Annual*, 9: 641–44

Pasqualino, C. 1995. 'Dire le Chant: Anthropologie Sociale des Gitans de Jerez de la Frontera' (unpublished doctoral thesis, Paris: École des Hautes Études en Sciences Sociales)

Pensky, M. (ed.). 1997. *The Actuality of Adorno* (Albany: State University of New York Press)

Perks, R. and Thompson, A. 1998. *The Oral History Reader* (London: Routledge)

Planell, D. 1998. *Bazar* (Jerez de la Frontera: Hogar Sur)

Pohren, D. 1988. *Lives and Legends of Flamenco* (Madrid: Gráficas)

Rabinow, P. 1977. *Reflections on Fieldwork in Morocco* (Berkeley: University of California Press)

Rachman, J. (ed.). 1995. *The Identity in Question* (London: Routledge)

Rama, A. 1982. *Transculturación narrativa en América Latina* (Madrid: Siglo XXI)

Rapport, N. and Overing, J. 2000. *Social and Cultural Anthropology: The Key Concepts* (London: Routledge)

Redfield, R. 1960. *The Little Community and Peasant Society and Culture* (Chicago: Chicago University Press)

Ricoeur, P. 1981. *Hermeneutics and the Human Science*, ed. and trans. by J.B. Thompson (Cambridge: Cambridge University Press)

——, 1984, 1985. *Time and Narrative*, trans. by K. Mclaughlin and D. Pellauer, 3 vols (Chicago and London: University of Chicago Press)

——, 1995. *Figuring the Sacred*, ed. by M. I. Wallace, trans. by D. Pellauer (Minneapolis: Fortess Press)

Richards, M. ' "Terror in Progress": Industrialization, Modernity and the Making of Francoism', in *Spanish Cultural Studies: The Struggle for Modernity*, 173–95

Riera, M. 1989. 'El tópico hecho añicos: entrevista con Benardo Atxaga', *Quimera*, 94: 12–18

Ritzer, G. 1996. *Modern Sociological Theory* (Singapore: The McGraw-Hill Companies, Inc.)

Rowe, W. and Schelling, V. 1991. *Memory and Modernity: Popular Culture in Latin America* (London: Verso)

San Román, T. 1984. *Gitanos de Madrid y Barcelona: ensayos sobre aculturación y etnicidad* (Barcelona: Universidad Autónoma de Barcelona)

——, 1997. *La diferencia inquietante: viejas y nuevas estrategias culturales de los gitanos* (Madrid: Siglo XXI)
Sánchez, A. 1995–96. 'Reivindicación de la memoria perdida', *Journal of Hispanic Research*, 4: 115–31
Sherman, S. 1998. *Documenting Ourselves* (Kentucky: University Press of Kentucky)
Sieburth S. 1994. *Inventing High and Low: Literature, Mass Culture and Uneven Modernity in Spain* (London and Durham: Duke University Press)
Smith. A. 1995–96. 'Entrevista con Bernardo Atxaga', *Letras Peninsulares*, 8: 415–24
Smith, P. J. 2000. *The Moderns: Time Space and Subjectivity in Contemporary Spanish Culture* (Oxford: Oxford University Press)
Solares, M. 1997. 'Noticia de Obaba y otros territorios', *Vuelta*, 252: 31–34
Steingress, G. 1991. *Sociología del cante jondo* (Jerez de la Frontera: Centro Andaluz de Flamenco)
Stokes, M. (ed.). 1997. *Ethnicity, Identity, Music* (Oxford: Berg)
Strauss, L. 1975. *Political Philosophy: Three Essays by Leo Strauss* (Indianapolis: Bobs-Merrill)
Sullivan, J. 1988. *ETA and Basque Nationalism* (London: Routledge)
Tierney, J. 1996. *Criminology: Theory and Context* (Hertfordshire: Harvester Wheatsheaf)
Tomlinson, J. 1999. *Globalization and Culture* (Oxford: Polity Press)
Torfing, J. 1999. *New Theories of Discourse: Laclau, Mouffe and Zizek* (Oxford: Blackwells)
Tucker, Jr, K. H. 1998. *Anthony Giddens and Modern Social Theory* (London: Thousand Oaks; New Delhi: Sage)
Valdés, M. (ed.). 1991. *A Ricoeur Reader: Reflection and Imagination* (Hertfordshire: Harvester Wheatsheaf)
Washabaugh, W. 1996. *Flamenco: Passion, Politics and Popular Culture* (Oxford: Berg)
Werbner, P. and T. Modood (eds). 1997. *Debating Cultural Hybridity: Multi-Cultural Identities and the Politics of Anti-Racism* (London and New Jersey: Zed Books)
Williams, R. 1976. *Keywords* (London: Fontana)
Zaldívar, A. and Castells, M. 1992. *España, fin de siglo* (Madrid: Alianza)
Zamora, L. P. and W. B Farris (eds). 1995. *Magical Realism: Theory, History, Community* (London and Durham: Duke University Press)

REVIEWS AND REPORTS

Andreu, N., Introduction to Trencant Fronteres Exhibition, single sheet, 1998
Buisef, D., *Tres años del Proyecto Xenofilia de acogida y sensibilización*, *Memoria*, commissioned by the Dirección General de Migraciones, España, 1996
Catalá Domenech, J., Review of Trencant Fronteres Exhibition, single sheet, 1998
Proyecto Barañí, *Mujeres gitanas y sistema penal*, date and place unknown
Conference Proceedings: *Creative Time*, the 2nd European Conference on Theatre and Prison, Manchester University, April 1996
Unit for Arts and Offenders, *Music in Criminal Justice Settings*, Seminar Papers, 1996

PRESS ARTICLES

Barrios, Nuria, 'Amara Carmona', *El País de las Tentaciones*, 12 May 1995, p. 6
Cortázar, Beatriz, 'Alma gitana: un estreno con duende', *ABC-Madrid*, 30 January 1996, p. 114
Delgado, Gema, 'Amores Difíciles', *Cambio 16*, 13 March 1995, p. 84
Gil, Cristina, 'Los *gitanos* tenemos que luchar para que se nos conozca de verdad', *Ya-Madrid*, 30 January 1996, p. 51
Lee-Six, Abigail, 'Review of *The Lone Man*', *Independent on Sunday*, 6 October 1996
Montero, Rosa, 'Entre *gitanos*', *El Pais Semanal*, 25 February 1996, p. 12
Muñoz, Diego, 'El cine español se pone flamenco con "Alma Gitana", de Chus Gutiérrez', *La Vanguardia*, 5 February 1995, p. 54
Noceda, Nuria, 'El "alma gitana" de Chus Guitérrez', *Diario 16*, 30 January 1996, p. 42
Peñate Rivero, Julio, Interview with Atxaga, *Cambio 16*, 6 November 1995, pp. 1–15

INDEX